VALUES IN CONFLICT

VALUES IN CONFLICT
Funding Priorities for Higher Education

Edited by

MARY P. McKEOWN
Maryland State Board for Higher Education
Annapolis, Maryland

and

KERN ALEXANDER
Western Kentucky University
Bowling Green, Kentucky

Seventh Annual Yearbook of the
American Education Finance Association
1986

BALLINGER PUBLISHING COMPANY
Cambridge, Massachusetts
A Subsidiary of Harper & Row, Publishers, Inc.

International Standard Book Number: 0-88730-102-9

Library of Congress Catalog Card Number: 86-20597

Printed in the United States of America

Library of Congress Cataloging-in-Publication Data

Values in conflict.

(Annual yearbook of the American Education Finance Association ; 7th)
  Bibliography: p.
  Includes index.
  1. Education, Higher—United States—Finance.
I. McKeown, Mary P. II. Alexander, Kern. III. Series.
LB2342.V34 1986   379.1'214'0973   86-20597
ISBN 0-88730-102-9

CONTENTS

LIST OF FIGURES

LIST OF TABLES

PREFACE

In the 1980s educational reform has focused on both higher education and elementary and secondary education. Facing the need for improved quality of higher education, increased competition for resources at the state and federal levels, and declining enrollments at many institutions, institutions of higher education, state coordinating and governing boards, legislators, and others have been forced to reexamine the roles and missions of institutions of higher education. Critical issues include the sources of funding, the levels of funding, and the very existence of the institutions. Because education is a key contributor to continued U.S. economic growth and to maintaining the current U.S. position in the world economy, it is appropriate that this seventh annual yearbook of the American Education Finance Association focus on issues related to the funding of higher education.

While this yearbook was being written, the higher education community was saddened by the death of one of the foremost authorities on the funding of higher education, M.M. Chambers of Illinois State University. His seminal work in the finance of higher education was dedicated to the timely reporting of data that could be used in public policy decisions. Dr. Chambers's wise counsel will be missed by all of us. This yearbook is dedicated to his memory.

The work of M.M. Chambers is continued by John McCarthy and Edward Hines of Illinois State University, who in Chapter 1 of this yearbook establish the historical context of funding for higher education. In this opening chapter, they review the history of funding for higher education in the United States from the early beginnings of public and private colleges. In order to place current concepts within the context of this historical evolution, special attention has been given to the various sources of revenues for institutions and the ways in which their relative shares have changed over time. This first chapter is followed by a discussion of demographic trends and their impact on the financing of higher education prepared by Carol Frances of Washington Resources, Inc. Enrollment stabilization and decline, nontraditional enrollments, and the competing demands for resources from other social services are placed in the context of changes in the economy as a whole.

The financial structure of higher education is described in Chapter 3 by O. Homer Erekson of Miami University, who analyzes the trends in the various sources of revenues for public and private universities and colleges and the uncertainties faced by financial planners in higher education.

Mary P. McKeown of the Maryland State Board for Higher Education discusses in Chapter 4 the funding formulas used by states in the budgeting or resource allocation process. She examines the advantages and disadvantages of formula use and what formulas are and how they are used. The discussion of institutional support is continued in Chapter 5 by Sandra Allard and Lucie Lapovsky of the Maryland State Board for Higher Education, who present a description of current state programs and practices for providing various types of assistance to private higher education institutions and students. They conclude that, in a time of scarce resources and competing demands for public funds, states may eliminate or restrict programs that benefit private higher education.

Issues related to tuition and student assistance are addressed in the next three chapters. Tuition and fee pricing strategies are discussed in Chapter 6, by Richard A. Yanikoski of DePaul University. The discussion includes nontraditional pricing strategies varying from peer pricing to inflation indexing; these alternatives are examined in the context of the goal of tuition charges. In the next chapter, Terry W. Hartle of the American Enterprise Institute and James B. Stedman of the Congressional Research Service review the federal role in funding higher education. Hartle and Stedman posit that questions of cost, minority participation, and quality during the 1980s may significantly alter the federal commitment to equal opportunity through aid to individuals that has been the heart of federal aid to higher education in the 1960s and 1970s. Chapter 8, by Alan P. Wagner of the State University of New York at Albany, examines issues related to student financial aid programs. Wagner discusses the issues of access and choice, and who should pay for a college education, from the perspective of the public policy goals thought to be the focus of current financial aid programs.

In Chapter 9 Elchanan Cohn of the University of South Carolina and Terry G. Geske of Louisiana State University further explore the issues of the private and social benefits related to the cost of attending institutions of higher education. Cohn and Geske raise the issue of "overinvestment" in higher education, from both societal and individual perspectives, and indicate that no definitive conclusion has been reached yet.

Capital funding in higher education is discussed in Chapter 10 by Douglas R. Sherman and Ralph Nichols from the University of Michigan. Their chapter focuses on the methods by which public and private institutions secure funds for construction, remodeling, and renovation of facilities. Changes in student program preferences, technological changes, and aging campus buildings have contributed to crisis conditions for many campus physical plants. The authors suggest that focusing on specific needs and providing incentives for good management could help solve many problems in the next decade.

Background information and issues related to research and development funding for higher education are provided in Chapter 11 by Howard Gobstein of the U.S. General Accounting Office. Gobstein highlights the state of research and development funding at colleges and universities, including the competition for funds, and raises interesting questions about the future of research and development funding.

The concluding two chapters address major current issues confronting higher education. The recent reports calling for the reform in higher education are examined in Chapter 12 by Frances Kemmerer of the State University of New York at Albany. Her analysis raises the important issue of who should pay for reform of higher education and how reforms will affect the cost of and access to higher education. The concluding chapter by John D. Millett, president emeritus of Miami University and chancellor emeritus of the Ohio Board of Regents, focuses on the trends and emerging issues that relate to the funding of higher education. Millett examines various societal, demographic, governmental, and economic trends and asks whether U.S. society will continue to support and be served by U.S. higher education.

The editors wish to express their appreciation to the numerous individuals who participated in the completion of the 1986 yearbook, especially each of the authors, who contributed their time and energy to make this book possible. Special thanks are extended to James Phelps, 1985–86 AEFA president, and to the AEFA board of directors for their interest and thoughtful criticism.

Mary P. McKeown
Kern Alexander

Annapolis, Maryland
April 1986

1 PUBLIC AND PRIVATE FUNDING OF U.S. HIGHER EDUCATION, 1840-1985

John R. McCarthy and Edward R. Hines

Many noted authors have ventured into the debate about the intent and level of public funding of higher education. Public funding of higher education has been posed as an economic issue, a political issue, an equity issue, and a fundamental right in a democratic society. The debate continues.

The historical data presented in this chapter can be placed in various frames of reference for formulating hypotheses and making observations, and so some explanations are called for. The data came from a variety of sources: (1) *Census of the United States* (various years), (2) *Annual Report of the United States Commissioner of Education* (1867-1978), (3) *Statistical Abstract of the United States* (various years), and (4) *Historical Statistics* (various years). The attempt was made to avoid juxtaposing more refined against less refined data. All data, for comparative purposes, were collected under the same governmental authority using the same procedures. As with many data collections and macroanalyses, the data are better viewed as a directional trend rather than a precise instrument of measurement. These cautionary statements, however, should not be misconstrued because the greatest fluctuation among data sources range only within plus or minus 5 percent.

1

GOVERNMENT SUPPORT FOR U.S. HIGHER EDUCATION, 1790–1910

Neither the state governments nor the federal government has eagerly sought responsibility for financing higher education. With the historic Morrill Land Grant Act of 1862, the federal government believed that it had endowed an educational system that eliminated the need for continued funding from federal or state government. Systematic funding of state colleges and universities is largely a twentieth-century phenomenon in the United States. As shown in Table 1-1, less than 6 percent of the total income in 1860 for the 467 institutions of higher education came from government sources. The 1850 census indicates that of the $200,034 coming from "public funds," only $15,485 or almost 8 percent of the total came from direct taxation. The remaining $184,549 or 92 percent of the total came from direct grants from a variety of mostly local and state governments as one-time gifts—usually with the understanding that the gift was contingent on the school's promise never to approach that particular government for funds in the future. Of course, this promise was often given but seldom honored by the educational institution. In 1850 all colleges and universities received nearly 24 percent of their revenues from endowments; in 1860 they received 28 percent from endowments. The major source of funds for private institutions during this period was the category "other," which provided almost 66 percent of total income in 1850 and 67 percent in 1860. The major "other" source was religious congregations and individuals located usually in Europe. Many Europeans viewed the United States as a

Table 1-1. Number of Colleges and Students and Sources of Funding for 1850 and 1860.

	1850	*1860*
Number of colleges	234	467
Number of students	27,158	56,120
Total income	$1,916,628	$3,176,717
Endowments	$452,314	$894,736
Public sources	$200,034	$159,822
Other sources	$1,264,280	$2,122,159

Sources: U.S. Bureau of the Census (1853: lx, 1872: 456).

vast wilderness filled with heathens, and therefore many churches sent missionaries to the United States. The need to train and educate U.S. ministers struck a responsive cord in the evangelical churches of Europe. Many U.S. college presidents spent more time in Europe seeking funds than they did on their own campuses.

External funding for U.S. higher education was not limited to religious groups, however. In 1807 the British parliament abolished slavery throughout the empire, and the political instruments that had mobilized public opinion in Great Britain soon turned their talents and funds to abolish slavery in the United States. By the 1840s and 1860s the support of U.S. abolitionists and antislavery institutions of higher education was an effective way to combine religion, education, and moral indignation into one political instrument. Some European power bases responded by supporting proslavery institutions of higher education. The Civil War ended the debate and also this European source of funding for U.S. higher education.

INCOME, EXPENDITURE, AND STUDENT ENROLLMENT IN U.S. HIGHER EDUCATION, 1910–82

Data on sources of income for institutions of higher education from 1860 to 1910 do not identify specific funding sources. As shown in Table 1–2, in 1920 only 7 percent of total income came from the federal government, and 31 percent of the total income came from state and local governments combined; over 62 percent came from sources other than federal, state, and local governments. The highest level of support of higher education ever provided by the federal government was 22 percent of total income in 1950 and 18 percent in 1960. Federal support, based on data reported in Table 1–2, averaged almost 12 percent from 1920 through 1982.

It is clear that since 1920 state governments have been increasing their support for higher education. In 1920 the combined support of higher education by both state and local government was 31 percent of total income. In 1982 state support alone accounted for 30 percent of all income of institutions of higher education.

Local governmental support for institutions of higher education has remained relatively constant since 1920. In 1970 the local government share peaked with a 3.6 percent contribution to the total

Table 1–2. Sources of Income of Institutions of Higher Education: Public and Private Institutions Combined (*in thousands of dollars and in percentages*).

Year	Total	Federal	State	Local	Other
1982	$72,191	$8,320 (12%)	$21,849 (30%)	$1,938 (3%)	$40,084 (55%)
1980	58,520	7,772 (13%)	18,378 (31%)	1,558 (3%)	30,812 (53%)
1970	21,518	2,682 (12%)	5,788 (27%)	775 (4%)	12,270 (57%)
1960	5,786	1,037 (18%)	1,374 (24%)	152 (3%)	3,223 (55%)
1950	2,375	524 (22%)	492 (21%)	61 (3%)	1,298 (54%)
1940	715	39 (5%)	151 (21%)	24 (3%)	501 (71%)
1930	555	21 (4%)	S/L = 151 (27%)	—	383 (69%)
1920	200	13 (7%)	S/L = 62 (31%)	—	125 (62%)
1910	68	—	—	—	—
1900	35	—	—	—	—
1890	21	—	—	—	—

Sources: Compiled from U.S. Bureau of the Census (1975: 384, 1983: 164–65, 1984: 154–55).

Table 1-3. Governmental and Other Sources of Income of Institutions of Higher Education (*in thousands of dollars and in percentages*).

Year	Government	Other
1982	$32,107 (44%)	$40,084 (56%)
1980	27,708 (47%)	30,812 (53%)
1970	9,245 (43%)	12,270 (57%)
1960	2,563 (44%)	3,223 (56%)
1950	1,077 (45%)	1,298 (55%)
1940	214 (30%)	501 (70%)
1930	172 (31%)	383 (69%)
1920	75 (38%)	125 (62%)
1910	—	—
1900	—	—
1890	—	—

Sources: Compiled from U.S. Bureau of the Census (1975: 384, 1983: 164-65, 1984: 154-55).

income of higher education, and local government support has averaged almost 3 percent since 1920.

Since 1920 the "other" category has continued to be the major source of income for institutions of higher education. The "other" category includes interest from endowments, contributions, scholarships, and the mainstay—tuition and fees. Since the 1840s the "other" category has averaged 60 percent of the total income of institutions of higher education in the United States.

Table 1-3 is a composite of all governmental support for U.S. higher education in one column juxtaposed against the "other" column. The aggregate support of all governments has never reached 50 percent of the income of all institutions combined, but the various governments have averaged over 40 percent of the income of institutions of higher education since 1920. Most government support has come from state governments; support from other sources has ranged from a high of 70 percent of the total income in 1940 to a low of 53 percent in 1980.

As depicted in Table 1-4, the number of students enrolled in higher education increased by 5,230 percent from 1900 to 1982. During the same period, cost per student increased by 3,952 percent, and the cost per capita increased 66,633 percent. The greatest percentage increase in enrollment occurred between 1960 and 1970, when there

Table 1-4. Enrollment in Institutions of Higher Education and Expenditure per Student and Cost per Capita from 1890 to 1982 (*including percentages*).

Year	Number of Students		Expenditures per Student		Cost per Capita	
1982	12,426,000	(7.01%)	$5,809	(15.25%)	$305.12	(18.62%)
1980	11,611,000	(62.48%)	5,040	(67.38%)	257.00	(144.97%)
1970	7,146,000	(122.22%)	3,011	(67.37%)	104.91	(225.91%)
1960	3,216,000	(20.94%)	1,799	(101.45%)	32.19	(106.47%)
1950	2,659,000	(77.95%)	893	(86.62%)	15.59	(189.23%)
1940	1,494,203	(35.74%)	478	(−5.34%)	5.39	(19.77%)
1930	1,100,737	(84.10%)	505	(51.19%)	4.50	(139.36%)
1920	597,880	(68.34%)	334	(74.86%)	1.88	(144.05%)
1910	355,215	(49.50%)	191	(29.93%)	.77	(67.39%)
1900	237,592		147		.46	

Sources: Compiled from U.S. Bureau of the Census (1975: 383–84, 1983: 164–65, 1984: 6, 126, 152–55).

was over a 122 percent increase in student enrollment. The greatest increase in per capita cost (226 percent) occurred during the same decade, with an average increase of over 22 percent per year. The cost per student, however, increased only by 67 percent, for an average of almost 7 percent increase per year, which was the lowest percentage increase per decade since 1940.

The lowest percentage increase (21 percent) in enrollment was in the decade from 1950 to 1960. During the same decade, student cost increased at the highest rate, averaging 10.1 percent per year. The cost per capita increased at approximately the same percentage rate (10.6 percent) but was the lowest percentage increase for the decades between 1940 and 1980.

INCOME, EXPENDITURE, AND STUDENT ENROLLMENT IN PUBLIC AND PRIVATE INSTITUTIONS OF HIGHER EDUCATION

The data on funding recipients presented in Tables 1–5 and 1–6 were collected by the U.S. Census Bureau, and the level of error should be relatively consistent in all the data. In this sense the data are comparable and reflect the total amount of expenditures by

Table 1-5. Expenditures for Private Higher Education, Total Expenditures for All Higher Education, and Total Number of Students per Year Enrolled in Private Higher Education (*in thousands of dollars and in percentages*).

Year	Total	Private		Students	
1982	$70,339,000	$24,120,000	(34%)	2,730,000	(22%)
1980	56,914,000	21,300,000	(37%)	2,487,000	(21%)
1970	21,403,000	8,200,000	(38%)	2,024,000	(28%)
1960	6,617,000	2,864,000	(43%)	1,384,000	(43%)
1950	2,123,275	949,150	(45%)	1,304,119	(49%)
1940	605,755	273,162	(43%)	697,672	(47%)
1930	632,249	343,340	(54%)	568,090	(42%)
1920	216,366	100,769	(47%)	282,498	(47%)
1910	—	—		188,655	(53%)
1900	—	—		146,903	(62%)

Sources: Compiled from U.S. Bureau of the Census (1954: 132-33, 1964: 106-107, 1981: 164, 1984: 126-27, 154-55).

Table 1-6. Expenditures for Public Higher Education, Total Expenditures for All Higher Education, and Total Number of Students per Year Enrolled in Public Higher Education (*including percentages*).

Year	Total	Public		Students	
1982	$70,339,000	$46,219,000	(66%)	9,696,000	(78%)
1980	56,914,000	41,400,000	(63%)	9,124,000	(79%)
1970	21,403,000	14,600,000	(62%)	5,122,000	(72%)
1960	6,617,000	3,753,000	(57%)	1,832,000	(57%)
1950	2,213,275	1,174,125	(55%)	1,354,902	(51%)
1940	605,000	332,592	(57%)	796,531	(53%)
1930	632,249	288,909	(46%)	532,647	(58%)
1920	216,366	115,587	(53%)	315,382	(53%)
1910	—	—		166,560	(47%)
1900	—	—		90,689	(38%)

Sources: U.S. Bureau of the Census (1954: 132-33, 1964: 106-07, 1981: 164, 1984: 126-27, 154-55).

private higher education and public higher education for the times indicated. As shown in Table 1-5, the number of students and the expenditures of funds to educate those students have continued to rise since 1900. However, the percentage share of the students and of the expenditures of funds by private higher education has continued to drop throughout the twentieth century. From a high of 62 percent of all students in 1900, the percentage has dropped to approximately 22 percent in 1982. In 1920 private higher education enrolled 47 percent of the students and expended 47 percent of total dollars for higher education. This pattern was repeated in 1960 with 43 percent of the students and 43 percent of the dollars in private higher education. In 1982 private higher education expended 37 percent of all education dollars to educate 22 percent of the students enrolled. The data presented in Table 1-5 show that the only time that private higher education spent a lesser percentage than their percentage share of the student population was in 1940 and 1950.

Table 1-6 shows a different trend for public higher education expenditures and enrollment through time. Student enrollment in institutions of public higher education has gone from 38 percent of the total student enrollment in 1900 to more than 78 percent in 1982. With few aberrations of the data in terms of percentage share, there has been a continuing shift from private to public higher education in the United States. In 1960 the percentage of students enrolled in public higher education and the percentage of expenditures of institutions of higher education were equal, at 57 percent for both categories.

Only in 1940 and 1950 did the percentage of funds expended exceed the percentage of student enrollment, and then only by less than 5 percent. In 1980 the negative percentage differential between these two percentages was over sixteen percentage points; by 1982 the gap had been reduced to less than eleven percentage points. Compared to the private institutions of higher education, the situation was almost reversed; in 1982 there was a positive differential between these two of more than ten percentage points. In 1980 the positive differential was in excess of sixteen percentage points. There is no evidence to support or deny the view that there should be a balance between percentage of enrollment and percentage of students. As indicated earlier, macrodata are examined to identify possible trends for further analysis.

Table 1-7. Percentage of Students Enrolled in Public and Private Institutions of Higher Education with Expenditure per Student per Year Based on Recorded Expenditures of Both Types of Institutions.

Year	Public Institutions		Private Institutions	
	Percentage Enrolled	Expenditures per Year	Percentage Enrolled	Expenditures per Year
1982	78%	$4,766 (5%)	22%	$8,835 (3%)
1980	79%	4,537 (59%)	21%	8,564 (111%)
1970	72%	2,850 (39%)	28%	4,051 (196%)
1960	57%	2,048 (136%)	43%	2,069 (185%)
1950	51%	867 (108%)	49%	727 (85%)
1940	53%	417 (-30%)	47%	392 (-35%)
1930	58%	542 (48%)	42%	604 (65%)
1920	53%	367	47%	365
1910	47%	—	53%	—
1900	38%	—	62%	—

Sources: Compiled from U.S. Bureau of the Census (1954: 132-33, 1964: 106-07, 1975: 383-84, 1981: 164, 1984: 126-27, 152-55).

The need for additional analysis, however, may be demonstrated by data in Table 1-7. In Table 1-7 the total expenditures of both private and public institutions are divided by the number of students enrolled in each sector. The data were collected by the federal government concurrently from both types of institutions; the same questions were asked of all institutions, and all the data were collected and analyzed typically in the same way. The data presented in Table 1-7 should be viewed as measures of direction and trends rather than absolutes because, over time, techniques change, categories change, and classifications may be altered due to methodological improvements by the U.S. Bureau of the Census. With these reservations, the data in Table 1-7 may need to be scrutinized carefully from a variety of perspectives.

Expenditures per student by the public and private sectors were relatively equal prior to 1960. In 1920, 1940, and 1950, the expenditure per student was actually less in the private sector than in the public sector; in 1960 the expenditure per student in private higher education was only $21 more than expenditure per student at public institutions. Expenditure per student increased 118 percent in private institutions between 1970 and 1982. During the same period, however, expenditure per student increased only 67 percent in public higher education. During this same time frame, student enrollment in public institutions increased 89 percent, while the private sector increased expenditures per student by 118 percent to deal with a 34 percent increase in enrollment; public higher education, for the same period, increased expenditure per student by 67 percent to contend with a 89 percent enrollment increase.

Whatever the cause, in 1982 private institutions of higher education were spending 85 percent more per student than were public institutions of higher education. If the student enrollment was categorized as doctoral, master's, and bachelor's degree-seeking students, the differences might even be more extreme because advanced degrees are more costly. Since most advanced degrees are produced in public higher education, the differences between expenditures of public and private higher education are even more discernible.

If the data presented thus far were evaluated solely from the efficiency and effectiveness standard, two interpretations could be possible: (1) Private higher education is producing a better product because it spends more per student than public higher education does, or (2) private higher education is more expensive because it is not at production capacity, and the expenditure per student by public higher education may reflect better utilization of capacity. If the expenditure differential between public and private higher education is caused by underutilized capacity in the private sector, then the private sector could absorb substantially more students than it is now serving without the need for any additional expenditures. Private higher education is possibly operating at 50 percent of its capacity. For public higher education to expend the same level of dollars per student, it would have to increase expenditures by $39 billion on an annual basis or reduce current enrollment by almost half to approximately 4,445,000 students.

The above interpretations are highly speculative and ignore the cautions about generalizations based on macrodata. The differences between public and private higher education could be explained by a variety of factors unrelated to efficiency and effectiveness measures. Differences in missions, goals, objectives, students, and so forth could predict, if not require, such differences in expenditure per student between the two sectors. A more conservative interpretation of the data would be that until 1960 expenditures per student in bot sectors were relatively equal. Since 1960 the emergence of public community colleges that educate large numbers of students has discernibly affected average expenditures per student.

BUDGETARY EXPENDITURES BY CATEGORY IN U.S. HIGHER EDUCATION, 1930–82

In an attempt to isolate the cause for the differences between public and private higher education expenditures, budget categories from 1930 to 1982 shall be examined. In the data reported for the period of 1930 through 1970, the U.S. census used three broad budget categories for expenditures: (1) educational and general, (2) auxiliary enterprises, and (3) student aid. Examining the percentage of expenditures in these three categories since 1930 may help identify and develop a benchmark to identify unanticipated variations in the data. These data are presented in Table 1–8.

As shown in Table 1–8, the percentage of total expenditures represented by the category "educational and general" has fluctuated from a high of 81 percent of total institutional expenditures in 1960 to a low of 70 percent in both 1982 and 1980. This category has averaged 75 percent of total expenditures from 1930 to 1982. For the education and general fund to have received 81 percent of the

Table 1–8. Current Expenditures by Category of Higher Education from 1930 to 1982 (*including percentages*) (*in millions of dollars*).

Year	Total	Education and General	Auxiliary	Student Aid
1982	$70,339	49,176 (70%)	$7,998 (11%)	2,685 (4%)[a]
1980	56,914	39,794 (70%)	6,486 (11%)	2,200 (4%)[a]
1970	21,043	15,789 (75%)	2,769 (13%)	2,485 (12%)
1960	5,601	4,513 (81%)	916 (16%)	172 (3%)
1950	2,246	1,706 (76%)	87 (4%)	453 (20%)
1940	675	522 (77%)	35 (5%)	121 (18%)
1930	507	378 (75%)	3 (1%)	126 (24%)

a. These data were adjusted to be compatible with the other data presented in this table and percentages for 1980 and 1982 will not equal 100 percent.

Sources: Compiled from U.S. Bureau of the Census (1975: 384, 1983: 164–65, 1984: 154–55).

:d in 1982 in these categories rather than the 70
it did receive would have required an additional
ɔ be placed in the "educational and general" category.
enterprise expenditures peaked in 1960 when 16 percent
ʟutional expenditures were represented by auxiliary enter-
⸻ ⸤penditures for auxiliary enterprises in 1930 consumed
barely ⸳ percent of expenditures; the percentage has averaged 9.2
percent between 1930 and 1982, but the trend is definitely that
auxiliary enterprises represent a greater share of expenditures. Auxiliary enterprises represented 13 percent of total institutional expenditures in 1970, and 11 percent in 1980 and again in 1982.

The trend in institutional student aid seems to be opposite that
shown by auxiliary enterprises. Of these three categories, 24 percent
of all expenditures in 1930 was for student aid. The low point was
reached in 1960 when only 3 percent of expenditures were for student aid. In 1980 and 1982 only 4 percent of these expenditures
were for student aid. The decreasing institutional expenditures for
student aid probably reflect the use of federal funds for student aid
as the first line of aid.

In summary, the longitudinal analyses of these three broad categories identify trends and give directions. In terms of all expenditure
categories, the category of "educational and general" is the one that
is most directly related to the instructional cost of any particular
institution. For this reason, the subsystems of this category are also
examined. The subcategories include (1) administration and general
expense, (2) instruction and departmental research, (3) organized
research, (4) libraries, (5) plant operation and maintenance, (6)
organized activities related to instructional departments, and (7)
extension and public services. To identify discernible differences
between expenditures per student between the two sectors, these
subcategories were examined to determine fluctuation and variations of expenditure patterns in order to refine the bench mark for
analysis.

In Table 1–9 the broad category of "educational and general"
expenditures is compared within and across years since 1930. The
percentage of expenditures used to administer higher education has
gone from a low of 11 percent in 1930 to a high of 17 percent in
1970. Since 1930 an average of 13 percent of this broad category has
been expended for administrative costs.

Table 1-9. Expenditures in the Category of "Education and General" in Higher Education Budgeting from 1930 to 1982.

Year	Total	Administration	INDR	Research	Library	Plant	Support	Service
1982[a]	48,203	6,471 (13%)	22,963 (47%)	5,930 (12%)	1,922 (4%)	5,979 (12%)	2,734 (5%)	2,204 (4%)
1980[a]	39,043	5,054 (12%)	18,497 (44%)	5,099 (12%)	1,624 (4%)	4,700 (11%)	2,252 (5%)	1,817 (4%)
1970	15,789	2,628 (17%)	7,653 (48%)	2,144 (14%)	653 (4%)	1,542 (10%)	648 (4%)	521 (3%)
1960	4,513	583 (13%)	1,793 (40%)	1,022 (23%)	135 (3%)	470 (9%)	303 (7%)	206 (5%)
1950	1,706	213 (12%)	781 (46%)	225 (13%)	56 (3%)	225 (13%)	119 (7%)	87 (6%)
1940	522	63 (12%)	280 (54%)	27 (5%)	19 (4%)	70 (13%)	27 (5%)	35 (7%)
1930	378	43 (11%)	221 (58%)	18 (5%)	10 (3%)	61 (16%)	—	25 (7%)

a. Totals were adjusted for 1980 and 1982; percentages for 1980 and 1982 will not equal 100 percent.
Sources: Compiled from U.S. Bureau of the Census (1975: 384, 1983: 164–65, 1984: 154–55).

Instruction and departmental research (INDR) represented the majority of the funds in 1930 and 1940; in 1960 INDR garnered only 40 percent of total funds. The average expenditure on INDR since 1930 has been over 48 percent. In 1980 the percentage share dropped to the second-lowest point since 1930, but in 1982 the INDR expenditure increased to over 47 percent.

In 1930 and in 1940 organized research expended only 5 percent of total expenditures. The highest level of expenditure for research occurred in 1960, when 23 percent of all expenditures went for this purpose. The average percentage expended for research since 1920 has been 12 percent; in 1980 and in 1982 the percentage expended was 12 percent.

The percentage of expenditures supporting libraries has been consistent since 1930. The average percentage rate of investment in libraries has averaged nearly 4 percent; there have been no large fluctuations.

Plant operations and maintenance have averaged 12 percent of expenditures since 1930. Since 1960, however, this operation has increased its percentage share of the budget by 1 percent per decade. The highest percentage investment in the physical plant and operations occurred in 1930.

Support activities related to the academic departments averaged 5 percent since 1930. The high points were in the decades of the 1940s and the 1950s, when 7 percent of the total went into support activities. The lowest point of investments was in 1970.

Public service was the only area examined where the percentage of expenditure seems to be on a downward slope. The highest percentage expenditure was in 1920 and 1930, and the lowest point of expenditure was in 1970. The degree of recovery is minimal because both in 1982 and 1980 it was necessary to round off to raise the level of investment up to 4 percent.

In terms of combined data analysis, in 1930 and 1960 63 percent of expenditures were in organized research and in instruction and departmental research. More than 62 percent of total expenditures were in these two items in 1970, and 59 percent of the total was expended in these two line items in 1930 and 1940. The lowest point was in 1980, with a combined percentage of 56 percent followed by 57 percent in 1982. The percentage of total funds available to this category has been declining since 1960. In 1960, 81 percent of all expenditures in higher education was for this category; in 1970 the percentage dropped to 75 percent followed by a 70 percent share in 1980 and 1982. If 81 percent of all 1982 funds for higher education had been for the "educational and general" category, an additional $8.7 billion would have been available.

A general conclusion could be that the data in Tables 1-8 and 1-9 present no dramatic fluctuations. However, as demonstrated above, the percentage share in almost every category dropped from 1970 to 1980 with marginal, if any, recovery in 1982. Positing the categorical data of private and public institutions against the aggregate data presented in Tables 1-8 and 1-9 may help identify trends that indicate directions for research into the growing disparity between the sectors in total expenditures per student.

REVENUE AND EXPENDITURES OF PUBLIC AND PRIVATE INSTITUTIONS OF HIGHER EDUCATION, 1975-82

Isolation of differences and identification of trends in public and private support for higher education require examining revenues as well as expenditures. This examination of both public and private institutions of higher education in 1975, in 1980, and in 1982 attempts to determine whether the data found for both sectors mirror the findings of the aggregate data presented in the previous tables.

Even though public higher education enrolled 78 percent of all students in 1982, as shown in Tables 1-6 and 1-10, it expended approximately 69 percent of all "educational and general" funds in 1982, 1980, and 1975. Within the subcategories of "educational and general," percentage expenditures remain within one or two percentage points of each other. During this same period, public higher education received approximately 66 percent of all higher education revenue. Fund revenue, as measured in percentages, was even more stable than expenditures in both broad categories and subcategories. An examination of the data from 1975 to 1982 in terms of percentage change and absolute change reveals no indications of shifts of income or expenditure patterns that would suggest the dramatic change in expenditure per students as reported in Table 1-7.

As shown in Tables 1-5 and 1-11, from 1975 private higher education expended approximately 34 percent of all expenditures per year while the percentage share of students dropped from 28 percent

Table 1-10. Revenues and Expenditures of Public Institutions of Higher Education, by Category and Percentage for 1982, 1980, and 1975.

	1982		1980		1975	
	Total	Public	Total	Public	Total	Public
Fund revenues	$72,191[a]	$47,271 (65%)	$58,520[b]	$38,824 (66%)	N/A	N/A
Tuition and fees	15,774	6,395 (41%)	11,930	4,860 (41%)	—	—
Federal government	8,320	5,296 (64%)	7,772	5,012 (64%)	—	—
State government	21,849	21,397 (98%)	18,378	17,974 (98%)	—	—
Local government	1,938	1,757 (91%)	1,588	1,436 (90%)	—	—
Endowment earning	1,597	244 (15%)	1,177	191 (16%)	—	—
Gifts/contracts	3,564	1,277 (36%)	2,806	979 (35%)	—	—
Related activities	1,583	1,072 (68%)	1,239	819 (66%)	—	—
Auxiliary enterprises	8,122	5,123 (63%)	6,481	4,089 (63%)	—	—
Other revenue	9,446	4,710 (50%)	7,146	3,464 (48%)	—	—
Plant funds	5,185	3,480 (67%)	4,382	3,166 (72%)	—	—
Income in fund balance	2,224	462 (21%)	2,153	437 (21%)	—	—
Endowment	2,030	415 (20%)	1,874	344 (18%)	—	—
Annuity/life income	49	7 (14%)	64	3 (5%)	—	—
Loans	145	40 (28%)	215	90 (42%)	—	—
Current expenditures	70,339[a]	46,219 (66%)	56,914[b]	37,768 (66%)	$35,058[b]	$28,635 (67%)
Education and general	54,849	37,171 (68%)	44,543	30,627 (69%)	27,548	19,092 (69%)
Instruction	22,963	16,348 (71%)	18,497	13,319 (72%)	11,798	8,574 (73%)
Instructional support	6,471	3,957 (61%)	5,054	3,156 (63%)	3,057	1,917 (63%)
Research	5,930	4,005 (68%)	5,099	3,409 (67%)	3,132	2,042 (65%)
Plant operations	5,979	4,104 (69%)	4,700	3,267 (70%)	2,787	1,935 (69%)

Academic support	4,656	3,298 (71%)	3,876	2,786 (72%)	2,256	1,612 (71%)
Libraries	1,922	1,288 (67%)	1,624	1,114 (69%)	1,002	680 (68%)
Student services	3,177	2,086 (66%)	2,567	1,715 (67%)	1,439	985 (68%)
Scholar/fellowships	2,685	1,089 (41%)	2,200	970 (44%)	1,450	719 (50%)
Unrestricted	1,236	375 (30%)	905	324 (36%)	632	267 (42%)
Restricted	1,449	714 (49%)	1,296	646 (50%)	818	452 (55%)
Public service	2,204	1,812 (82%)	1,817	513 (83%)	1,098	924 (84%)
Mandatory transfers	784	471 (60%)	732	473 (65%)	532	386 (73%)
Auxiliary enterprises	7,998	5,070 (63%)	6,486	132 (64%)	4,074	2,537 (62%)
Hospitals	6,234	3,902 (63%)	4,757	2,948 (62%)	2,351	1,369 (58%)
Independent operations	1,259	76 (6%)	1,128	61 (5%)	1,087	492 (45%)

a. Source: U.S. Bureau of the Census (1984: 154–55).
b. Source: Compiled from U.S. Bureau of the Census (1981: 164).

Table 1-11. Revenues and Expenditures of Private Institutions of Higher Education, by Category and Percentage for 1982, 1980, and 1975.

	1982		1980		1975	
	Total	Private	Total	Private	Total	Private
Fund revenues	$72,191[a]	$24,920 (35%)	$58,520[b]	$19,696 (34%)	N/A	N/A
Tuition and fees	15,774	9,379 (59%)	11,930	7,070 (59%)	—	—
Federal government	8,320	3,023 (36%)	7,772	2,759 (36%)	—	—
State government	21,849	452 (2%)	18,378	404 (2%)	—	—
Local government	1,938	181 (9%)	1,588	151 (10%)	—	—
Endowment earning	1,597	1,353 (85%)	1,177	986 (84%)	—	—
Gifts/contracts	3,564	2,287 (64%)	2,806	1,829 (65%)	—	—
Related activities	1,583	511 (32%)	1,239	420 (44%)	—	—
Auxiliary enterprises	8,122	2,999 (37%)	6,481	2,393 (37%)	—	—
Other revenue	9,446	4,736 (50%)	7,146	3,682 (52%)	—	—
Plant funds	5,185	1,704 (33%)	4,382	1,216 (28%)	—	—
Income in fund balance	2,224	1,761 (79%)	2,153	1,718 (79%)	—	—
Endowment	2,030	1,615 (80%)	1,874	1,531 (82%)	—	—
Annuity/life income	49	41 (86%)	64	62 (95%)	—	—
Loans	145	105 (72%)	215	125 (58%)	—	—
Current expenditures	70,339[a]	24,120 (34%)	56,914[b]	19,146 (34%)	$35,058[b]	$11,568 (33%)
Education and general	54,849	17,678 (32%)	44,543	13,915 (31%)	27,548	8,455 (31%)
Instruction	22,963	6,614 (29%)	18,497	5,178 (28%)	11,798	3,224 (27%)
Instructional support	6,471	2,514 (39%)	5,054	1,919 (37%)	3,057	1,140 (37%)
Research	5,930	1,925 (32%)	5,099	1,691 (33%)	3,132	1,090 (35%)
Plant operations	5,979	1,875 (31%)	4,700	1,433 (30%)	2,787	852 (31%)

Academic support	4,656	1,358 (29%)	3,876	1,091 (28%)	2,256	644 (29%)
Libraries	1,922	635 (33%)	1,624	509 (31%)	1,002	322 (32%)
Student services	3,177	1,091 (34%)	2,567	812 (33%)	1,439	454 (32%)
Scholar/fellowships	2,685	1,596 (59%)	2,200	1,230 (66%)	1,450	731 (50%)
Unrestricted	1,236	861 (70%)	905	581 (64%)	632	365 (68%)
Restricted	1,449	735 (51%)	1,296	649 (50%)	818	366 (45%)
Public service	2,204	392 (18%)	1,817	304 (17%)	1,098	147 (16%)
Mandatory transfers	784	313 (40%)	732	259 (35%)	532	147 (27%)
Auxiliary enterprises	7,998	2,928 (37%)	6,486	2,354 (36%)	4,074	1,537 (48%)
Hospitals	6,234	2,332 (37%)	4,757	1,810 (38%)	2,351	982 (42%)
Independent operations	1,259	1,182 (94%)	1,128	1,067 (95%)	1,087	594 (55%)

a. Source: U.S. Bureau of the Census (1984: 154–55).
b. Source: Compiled from U.S. Bureau of the Census (1981: 164).

in 1970 to 21 percent in 1982. Even within the subcategories of expenditures, there is little evidence of dramatic shifts. Mirroring the pattern found in public higher education revenue, private education revenue was marked with little percentage variation among the subcategories of income

Nothing in the data can explain the growing difference between the private sector's expenditure per student compared with the public sector's expenditure. No dramatic shift in the data or in the percentage of revenue or expenditures can be found to explain the changes. It should be noted the student enrollment in private and public higher education has shown a consistent increase for each decade examined. Thus the proportionate increase in expenditures by private institutions cannot be summarily dismissed on the basis of declining enrollment in the private sector and increasing enrollment in the public sector. While the revenue, expenditures, and student enrollment were reported in the same way, the definition of a full-time student may vary from campus to campus. The nontraditional part-time student is more likely to be found in a public community college than in a private liberal arts college. The propensity to find more traditional college students in the private sector and more nontraditional students in the public sector may help obviate some of the disparity between expenditures. No evidence was found that one sector was delaying plant maintenance at a greater rate than the other sector.

FEDERAL FINANCIAL AID TO STUDENTS

The federal program that gives dollars directly to students started on a large scale after World War II when various benefits were given to armed services veterans. Although fugitive sources of data go back to this period, it is difficult to compare the data over a long period of time. Since 1970, however, there has been a movement toward comparability of data. Even so, the data are not broken out between students attending private and public institutions of higher education. Analysis is further impeded by the fact that most federal financial aid is need based. Since this analysis examines macrodata for directional trends, the data presented in Table 1–12 show that federal financial aid to students amounted to $10.2 billion in 1982. Thus, the funds paid to students in higher education through federal

Table 1-12. Major Student Financial Assistance Programs, 1975–82
(*in millions of dollars*).

Year	Amount	Percentage of Total Expenditures
1982	$10,269	14.59%
1980	8,932	15.69%
1975	2,590	7.38%

Source: Compiled from U.S. Bureau of the Census (1984: 154–55).

financial aid in 1982 equaled almost 15 percent of all expenditures by private and public higher education during that year. There were 7,564,200 recipients of federal aid during this period. In 1980 federal aid to students was $8.9 billion or almost 16 percent of the total expenditures for higher education. In 1975, $2.5 billion was spent on federal financial aid. This amount equaled a little over 7 percent of the total expenditures for higher education during that year. Thus in the critical period from 1975 to 1982 federal aid measured in dollars increased by 396 percent and measured in terms of percentage of total expenditures by higher education increased by 100 percent. The number of recipients increased from 3,208,000 in 1975 to 7,561,200 students in 1982. There is no assurance, however, that federal financial aid goes directly to institutions of higher education.

SUMMARY

In terms of public support of higher education, the role of the state governments seems to be consistent; since the 1920s income for institutions of higher education has averaged around 27 percent, and the direction of that support has been upward. Income derived from the federal government, however, has been sporadic and inconsistent. Since 1920 federal support has averaged around 12 percent. In 1950 the percentage income from the federal government peaked at 22 percent and has declined since. The single greatest source of income of institutions of higher education continues to be tuition, fees, and private contributions. Since 1920 this source has averaged 60 percent of the total income of institutions of higher education. From a macro perspective, the most unpredictable partner in the funding of higher education is the federal government, which seems to approach funding of higher education as a pragmatic process based on political considerations rather than comprehensive long-range planning. Higher education is not a high priority for the federal government unless political pressures make it so.

In terms of expenditures by categories since 1930, there have been no dramatic shifts. There have been small incremental changes through time, but the consistency of percentage per category is more impressive than the small changes even over the fifty-two-year time period examined.

The most dramatic change noted in the data was found in the cost per student in public institutions as compared to private institutions. Expenditures in both sectors remained relatively the same from 1900 through 1960. By 1970, however, there was almost a two-to-one ratio between private and public institutions. That ratio has remained relatively constant through 1982. Additional research needs to be undertaken to examine this differential in expenditure per student.

REFERENCES

U.S. Bureau of the Census. 1853. *The Seventh Census of the United States: 1850*. Washington, D.C.: Robert Armstrong, Public Printer.

_____. 1872. *The Ninth Census of the United States: 1870*. Washington, D.C.: U.S. Government Printing Office.

_____. 1954. *Statistical Abstract of the United States: 1954*, 75th ed. Washington, D.C.: U.S. Government Printing Office.

_____. 1964. *Statistical Abstract of the United States: 1964*, 85th ed. Washington, D.C.: U.S. Government Printing Office.

_____. 1975. *Historical Statistics of the United States: Colonial Times to 1970*, pt. I. Washington, D.C.: U.S. Government Printing Office.

_____. 1981. *Statistical Abstract of the United States: 1982–1983*, 103d ed. Washington, D.C.: U.S. Government Printing Office.

_____. 1983. *Statistical Abstract of the United States: 1984*, 104th ed. Washington, D.C.: U.S. Government Printing Office.

_____. 1984. *Statistical Abstract of the United States: 1985*, 105th ed. Washington, D.C.: U.S. Government Printing Office.

2 CHANGING ENROLLMENT TRENDS
Implications for the Future
Financing of Higher Education[1]

Carol Frances

Higher education is changing at an ever-quickening pace, and its outcome is being shaped by forces that are difficult to predict. Within this changing context, however, one feature remains constant: Higher education continues to adapt to change more easily than either its inside defenders or its outside critics have foreseen. The widespread institutional closings and enrollment decreases that were predicted have not occurred.

The dangers of assuming that population trends are reliable predictors of college enrollments are illustrated by comparing the recent data on college age population and college enrollments. The population for ages 18 to 21 peaked in 1980 and is predicted to decline steadily until about 1995. As shown in Table 2–1, the reversal of the trend for the ages 18 to 24 cohort is not expected to begin until a few years later. After the 1980 population peak, college enrollments did not decline as expected. In fact about 150,000 more students were enrolled in 1985 than were enrolled in 1980. Higher education enrollments for the 1985–86 academic year have been estimated to be 12.3 million students. This represents a decline of 218,000 students, or 1.8 percent, from the 1982–83 peak of 12.5 million. Enrollment data for the years from 1970 through 1985 are displayed in Table 2–2.

As an enterprise, higher education has proved to be very resilient, and its current picture appears to be brighter than the pessimists

Table 2-1. Trends in the College-Age Population (*in thousands*).

Year	Ages 18–21	Ages 18–24	Year	Ages 18–21	Ages 18–24
1979	17,156	29,299	1991	14,334	25,337
1980	17,533	30,345	1992	13,763	24,880
1981	17,446	30,410	1993	13,264	24,583
1982	17,306	30,561	1994	13,054	24,139
1983	16,910	29,922	1995	13,069	23,702
1984	16,384	29,374	1996	13,191	23,250
1985	15,669	28,739	1997	13,373	23,278
1986	15,057	27,838	1998	13,817	23,627
1987	14,710	27,248	1999	14,185	24,127
1988	14,709	26,784	2000	14,612	24,600
1989	14,828	26,375	2005	15,629	26,981
1990	14,684	25,794			

Source: U.S. Bureau of the Census (1984a, 1985).

Table 2-2. Trends in College Enrollment, 1970–85 (*opening fall enrollment, numbers in thousands*).

Year	Total	Men	Women
1970	8,581	5,044	3,537
1971	8,949	5,207	3,742
1972	9,215	5,239	3,976
1973	9,602	5,371	4,231
1974	10,224	5,622	4,601
1975	11,185	6,149	5,036
1976	11,012	5,811	5,201
1977	11,286	5,789	5,497
1978	11,259	5,640	5,619
1979	11,570	5,683	5,887
1980	12,097	5,874	6,223
1981	12,372	5,975	6,397
1982	12,426	6,031	6,394
1983	12,465	6,023	6,441
1984	12,241	5,864	6,378
1985	12,247	5,996	6,251

Source: U.S. Department of Education, Center for Statistics (1986).

predicted or the optimists anticipated. Overall, enrollments have remained relatively stable as the college-age cohort has declined, and
institutions have been more responsive to changing demands than
anticipated. However, careful examination by perceptive observers
suggests shadows across the landscape that portend a darker future.

Making demographic projections related to future higher education enrollments has become more of an art than a science. Past
experiences have proved to be insufficient in projecting changes
brought about by student decisions to attend college, student choice
of institution, family preferences, economic growth, and institutional
responsiveness.

This chapter begins by reviewing economic and enrollment trends
and then analyzes changing enrollment trends by age, gender, and
type of institutional control. Interpretations of these data focus on
detecting the direction and momentum of change in higher education
enrollments. It is hoped that these interpretations will prove more
accurate in predicting the future environment of higher education
institutions and their financing than mechanistic extrapolations of
past enrollments and routine demographic projections.

IMPACT OF ECONOMIC CONDITIONS

In analyzing how economic trends affect higher education enrollments, efforts should be made to separate the effects of (1) long-
term trends, (2) short-term economic cycles, and (3) one-time
events. Over the long run, the demand for higher education has increased with the growth of population and income, and in response
to economic and social needs. The land grant universities were created in the latter half of the nineteenth century to support agricultural and industrial development. The community colleges and the
urban universities were established, most in the last thirty to forty
years, to broaden access to higher education and to support urban
and economic development. A forty-year chronology of economic
cycles and political events that have affected higher education enrollments is shown in Figure 2–1.

Even though the long-term patterns show higher education enrollment growth, short-term business expansions and recessions affect
enrollments in some interesting ways. Over the short-term business

Figure 2-1. Chronology of Economic Cycles and Political Events That Affect College Enrollments.

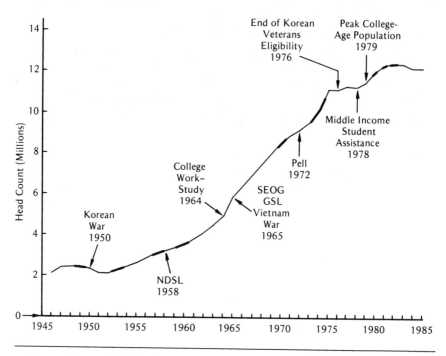

Source: Frances (1986).

cycles, higher education enrollments are countercyclical. For example, during declines in economic activity and increases in unemployment, higher education enrollments generally increase. The enrollment patterns during the eight recessions in the U.S. economy between 1945 and 1985 are indicated in Figure 2-1. The heavier segments of the trend line mark the period from the peak to the trough of the business cycles. (The time periods for the recessions are shown in Table 2-3.) In at least six of these recessions, college enrollment increased. During these periods, total enrollment increased, but the growth was most evident in those colleges and universities that serve part-time students, particularly in the two-year colleges.

The current economic expansion and decline in unemployment rates, which date from 1982, provide partial explanation for the decreases in higher education enrollment over the past few years. As might have been anticipated, the decline has been most noticeable

Table 2-3. Economic Recessions

Peak	Trough	Peak	Trough
November 1948	October 1949	December 1969	November 1970
July 1953	May 1954	November 1973	March 1975
August 1957	April 1958	January 1980	July 1980
April 1960	February 1961	July 1981	November 1982

in two-year colleges. Following this premise, continued economic expansion will put further downward pressure on higher education enrollments, particularly for those students who leave school for full-time employment because of the increased opportunity cost of remaining in school as measured by forgone income.

One-time events that provide some insights into changes in higher education enrollments also are shown in Figure 2-1. For example, the congressional passage of the college work-study program as a part of the federal antipoverty program in 1964, the enactment of equal opportunity programs in 1965, and the expansion of those programs in 1972 clearly preceded increases in higher education enrollment that were greater than the underlying increases in the college-age population. Another one-time event is illustrated by the upsurge of higher education enrollments in 1975 that appear to have been the result of the anticipated termination of education benefits for Korean veterans. Following this upsurge, enrollments flattened in the late 1970s, and analysts, ignoring the impact of the these intervening events, incorrectly interpreted the slowed rate of increase as the beginning of a major downward trend in higher education enrollments.

Congressional actions again appear to have contributed to an increase in higher education enrollments following the extension of subsidized federal guaranteed student loans to middle-income students with the enactment of the Middle Income Student Assistance Act in 1978. Following this increase, higher education enrollments have decreased slightly between 1983 and 1985; contributing events appear to have been the retargeting of federal student financial assistance on lower-income students, decreases in unemployment, and decline in the overall college-age population. The following discussion examines several important developments that may explain why the predicted enrollment decline has been later and far less severe than originally predicted.

EFFECT OF DEMOGRAPHIC CONDITIONS

Higher education enrollment projections based on population projections generally are expected to be the most "certain" projections that can be made; the subjects of the projections, after all, are already born. However, this level of "certainty" often leaves planners unprepared for unexpected new developments brought about by unanticipated events.

For the years 1980 through 1985 revised estimates and projections have been about 400,000 persons higher than the original estimates of the population for ages 18 to 24. The 1985 estimates in the Series P-25 reports published by the U.S. Bureau of the Census were 2.6 percent higher than the projections for the same years published in 1983. These new estimates also moved the peak year in the college-age population from 1979 to 1980.

At least two factors contributed to the new estimate. First, the 1980 population count was higher than the earlier estimates based on year-to-year incremental updates of the population count from the 1970 census. The 1983 estimates had been published before the results of the 1980 census became available.

The second factor was immigration. More than 3 million persons immigrated legally into the United States between 1980 and 1985. In fact, this legal immigration accounted for about one-third of the total population increase in 1984. Conservative estimates suggest that this immigration has resulted in perhaps 200,000 additional higher education students. The assumption is (1) that these immigrants have pursued higher education to gain the language skills necessary for them to apply their previously acquired professional skills and (2) that they also likely will follow the traditional American route of using education to facilitate economic advancement and social assimilation.

Increases in the College-Going Rates

Since 1980 increases have been noted in the proportion of the total population attending higher education institutions, the college-going rate. The college-going rates in the 18 to 21 age group have increased enough to more than offset the assumed decline in college enrollment based on the reduced number of persons in the college-age

Table 2-4. Trends in College-Going Rates, by Age, 1972-84.

Year	Ages 14-17	Ages 18-21	Ages 22-24	Ages 18-24	Ages 25-29	Ages 30-34	Ages 35 and Over
1972	1.8	31.0	13.8	24.0	8.1	4.3	.9
1973	1.2	28.9	13.7	22.7	8.1	4.2	.9
1974	1.8	29.4	14.0	23.2	9.0	5.3	1.2
1975	1.7	31.5	14.9	24.8	9.4	6.0	1.3
1976	1.6	31.4	15.9	25.1	9.2	5.5	1.3
1977	1.6	31.0	15.1	24.5	9.9	6.3	1.5
1978	1.6	29.9	14.7	23.6	8.7	5.8	1.4
1979	1.9	29.7	14.3	23.3	8.8	5.9	1.5
1980	1.5	30.5	14.6	23.8	8.3	6.0	1.3
1981	1.5	32.6	15.3	25.0	8.4	6.4	1.4
1982	1.7	32.5	15.9	25.4	9.0	6.0	1.4
1983	1.8	32.1	15.7	25.0	9.1	6.1	1.5
1984	1.7	33.3	16.4	25.8	8.7	5.9	1.4

Source: Calculated from U.S. Bureau of the Census (1985, 1984b).

segment of the total population (see Table 2-4 and Figure 2-2). The proportion of the 18 to 21 age group in the total population enrolled in higher education institutions increased from a recent low of 29.7 percent in 1979 to a new high of 33.3 percent in 1984.

This actual increase in college-going rates is in contrast to the widely predicted enrollment decrease that was projected because of the diminished real dollar value of federal student assistance programs and the increases in the costs of attending college. While the 2.6 percentage point increase in the college-going rate of those aged 18 to 21 may not appear to be large, the increase is sufficiently large to more than offset the predicted decline in higher education enrollments based on the predicted decline in the college-age population.

The college-going rates reported in Tables 2-4 and 2-5 and in Figures 2-2 and 2-3 have been calculated as straight percentages of the total population enrolled in college. Adjustments have not been made for the number of persons in the age group who have already completed college or for the number of persons who dropped out of high school and are not generally eligible for admission to higher education institutions. From 1980 to 1984 both the traditional college-age and older population groups contributed to the increase in higher education enrollments.

Figure 2-2. Trends in the College-Going Rate.

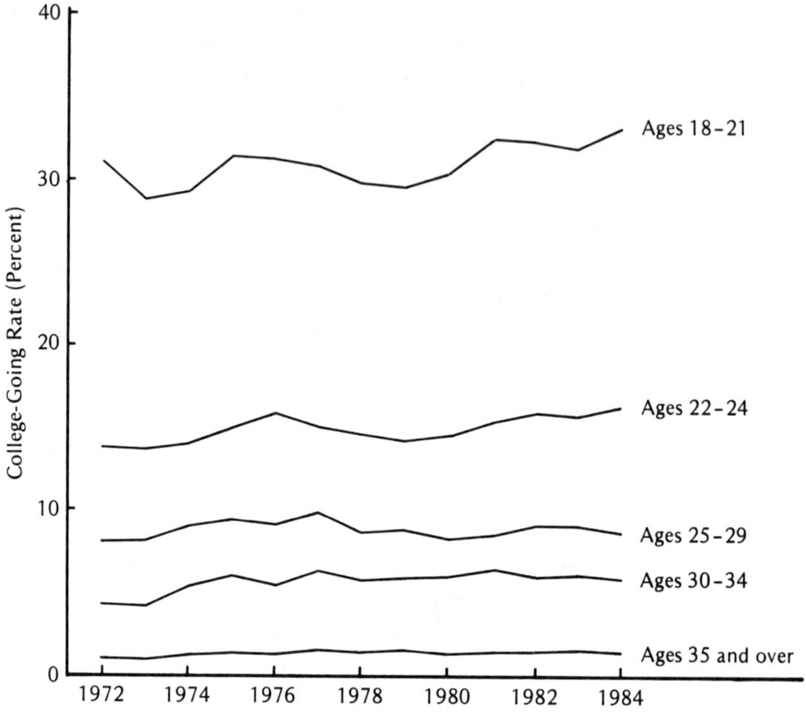

Source: U.S. Bureau of the Census (1984b, 1985).

As shown in Figure 2-3, the college-going rates of both men and women in the 18 to 24 age group increased from 24 percent in 1972 to over 25 percent in 1984. Over the same period of time, the percentage of women attending college in the 18 to 24 age group increased from 21 percent to over 27 percent. In contrast, the proportion of males attending college declined from 27 percent to slightly more than 26 percent.

Between 1980 and 1984, the college-going rates of those ages 25 and over increased even though the rates declined slightly from the midperiod peaks (see Tables 2-4 and 2-5). During this period, both the traditional college-age and older population groups contributed to the increase in higher education enrollments.

Figure 2-3. Trends in the College-Going Rate, Ages 18–24, by Gender.

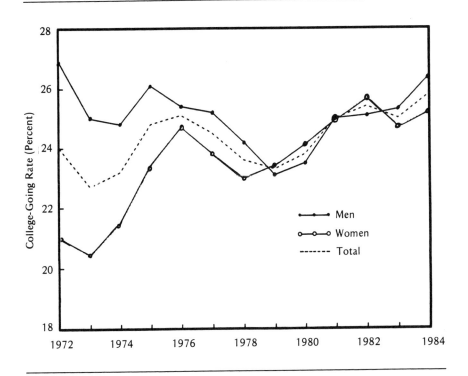

Source: U.S. Bureau of the Census (1984a, 1984b, unpublished data).

Trends in Enrollment by Gender and Age

Dramatic changes have occurred in the composition of higher education enrollment in recent years. An analysis of enrollment increase data by gender indicates that from 1972 to 1980 women accounted for 91 percent of the increase in enrollment and men accounted for only 9 percent (see Table 2-6). In contrast, from 1980 to 1983 (the latest year for which enrollment data by gender and age were available) women accounted for only 38 percent of the increase, while men accounted for 62 percent (see Table 2-7).

Table 2-5. Trends in Population and in College-Going Rates, by Age Group, 1980-84.

	Ages 14–17	Ages 18–21	Ages 22–24	Ages 25–29	Ages 30–34	Ages 35 and Over
Population						
1980	16,139	17,533	12,812	19,795	17,814	96,074
1984	14,707	16,384	12,999	21,434	19,674	103,510
College-going rates						
1980	1.5	30.5	14.6	8.3	6.0	1.3
1984	1.7	33.3	16.4	8.7	5.9	1.4
Percentage change, 1980–84						
Population	−8	−6	+1	+8	+10	+7
College-going rates	+13	+9	+12	+4	−0.1	+7

Source: Calculated from U.S. Bureau of the Census (1984a, 1984b).

Table 2-6. Distribution of the Increase in College Enrollment by Gender and Age, 1972-80.

Age Group	Number (thousands)			Percentage		
	Total	Men	Women	Total	Men	Women
All age groups	2,291	212	2,080	100	9	91
Below college age						
14-17	-46	-45	-1	-2	-2	—
College age						
18-21	562	79	483	24	3	21
22-24	409	-9	418	18	—	18
18-24	971	70	901	42	3	39
Over college age						
25 and over	1,367	187	1,181	60	8	52

Source: U.S. Bureau of the Census (1984b: 17).

Table 2-7. Distribution of the Increase in College Enrollment by Gender and Age, 1980-83.

Age Group	Number (thousands)			Percentage		
	Total	Men	Women	Total	Men	Women
All age groups	933	580	353	100	62	38
Below college age						
14-17	11	12	-1	2	2	—
College age						
18-21	79	35	44	8	3	4
22-24	172	181	-9	18	20	-1
18-24	251	216	35	26	23	3
Over college age						
25 and over	673	352	319	72	37	34

Source: U.S. Bureau of the Census (1984b: 7).

Analysis of the 1972–80 enrollment increase data by age showed that students ages 25 and over accounted for 72 percent of the increase in enrollment, while students ages 24 and under accounted for 28 percent of the increase. In contrast, between 1980 and 1983 the share of the enrollment increase accounted for by students ages 25 and over dropped from 72 to 60 percent, and the increase attributable to students ages 24 and under increased from 28 to 40 percent.

When the age and gender data were integrated, the share of the enrollment increase accounted for by women older than the 18 to 24 age group was 52 percent from 1972 to 1980 but dropped to 34 percent from 1980 to 1983. In contrast, the share of the enrollment increase attributable to men older than the traditional college age group increased from 8 to 37 percent. Thus, one major new trend in college enrollments is that male students ages 25 and over constituted the largest source of enrollment increase from 1980 to 1983.

Nontraditional Students

Nontraditional students continue to account for the preponderant share of the growth in enrollment at traditional higher education institutions. Of the increase in higher education enrollments from 1976 to 1983, two-thirds of the enrollment was attributable to students ages 25 and over. (In contrast, students in the traditional college-age group account for a sizable share of the growth in the nontraditional proprietary institutions.)

Nontraditional students often are defined to include students in the traditional college-age group who are attending college on a part-time basis, and students older than the traditional college-age group whether attending college full-time or part-time. One question for higher education is whether the enrollment decisions of nontraditional students are driven by academic or financial considerations, or by a combination of the two. Because college costs are rising faster than the ability of students to pay for college, the enrollment decisions of nontraditional students are probably constrained primarily by financial necessities.

Few institutions have gathered and analyzed data about the motivations, college attendance patterns, or career aspirations of their nontraditional students. Some students may be pursuing avocational interests, but others may be enrolled in job-related courses or may be seeking to acquire skills that will enable them to enter a more rewarding occupation.

Enrollment Splicing

Some institutions may be experiencing enrollment fluctuations for economic reasons. The availability of higher education courses at various prices appears to have contributed to the development of a new practice referred to as "enrollment splicing." Some students appear to be dropping out of their primary institution and enrolling for general education courses or electives at community colleges or other lower-cost institutions. On completion of the courses, they then reenroll in their primary institution and transfer the credits. This practice is in contrast to those students who enroll for one or two years in a community college or low-tuition public university and then transfer to a more prestigious institution to complete their degree.

These students are engaged in innovative financial and educational strategies designed to increase the likelihood of achieving their educational goals. Not only can they "splice" lower-cost courses into their degree program, but they also can "shop" for courses that are more compatible with their interests.

Enrollment Trends by Sector

Private higher education institutions were predicted to bear the brunt of the enrollment decline projected for the late 1970s. The contention was that the impact on the public institutions would be reduced because of their public support base. As shown in Table 2–8, comparative rates of enrollment increases from 1976 through 1983 were greater in four-year private institutions than in four-year public institutions.

The enrollment increases in private institutions were greater in all types of student counts, for both men and women, and at all levels of study. Among public institutions, an actual decline was reported in the enrollments of graduate and unclassified students. The data suggest a shift of graduate students from public to private universi-

Table 2-8. Comparative Rates of Increase in Enrollment by Sector, 1976-83 (*opening fall enrollment*).

	Four-Year Institutions	
	Public	*Private*
Head count	6.8	14.7
Full-time equivalent	7.0	12.6
Full-time	7.2	11.2
Part-time	6.0	24.2
Men	0.9	4.6
Women	13.4	27.3
Undergraduate	10.0	13.8
Graduate	-4.8	16.4
First professional	12.2	15.5
Unclassified	-1.4	18.4

Source: Frances (1986). Based on computerized data generated by Paula Knepper, Applied Systems Institute, using HEGIS data.

ties. From 1976 to 1983 graduate student enrollment at public universities declined by 30,000, and graduate student enrollment at private universities increased by 50,000. Further analysis of these data might be beneficial because, as illustrated by the previous discussion, consistent trends were not maintained over the time period and differences were noted by the gender and age of the students. (See Chapter 5 for a more comprehensive discussion of private higher education.)

Enrollments in proprietary institutions are growing faster than in any other sector of postsecondary education. As new data become available on enrollments in proprietary institutions, analysts may find that higher education enrollment reports will be more meaningful if these institutions are treated as a third sector rather than included, without differentiation, as a subset of private institutions.

Proprietary institutions are working with the Department of Education in the development of the new Integrated Postsecondary Education Data System (IPEDS), which will expand the current data reporting system to include these institutions in the national surveys. Many long-established and successful proprietary institutions are relatively small when compared with other private or public institutions. Even though missions may differ among the different types of institutions, interesting research questions may be posed concerning minimum feasible size and economies of scale.

IMPLICATIONS FOR LONG-RANGE PLANNING FOR HIGHER EDUCATION

Long-range planning is not very useful in a turbulent world. Where it focuses attention inward on an institution's own aspirations instead of outward on the needs of the surrounding society, long-range planning can do more harm than good. As a result of their inward focus, planners in higher education do not have a very good record in making predictions. Instead of engaging in fruitless attempts to make predictions more accurate by refining models, it may be wiser to try to improve the ability to anticipate new developments. Institutional researchers could concentrate more usefully on scanning information about the outside world to pick up signals helpful in anticipating new developments. The colleges and universities then would be better able to respond, where appropriate, creatively—a style more characteristic of entrepreneurs than of planners. Organizationally, this may mean a management style that relies less on reporting structures and more on working relationships.

SUMMARY

In contrast to the predictions for higher education enrollments that were forecast for the 1980s, higher education institutions have maintained their enrollments. However, analyses of enrollment data reveal short-term shifts in the age and gender distribution of students. Further, this stability in higher education enrollments masks declines and increases in enrollments among the various types of public, private, and proprietary postsecondary education institutions.

Higher education enrollment changes suggest that the most profound influences may be external forces rather than institutional decisions or demographic cohorts. These forces include public policy decisions to form institutions and programs as a response to perceived national, political, or economic interests. The emergence since the mid-1960s of a complex set of federal student assistance programs provides a somewhat different example of the manner in which public policy decisions can affect higher education enrollments. Changes in the nation's industrial base and economic fluctuations also influence higher education enrollments.

Traditional projections of higher education enrollments based on demographic trends have concentrated on the decline in the total college-age population and have not considered increases in the population cohort ages 25 and over. Persons in the older group are entering college for the first time, and data suggest that the more that education people have, the more education they seek. Under this premise, increasing levels of educational attainment by the population do not lead to saturation of the demand for education but rather may expand the demand for education.

For over 100 years, changes in the employment needs of the U.S. economy have influenced higher education institutions in a variety of ways. For example, recent employment fluctuations in the aviation and space industry have contributed to periodic increases and declines in the demand for engineers. As the number of persons employed in "hard goods" industries declines and as the number employed in the service economy increases, some have predicted that the level of training required for emerging jobs may decline because of reduced demand for certain types of postsecondary education. These predictions likely will prove wrong.

The educational choices of persons ages 25 and over are important factors in the outlook for higher education. One scenario is that the period of higher education enrollment increases will soon be over because persons in this age group have fulfilled their educational aspirations. Another scenario is that women in the ages 25 and over group will continue to seek additional higher education as a means of achieving equality in the workplace. A third scenario is that the increasing number of women who are from two-income households or who are single parents will contribute to continuing efforts by women to pursue higher education. An additional scenario is that new persons who enter this age group will seek higher education to achieve upward employment mobility or personal fulfillment.

As they contemplate the future of their institutions, managers of higher education institutions are challenged to integrate current realities with external events. Increased enrollments, increased tuitions, and decreased inflation have eased financial pressure on colleges and universities since 1980. However, the longer-term financial outlook may be much darker, when deferred obligations become due. There are a growing number of these problems:

1. Although total enrollments have remained steady, enrollments of low-income and minority students have declined. This may further divide the "rich" and the "poor" in the United States.

2. Since 1980, more students have been required to borrow to finance their college educations. When debt burdens on students become excessive, institutions likely will respond by reducing costs to students, either by smaller tuition increases or by providing more institutionally funded student aid. This will put additional financial pressures on the institutions.

3. In terms of real purchasing power, faculty salary levels are below those of the early 1970s in terms of real purchasing power. Institutions will be pressured to increase salaries, and thus increase tuitions. Underfunded retirement systems will require a larger share of state resources, thus reducing funds available to the institutions.

All of these factors contribute to intergenerational shifts in fiscal responsibility for higher education. Thus, the future financing of higher education will depend not only on economics and demographics but also on politics and ethics.

NOTES

1. This chapter is based on a special report prepared by Carol Frances for the Postsecondary Education Statistics Division, Center for Statistics, U.S. Department of Education (March 1986).

REFERENCES

Frances, Carol. 1986. "New Trends in College Enrollments." Prepared for U.S. Department of Education, Center for Statistics, Washington, D.C.

U.S. Bureau of the Census. 1984a. "Projection of the Population of the United States by Age, Sex, and Race, 1983–2080." *Population Characteristics*, Series P-25, No. 952. Washington, D.C.: U.S. Government Printing Office.

_____. 1984b. "School Enrollment—Social and Economic Characteristics of Students." *Population Characteristics*, Series P-20, No. 394. Washington, D.C.: U.S. Government Printing Office.

_____. 1985. "Estimate of the Population of the United States by Age, Sex, and Race, 1980 to 1984." *Population Characteristics*, Series P-25, No. 965. Washington, D.C.: U.S. Government Printing Office.

3 REVENUE SOURCES IN HIGHER EDUCATION
Trends and Analysis

O. Homer Erekson

Financial decisionmakers in higher education are facing unsettling questions as they attempt to achieve financial stability for their institutions while maintaining vital academic programs. Financial concerns arise from uncertainties about all of the major sources of revenue for higher education.

With a 21 percent decline in the 18- to 24-year-old population expected over the next decade, enrollment in higher education is expected to decrease (Carnegie Foundation 1985), which will cause tuition revenue to decline. In addition, federal government support for higher education is likely to continue to decline because of federal deficit problems, necessitating greater support from state and local governments and from voluntary sources.

Careful financial planning in higher education can be facilitated by an understanding of the financial structure of higher education. This chapter describes the financial structure of higher education and analyzes trends in various sources of revenue. The basic sources of revenue in higher education are discussed, basic trends for each revenue source are examined, and then differences in sources of revenue for private and public institutions and for universities, other four-year colleges, and two-year institutions are examined. Each source of revenue is scrutinized for significant determinants and patterns for each source. Finally, summary remarks comment on the significant findings about the financial structure of higher education.

THE FINANCIAL STRUCTURE
OF HIGHER EDUCATION

Changes in the basic sources of revenue for institutions of higher education can be traced over time. The data for various types of institutions for this analysis were taken primarily from the Higher Education General Information Survey (HEGIS), the most comprehensive set of financial survey statistics for higher education. HEGIS information was used directly from the survey for the 1982 fiscal year and for several years as reported in a study by Nelson (1978).

Sources of Revenue

The sources of current-fund revenue for private and public institutions are reported in Table 3-1, which shows the percentage of total revenue contributed by each source. Sources are divided into tuition and fees (all tuition and fees assessed against students for current operating purposes, including tuition and fee remissions or exemptions); federal, state, and local government support (appropriations by a legislative body for current operating expenses and grants and contracts for specific research projects or other types of programs); gifts, grants, and contracts (private gifts, grants, and contracts directly related to instruction, research, or public service); endowment income (restricted and unrestricted income of endowment and similar funds); sales (revenues from sales of goods and services incidental to the conduct of instruction, research, or public service, revenues from the sales and services of hospitals operated by the institution, and other revenue not covered elsewhere); and auxiliary enterprise income (all revenues generated by the auxiliary enterprise operations of an institution).

Private Institutions. Private institutions of higher education traditionally have relied quite heavily on revenue from tuition and fees and, more recently, on income from the federal government. From 1939–40 to 1971–72 tuition and fees, state and local government support, and gifts, grants, and contracts accounted for a fairly steady share of the revenues of private institutions. Over this same period, private institutions relied increasingly on federal government support and income from sales, while relying less on endowment income and revenues from auxiliary enterprises.

Table 3–1. Current-Fund Revenue of Private and Public Institutions of Higher Education, by Source, as a Percentage of Total Revenue.

	1939–40[a]	1949–50[a]	1959–60[a]	1971–72[a]	1981–82[e] All	Sectarian	Nonsectarian
Private[b]							
Tuition and fees	40.4	41.6	32.8	35.7	55.6	47.8	62.5
Government, total	2.9	12.2	23.1	25.8	8.2	8.1	8.2
Federal[c]	0.7	8.6	19.4	19.8	6.4	6.6	6.2
State and local[c]	2.1	2.4	1.4	1.6	1.8	1.5	2.1
Gifts, grants, and contracts	9.8	8.7	11.7	9.6	11.2	15.4	7.4
Endowment	17.9	7.7	7.4	4.6	4.2	4.4	4.0
Sales	5.6	6.5	6.8	10.0	5.3	4.8	5.7
Auxiliary Enterprises	23.6	23.3	18.2	14.0	15.7	19.6	12.2
Public[d]							
Tuition and fees	15.5	18.5	10.2	13.6	17.3		
Government, total	57.6	52.3	63.6	64.3	68.2		
Federal[c]	10.3	9.6	16.6	15.4	6.8		
State and local[c]	40.5	37.4	41.3	40.9	61.3		
Gifts, grants, and contracts	1.4	1.6	2.6	1.8	1.0		
Endowment	1.9	0.7	0.6	0.3	0.2		
Sales	6.8	7.0	6.2	8.0	4.0		
Auxiliary enterprises	16.6	19.9	16.6	11.7	9.3		

a. Figures for 1939–40 to 1971–72 were taken from Nelson (1978).
b. 1,174 private institutions in the sample.
c. Federal and state and local categories for 1939–40 to 1971–72 do not include student income.
d. 1,421 public institutions in the sample.
e. Source: Higher Education General Information Survey (1982).

Over the next decade, some striking changes appeared in the financial structure of private institutions. Most notably, federal support declined from 19.8 percent of total revenue in 1971–72 to 6.4 percent of total revenue in 1981–82. Most of this decrease in federal support was offset by an increase in revenue from tuition and fees and to a lesser extent by income from auxiliary enterprises and private gifts. While private institutions received 35.7 percent of their revenue from tuition and fees in 1971–72, this figure had risen to 55.6 percent in 1981–82.

The reliance of nonsectarian private institutions on tuition and fees had risen to 62.5 percent in 1981–82. Although sectarian private institutions also experienced an increase in the reliance on tuition and fee income to 47.8 percent, increases occurred in private gifts, grants, and contracts (most likely from religious denominations) and in auxiliary enterprise income (which may reflect a slow movement back to the traditional model of a residential college at private religious institutions).

Public Institutions. Public institutions had a distinctly different financial structure than private institutions. Public institutions relied heavily on government appropriations (receiving two-thirds support from government) and significantly less on tuition and fees and on gifts, grants, and contracts. The other categories of support for public institutions—including gifts, grants, and contracts, endowment income, and sales income—have contributed fairly steady shares to current-fund revenue between 1939–40 and 1981–82. A rather steady decline occurred in the share of revenue from auxiliary enterprises. However, the most striking changes in revenue support occurred in government appropriations. State and local appropriations accounted for approximately 40 percent of public institution revenue from 1939–40 to 1971–72, while federal government appropriations rose from 10.3 percent in 1939–40 to 15.4 percent in 1971–72. Like the private institutions, public institutions experienced a significant decline in the share of revenue received from federal appropriations from 1971–72 to 1981–82; the federal share declined more than 50 percent. However, unlike the private institutions, the public institutions turned to increased state and local government support, which had risen to 61.3 percent of total revenue by 1981–82.

Type of Institution. Comparison of the financial structures of private and public institutions has identified important differences in their revenue sources. Other differences in the financial structures of these institutions are highlighted when institutions are grouped into universities, four-year colleges, and two-year institutions as shown in Table 3–2.

For private institutions, the share of revenue attributed to tuition and fees in 1981–82 was largest for two-year institutions, 68.4 percent of total revenue, and smallest for universities, 40.0 percent of total revenue. This pattern has remained relatively stable over the last thirty years. The pattern for government appropriations differed markedly among the different private institutions as well. Private universities and four-year colleges experienced significant growth in the reliance on federal government funding in the 1960s and have suffered significant declines in the share of federal government revenue during the most recent decade. The federal share of revenues for private universities has remained roughly double that for four-year colleges for the entire period shown. On the other hand, two-year institutions have relied increasingly on federal funds with the share of federal government rising from 0.9 percent in 1959–60 to 4.6 percent in 1981–82.

State and local funding was a much smaller part of revenue for all private institutions; four-year and two-year institutions increased their reliance on state and local funding slightly while universities kept basically a constant share. Reliance on private gifts and on endowment income has remained small for all three types of institutions. However, over the last decade, four-year colleges experienced an increase in the share of revenue attributable to gifts, while universities experienced an increase in the share of revenue from endowment income. While sales have been a fluctuating source of revenue for four-year colleges, universities and two-year institutions experienced significant growth in sales. In fact, private universities received 19.0 percent of their revenue from sales in 1981–82, making sales the second-largest source of revenue for private universities. This growth in the importance of sales for both of these types of institutions likely resulted from increased public service outreach and, for universities, from increased revenues resulting from rapidly rising costs for hospital and other health services. All three types of private institutions experienced a decrease in the revenue share

Table 3-2. Current-Fund Revenue of Private and Public Institutions of Higher Education, by Source, as a Percentage of Total Revenue.

	Universities[b]			Four-Year Colleges[c]			Two-Year Institutions[d]		
	1959-60[a]	1971-72[a]	1981-82[e]	1959-60[a]	1971-72[a]	1981-82[e]	1959-60[a]	1971-72[a]	1981-82[e]
Private									
Tuition and fees	28.1	26.8	40.0	36.3	43.9	51.9	48.3	50.0	68.4
Government, total	31.6	35.8	15.9	15.9	16.8	8.1	1.6	10.3	6.7
Federal	27.0	29.1	13.5	13.3	11.5	6.5	0.9	3.8	4.6
State and local	2.4	2.2	2.5	0.5	1.1	1.6	0.0	1.1	2.1
Gifts, grants, and contracts	9.6	8.9	8.0	13.6	10.3	12.6	14.0	11.9	8.1
Endowment	8.1	5.4	6.1	7.0	4.1	4.9	2.5	1.6	1.7
Sales	9.6	13.5	19.0	4.4	6.9	4.5	1.9	2.3	4.6
Auxiliary enterprises	12.7	9.6	10.9	22.6	18.1	18.0	31.5	24.0	10.6
Public									
Tuition	9.5	13.1	14.6	11.9	14.8	18.3	10.7	13.5	17.2
Government, total	62.6	60.2	56.7	63.6	64.8	62.3	75.1	79.1	71.9
Federal	20.3	19.9	12.9	10.8	11.1	6.4	1.4	6.3	6.4
State and local	40.0	37.9	43.8	48.1	47.2	55.8	73.2	70.2	65.5
Gifts, grants, and contracts	3.5	2.7	3.5	0.7	1.1	1.3	0.4	0.3	0.5
Endowment	0.8	0.5	0.7	0.1	0.1	0.3	0.2	0.1	0.1
Sales	7.9	11.3	9.7	3.1	4.9	3.7	1.4	1.3	3.6
Auxiliary enterprises	15.6	12.1	14.7	20.6	14.3	14.2	12.2	5.9	6.7

a. Figures for 1959-60 and 1971-72 were taken from Nelson (1978).
b. There were sixty-two private universities and ninety-four public universities in the sample.
c. There were 803 private four-year colleges and 399 public four-year colleges in the sample.
d. There were 309 private two-year institutions and 928 public two-year institutions in the sample.
e. Source: Higher Education General Information Survey (1982).

attributable to auxiliary enterprises. This decline may be related to a decline in the residential college as a model for higher education and the related entrance of the private sector into the food and housing market for college students.

For the public universities, notable differences existed in the funding structure for the three main types of institutions. For all three types of institutions, tuition and fees have become an increasingly important source of revenue, though significantly less so than for private institutions. The share of tuition and fees in 1981–82 varied from a minimum of 14.6 percent for universities to a maximum of 18.3 percent for four-year colleges. Naturally, for public institutions, government appropriations accounted for the main source of revenue for all three types of institutions, comprising more than 50 percent of total revenue.

When different levels of government support are examined, some clear similarities to the revenue structure of private institutions become apparent. The share of revenue attributable to federal appropriations decreased between 1959–60 and 1981–82 for universities and four-year colleges. However, the federal share increased for two-year institutions. Nonetheless, the federal share for universities was still approximately double that for four-year colleges or two-year institutions.

The major source of revenue for public institutions was state and local government appropriations; those appropriations increased for universities and four-year colleges and decreased slightly for two-year institutions over the past two decades. However, two-year institutions depended on state and local government appropriations for two-thirds of their revenue. Auxiliary enterprises represented a generally declining source of revenue for all three types of institutions over the past two decades. The other sources of revenue (gifts, endowment income, and sales) have been rather constant and small proportions of revenue for all types of institutions; the only significant source of revenue was sales for public universities. However, over the last decade even sales have been a declining source of revenue for universities.

Revenues per Student

The analysis above, which examines the financial structure of higher education in terms of the proportion of revenue from each source, prevents comparison of the level of dependence on each source by institutions of higher education. Table 3–3 presents revenues per student for the various categories of institutions for 1981–82 for several of the main sources of revenue presented above. Revenues per student may reflect better the ability of institutions to provide academic quality as this method controls for enrollment differences among types of institutions.

When all private and public universities are compared, the importance of controlling for enrollment differences becomes apparent. Mean total current-fund revenue for public universities in 1981–82 was $29,575,069, while the similar figure for private universities was $18,201,622. However, as shown in Table 3–3, revenue per student for public institutions was $3,820 while that for private institutions was $7,908. The higher revenue per student for private institutions was attributable to tuition and fees per student, which were more than five times larger for private institutions; to federal government revenue per student, which was two-and-one-half times larger for private institutions; to private gifts, grants, and contracts per student, which were approximately eighteen times larger for private institutions; and to endowment income per student, which was almost forty times larger for private institutions. The only category shown where public institutions received more was state and local government revenue per capita; public institutions received twelve times as much of this revenue per student. Religiously affiliated institutions had a similar pattern to the more comprehensive category of all private institutions.

Useful insights also can be gleaned from examining revenue per student for each of the three types of institutions. Whether the focus is on all institutions or private and public institutions, quite similar patterns emerged. Universities received significantly higher revenue per student than four-year colleges or two-year institutions. This difference can be attributed largely to significantly higher tuition and fees per student and higher federal government revenue per student.

Universities were able to charge higher tuition and fees as the demand for their services is likely to be tuition (price) inelastic. That is, as tuition increases there is not a statistically significant change in enrollment in universities. McPherson (1978) has offered empirical evidence to support this claim and has suggested that this inelasticity may be explained because universities have strong reputations in academic quality and employment placement, serve the high-income

Table 3-3. Revenue Sources per Student, by Type of Institution, 1981–82.

	Revenue	Tuition	Federal	State/Local	Gifts	Endowments
Public	3,820	594	316	2,206	55	15
Private	7,908	3,384	790	187	992	592
Religious	6,317	2,851	434	87	982	316
Universities	12,395	2,565	2,016	2,458	834	516
Four-year colleges	7,400	2,547	650	1,181	801	500
Two-year colleges	3,140	1,095	227	1,255	122	28
Private universities	17,616	4,670	3,184	406	1,588	1,192
Private four-year colleges	8,315	3,383	780	209	1,159	739
Private two-year colleges	4,900	3,127	333	86	438	92
Public universities	8,951	1,177	1,246	3,811	336	70
Public four-year colleges	5,557	866	388	3,136	79	21
Public two-year colleges	2,554	418	191	1,644	16	7

Source: Higher Education General Information Survey (1982).

student distribution, rely on a larger market area for their students, and tend to be located near areas of dense population concentration. Universities received larger revenue per student from the federal government to support the research mission of these institutions. In addition, universities benefitted from higher private gifts, grants, and contracts per student and higher endowment income per student. In comparison with the two-year institutions, the four-year colleges had a distinct advantage in every category. In fact, the only strong source of revenue for two-year public institutions was state and local government revenue and for two-year private institutions was tuition and fee revenue.

THE ROLE OF GOVERNMENT IN FINANCING HIGHER EDUCATION

Governments have provided significant proportions of revenue for public and private institutions of higher education. This support, however, has been relatively unstable because of the growth of public institutions, the declining importance of the private sector, and significant changes in the support of the federal government.

Government provision and support of higher education have been justified in two ways. First, in its pursuit of allocative efficiency, government must support higher education so that it is not underprovided. Understanding this argument requires identifying three main sources of benefits for higher education. First, students at colleges and universities receive consumption benefits from higher education when they attend those institutions. Second, students receive investment benefits from higher education from the returns to the human capital investment in that education. Both consumption and investment benefits include externalities such as increased social mobility, improved political leadership or good citizenship, and an improved and more highly employed labor force (Hansen and Weisbrod 1969). To the extent that individuals do not appropriate the full and exclusive benefits of higher education, there would be underprovision of higher education. According to the classic remedy the level of government that can capture the variation in voter preferences while internalizing the externalities subsidizes the good or service in question (Oates 1972). In this case, the best case can be made for having state and local governments subsidize higher education because the benefit region for the externalities is likely primarily limited to a state.

A third type of activity in higher education that produces significant externalities is research and development. Research in higher education presumably leads to increases in knowledge or to advancements in technology that often have attributes of a public good (that is, a good that is equally available to a large group of persons and whose returns are not always capable of being fully appropriated by the researcher); collective subsidization of the good is appropriate to achieve efficiency. Although at times this will take the form of private industry support, in some cases it would be necessary for the federal government or state and local governments to intervene.[1]

A second justification for government provision and support of higher education argues that higher education can be used to distribute income more equitably. According to this view lower-income students can achieve upward mobility through government subsidization of their education. Although the success of this redistributive objective is debatable, traditional fiscal federalism theory argues for federal government involvement in redistribution to discourage migration of wealthier individuals to avoid taxation (Oates 1972).

A more positive argument is that higher education sometimes is funded by government because legislators, particularly at the state level, increase their chances for reelection by supporting higher education. Coughlin and Erekson (1986) offer evidence consistent with this view; state aid to higher education seems to be significantly determined by improved quality attributes of an institution and redistributive efforts by a state legislature.[2]

Federal Government Financing

As noted earlier one striking change in the financial structure of higher education over the last quarter century has been the declining share of revenue from the federal government. For private institutions most of this decline has been replaced by tuition and fee income, while for the public institutions, state and local government revenue seem to have replaced the federal revenue.

One way to understand changes in federal government support of higher education is to examine federal government support of research and development at colleges and universities and federal student aid. Research support from the federal government has been an important, albeit unstable, source of support for higher education. Table 3-4 shows how dependent higher education has been on the federal government for research support. Federal government funding has accounted for approximately two-thirds of total expenditures for research and development by universities and colleges since 1953. However, the federal share has declined over the last twenty years from a peak average of 71.3 percent from 1963-72 to 65.4 percent in 1982. The same period has seen a steady increase in the share from institutional funds and industry.

Between 1979 and 1982 federal research and development funding decreased in real terms at an average annual rate of 3 percent. Between 1982 and 1985 funding increased at an average annual rate of 9 percent. However, federal funding for research and development is expected to decrease by about 5 percent between 1985 and 1986 (National Science Foundation 1985).

In addition to fluctuations in the level of federal support, changes occurred in the composition of that support. From 1967-68 to 1973-74 significant growth occurred in applied research support, while the share of basic research fell from 75.6 percent to 69.2 percent (Nelson 1978). In fact, over the decade 1975-85 federal research and development funds that went to basic research increased from half to nearly two-thirds (National Science Foundation 1985).

This change in the composition of support may have differential implications for public and private institutions. Nelson (1978) noted that from 1968 to 1973 there was a shift in federal research and development funds from the private sector toward the public sector. She hypothesized that the rapid growth in applied research, which was concentrated in public universities, may explain part of the shift.[3] With a semblance of revival in federal funding of basic research, there may be a coincident shift back to increased relative funding of the private sector.

The other major source of federal government aid to colleges and universities is student aid. During the early 1970s there was a major shift from federal funding for research, traineeships, and fellowships toward student aid. Excluding social security and the GI bill, federal student aid grew 294 percent between 1974 and 1981, while federal spending on research in higher education grew only 16 percent (O'Neill and Simms 1983). As shown in Table 3-5, two-thirds of federal student aid in 1983 went to two direct student aid programs:

Table 3-4. Research and Development Expenditures at Universities and Colleges, by Source of Fund, Fiscal Years 1953–82 (*dollars in millions*).

	1953–62		1963–72		1973–82		1982	
	Amount	*Percentage*	*Amount*	*Percentage*	*Amount*	*Percentage*	*Amount*	*Percentage*
Total	493	100.0	1,931	100.0	4,724	100.0	7,261	100.0
Federal government	299	60.6	1,376	71.3	3,160	66.9	4,749	65.4
State and local governments	67	13.6	183	9.5	418	8.8	586	8.1
Industry	33	6.7	53	2.7	177	3.7	326	4.5
Institutional funds	53	10.8	191	9.9	633	13.4	1,098	15.1
All other sources	42	8.5	128	6.6	337	7.1	503	6.9

Amounts shown are averages.
Source: National Science Foundation (1984: 322).

Table 3-5. Federal Student Assistance in Higher Education, Selected Fiscal Years 1974–83.

	Current Dollars in Billions			
	1974	1978	1981	1983[a]
Pell grants	0.0	1.6	2.5	2.3
Guaranteed loans	0.3	0.5	2.3	3.7
Campus-based[b]	0.5	0.8	1.4	1.1
Social security	0.8	1.4	2.0	0.8
Veterans	2.6	2.7	1.8	1.2
Total	4.3	7.6	10.0	9.1

a. Baseline projection based on policies in the Omnibus Budget Reconciliation Act of 1981 and assumptions by the Congressional Budget Office.

b. Includes supplemental opportunity grants, work-study, direct loans, and state student incentive grants.

Source: O'Neill and Simms (1983: table 11–5, 353).

Pell grants (Basic Educational Opportunity Grants) and Guaranteed Student Loan programs. These programs have the advantage that aid may be targeted to particular students, presumably low-income students.

However, in practice these programs have generously supported students from higher-income groups. Among four-year private institutions, 37 percent of undergraduates received Pell grants in 1979–80, while the corresponding number for public universities was 26 percent. Moreover, in 1979, 40 percent of Pell grants received by freshmen went to middle- and upper-income students (O'Neill and Simms 1983). The Guaranteed Student Loan program, initially targeted for students from families with incomes below $15,000 has been liberalized so that it too served large numbers of middle- and upper-income families.

The campus-based programs—Supplemental Education Opportunity Grants and National Direct Student Loan programs—provide aid to students through the institutions. The College Work-Study program is a public employment program. None of these programs is targeted toward low-income students. Moreover, the social security program and the veterans program are obviously not intended for use as redistributive programs favoring low-income students. Therefore, the effectiveness of past federal student aid programs might be questioned if their intention is to provide disproportionate educational opportunities for low-income students. A reasonable view is that much of federal aid in the past has resulted in a windfall gain in income to families of students who would attend college without federal aid.

In response to large federal deficits and in response to mistargeting of student aid, significant reductions in federal student aid and revisions in existing programs have been proposed. The Gramm-Rudman-Hollings Act calls for a reduction in federal spending of $11.7 billion in 1986 with a 4.3 percent reduction in nondefense programs. As a result federal spending on student aid would be reduced by approximately $244 million for federal fiscal year 1986, and 68,000 Pell grants targeted especially for middle-income students would be eliminated (Palmer 1986). In addition, revisions in the Guaranteed Student Loan program increased the origination fee required to secure a loan and would decrease some of the interest rate advantage currently given to lenders.

State Financing of Higher Education

Historically, state governments have been the major source of revenue for public higher education.[4] Although some funds support student aid programs, most funding goes for institutional support. The public higher education share of state tax revenues changed very little between 1977–78 and 1983–84 (Halstead 1984). As shown in Table 3–6, higher education received approximately 10.5 percent of total state budgets during most of this period. An examination of state support per student makes it more apparent that states have supported higher education at a stable level of approximately $1,200 per student (after adjusting for inflation) since 1979.

Examining nationwide averages, however, obscures important differences between states. Table 3–7 presents 1985–86 data by state on total expenditures for higher education, expenditures per $1,000 of personal income, and the ten-year percentage change in real expenditures. Considerable variation exists in these figures. Total expenditures were highest in California, which spent $4,209,000,000 on higher education, and lowest in Vermont, which spent only $44,618,000.

The maximum amount of support per $1,000 of income was $26.98 in Alaska and the minimum expenditure was $7.80 by Vermont. The largest increase in ten-year change occurred in Alaska

Table 3-6. State Support of Higher Education, 1978-84.

Year	Share of State Budget	State Support per Student	
		Nominal	Real[a]
1977-78	10.3%	$2,547	$1,303
1978-79	—	—	—
1979-80	10.6%	3,055	1,238
1980-81	11.0%	3,250	1,193
1981-82	10.9%	3,490	1,207
1982-83	10.4%	3,600	1,206
1983-84	10.4%	3,850	1,237

a. Real figures in 1967 dollars.
Source: Halstead (1984).

Table 3-7. State Appropriations to Higher Education, 1985-86.

	Total Amount (thousands)	Rank	Per $1,000 Personal Income		Ten-Year Percentage Change	
			Amount	Rank	Percentage[a]	Rank
Alabama	$ 625,641	16	$15.69	6	24%	22
Alaska	235,756	35	26.98	1	122	1
Arizona	432,342	25	11.96	16	25	20
Arkansas	299,224	33	12.99	12	44	8
California	4,209,000	1	11.34	18	36	13
Colorado	406,368	27	9.23	35	10	33
Connecticut	329,917	31	6.32	49	7	36
Delaware	91,411	47	10.90	25	9	35
Florida	1,129,778	6	8.07	42	37	12
Georgia	664,597	14	9.86	33	29	17
Hawaii	208,636	39	15.40	8	9	34
Idaho	121,835	41	12.06	15	-1	45
Illinois	1,314,353	4	8.27	39	2	42
Indiana	607,341	17	9.43	34	4	41
Iowa	385,260	29	11.25	20	5	39
Kansas	349,500	30	10.89	26	14	28
Kentucky	433,065	24	11.29	19	26	19
Louisiana	572,657	19	11.87	17	42	9
Maine	100,927	45	8.07	41	11	30
Maryland	532,510	21	8.47	37	11	31

Table 3-7. continued

	Total Amount (thousands)	Rank	Per $1,000 Personal Income		Ten-Year Percentage Change	
			Amount	Rank	Percentage[a]	Rank
Massachusetts	711,102	13	8.30	38	69	2
Michigan	1,145,966	5	10.02	32	1	43
Minnesota	722,805	12	13.11	11	16	25
Mississippi	398,902	28	17.49	3	33	14
Missouri	453,882	23	7.46	46	6	38
Montana	108,184	44	12.45	13	21	24
Nebraska	214,951	38	10.77	27	7	37
Nevada	94,410	46	7.78	45	25	21
New Hampshire	50,265	49	3.90	50	12	29
New Jersey	847,673	10	7.31	47	33	15
New Mexico	234,564	36	16.06	5	55	4
New York	2,545,546	2	10.02	31	1	44
North Carolina	1,078,822	8	16.13	4	46	6
North Dakota	124,430	40	14.68	10	27	18
Ohio	1,085,255	7	8.17	40	22	23
Oklahoma	425,877	26	11.08	22	66	3
Oregon	312,194	32	10.05	30	-2	47
Pennsylvania	1,063,638	9	7.26	48	-16	50
Rhode Island	110,416	42	8.95	36	15	26
South Carolina	505,149	22	15.13	9	14	27
South Dakota	61,971	48	7.93	43	-13	49
Tennessee	547,788	20	11.15	21	47	5
Texas	2,204,354	3	10.97	24	32	16
Utah	249,399	34	15.52	7	41	10
Vermont	44,618	50	7.80	44	10	32
Virginia	767,147	11	10.27	29	38	11
Washington	588,933	18	10.59	28	-5	48
West Virginia	233,057	37	12.27	14	5	40
Wisconsin	655,436	15	11.02	23	-2	46
Wyoming	110,377	43	17.65	2	45	7
Total U.S.	30,747,229		10.22		19	

a. These figures are ten-year changes adjusted for inflation using the Consumer Price Indices.

Source: Evangelauf (1985), citing M.M. Chambers and Edward R. Hines, *Appropriations of State Tax Funds for Operating Expenses of Higher Education, 1985–86.*

where expenditures grew 122 percent; the largest decrease occurred in Pennsylvania, where expenditures decreased 16 percent.

A comparison of these three variables shows that little relationship existed between total state expenditures and the other two variables. In fact, the simple correlation between total higher education expenditures and the other variables was not statistically different from zero.[5] On the other hand, state expenditures per $1,000 income and ten-year change have a correlation coefficient of .59. Thus, there is some evidence to suggest that states with the highest tax effort also have experienced the most rapid growth.

There is little systematic analysis of the determinants of state support of higher education. In a study of major research universities, Coughlin and Erekson (1986) found that institutional quality, statewide demand for higher education, legislative concern for equity and institution effort, and success in intercollegiate athletics by an institution were positive significant determinants of state aid. A need exists for similar work to examine the determinants of state aid for a more broad-based sample of institutions of higher education.

ENDOWMENT INCOME IN HIGHER EDUCATION

Endowment income has been an important minor source of funding in higher education, especially for private institutions. Although public institutions depended on endowment income for less than 1 percent of their revenue, private institutions received closer to 5 percent of their revenues from this source.

Endowment income is a volatile source of revenue for colleges and universities. Total returns on endowments for all colleges and universities has varied as follows since 1982 (Desruisseaux 1986; Higher Education General Information Survey 1982):

Year	Total Return
1982	42.2 percent
1983	41.3 percent
1984	−2.8 percent
1985	25.4 percent

Significant positive rates of return may reflect general improvement in the performances of stocks and bonds held in university endowments or may reflect superior money management by university money managers. Returns on endowment income vary significantly by control of institution. In the HEGIS sample for 1982, reporting public institutions had a 77.1 percent mean increase in endowment market value, while private institutions had a 21.4 percent increase. Similar findings exist by type of institution; universities had a 4.9 percent increase; four-year colleges had a 16.5 percent increase; and two-year institutions had a 128.8 percent increase. This latter value must be viewed with caution as the base endowment market value for two-year institutions was quite small.

TRENDS IN VOLUNTARY SUPPORT OF HIGHER EDUCATION

To help ensure their vitality, institutions of higher education have turned increasingly to voluntary contributions as an important source of revenue. A century ago, private giving was the primary source of funding for higher education (Committee for Economic Development 1973). Currently, voluntary giving accounts for a considerably smaller share of higher education revenue.

In Table 3–8 various figures relating to voluntary support of higher education are presented. The sharp decline in real support per student after 1965–66 is striking. In fact, from 1977–78 to 1983–84 real support per student remained at approximately $140 per student (Council for Financial Aid to Education 1985). Moreover, from

Table 3-8. Voluntary Support of Higher Education.

Years	Total (in millions of dollars)	Support per Student Current	Real[a]	Average Annual Change from Previous Period (percentage)
1949–50	$ 240	90	126	—
1965–66	1,440	241	251	4.4%
1970–71	1,860	217	183	-6.1
1975–76	2,410	215	130	-6.6
1980–81	4,230	350	135	0.8
1983–84	5,600	449	147	2.9

a. Real changes expressed in 1967 constant dollars.
Source: Desruisseaux (1986), citing Council for Financial Aid to Education.

1965–66 to 1975–76 the annual change in voluntary support was an average decrease of over 6 percent.

If colleges and universities are to continue to rely on voluntary contributions, it will be necessary to carefully study their determinants of voluntary support. Historically, individuals have provided approximately 50 percent of all voluntary support, and foundations and corporations have provided another 40 percent. There has been little systematic analysis attempting to explain levels of voluntary support. One work by Leslie, Drachman, Conrad, and Ramey (1983) pointed to two important findings. Aggregate giving was significantly determined by changes in economic variables that captured the general state of economic activity, corporate profits, and personal savings. Moreover, individual donors and corporate donors seemed to be differently motivated in their giving. Leslie et al. (1983) hypothesized that individuals care more for institutional need and thus were more likely to give during economic slack periods. On the other hand, corporations seemed to respond to more traditional economic motives, increasing corporate giving as economic conditions improved. Proposing other differences in donor behavior, Coughlin and Erekson (1986) found corroborative evidence; giving for current programs and gifts by corporations seemed to be more affected by institutional quality and size than were giving for capital programs and gifts by alumni.

An important policy matter with potentially strong implications for voluntary support to higher education is federal tax reform. Higher education benefits from a large variety of tax advantages under existing federal tax laws.[6] Two of the more important advantages are deductibility of contributions to educational institutions and exclusion of capital gains on gifts and bequests of appreciated property. There are several proposals for tax reform and simplification before Congress, including the Bradley-Gephart proposal, the Kemp-Kasten proposal, and so-called Treasury I. Recent tax laws have raised the price of giving to higher education by lowering marginal tax rates and thus by lowering the benefit of deductibility of contributions to higher education. The proposals mentioned above all would raise further the price of giving to higher education. Through simulation, Auten and Rudney (1986) have compared the expected effects of various tax reform proposals and argue that higher education would receive significantly less voluntary giving with any of the reforms.

CONCLUSION

Financial planners in higher education face a number of uncertainties about continued support for all of the major sources of revenue for higher education. If institutions of higher education are to maintain vital academic programs, university and government officials must be sensitive to the revenue sources that are most likely to provide stable long-term revenues and must monitor those revenues that are likely to fluctuate.

NOTES

1. However, O'Neill and Simms (1983) argued that little increase in productivity can be attributed to research and development in higher education.
2. Coughlin and Erekson (1986) found that although tuition and state aid are inversely related, an institution's tuition relative to the state average is positively related to state aid.
3. Nelson (1978) noted that differences in indirect cost rates also may place private institutions at a competitive disadvantage since they must include these costs in their budgets.
4. Some state governments also provide limited support to private institutions. This aid is primarily in the form of student aid and is usually less than 3 percent of a state's expenditure on higher education (Nelson 1978).
5. This provides somewhat contrary evidence to the finding by Lindeen and Willis (1975) that population was a significant positive determinant of state support of higher education, since most of the highest expenditure states also have large populations.
6. See Sunley (1978) for a detailed analysis of these tax advantages.

REFERENCES

Auten, Gerald E., and Gabriel E. Rudney. 1986. "Tax Reform and Individual Giving to Higher Education." *Economics of Education Review* 5 (2): 142–60.

Carnegie Foundation. 1985. "Sustaining the Future." *Chronicle of Higher Education* 30 (June 5): 18–19.

Committee for Economic Development. 1973. *The Management and Financing of Colleges.* New York: Research and Policy Committee, CED.

Coughlin, Cletus C., and O. Homer Erekson. 1986. "Determinants of State Aid and Voluntary Support of Higher Education." *Economics of Education Review* 5 (2): 161–72.

Council for Financial Aid to Education. 1985. *Voluntary Support of Education.* Washington, D.C.: CFAE.

Desruisseaux, Paul. 1986. "Endowments Grew 25 Percent in Fiscal 1985." *Chronicle of Higher Education* 31 (January 8): 23.

_____. 1985. "Gifts to Higher Education Reach Record $5.6 Billion." *Chronicle of Higher Education* 30 (July 17): 10-12.

Evangelauf, J. 1985. "States Spending on Colleges Rises 19 Percent in 2 Years." *Chronicle of Higher Education* 31 (October 30): 12-14.

Halstead, D. K. 1984. *How States Compare in Financial Support of Higher Education, 1983-84.* Washington, D.C.: National Institute of Education.

Hansen, W. L., and B. A. Weisbrod. 1969. *Benefits, Costs, and Finance of Public Higher Education.* Chicago: Markham.

Higher Education General Information Survey. 1982. Washington, D.C.: U.S. Government Printing Office.

Leslie, Larry; Sally S. Drachman; Clifton F. Conrad; and Garey W. Ramey. 1983. "Factors Accounting for Variations over Time in Voluntary Support for Colleges and Universities." *Journal of Education Finance* 9 (2) (Fall): 213-25.

Lindeen, James W., and George L. Willis. 1975. "Political, Socioeconomic and Demographic Patterns of Support for Public Higher Education." *Western Political Quarterly* 28 (3) (September): 528-41.

McPherson, Michael S. 1978. "The Demand for Higher Education." In *Public Policy and Private Higher Education*, edited by David W. Breneman and Chester E. Finn, Jr., pp. 143-96. Washington, D.C.: The Brookings Institution.

National Center for Educational Statistics. 1982. *Higher Education General Information Survey.* Washington, D.C.: NCES.

National Science Foundation. 1984. *Academic Science/Engineering: 1972-83.* Washington, D.C.: NSF.

_____. 1985. *Federal Support to Universities, Colleges, and Selected Nonprofit Institutions.* Washington, D.C.: NSF.

Nelson, Susan C. 1978. "Financial Trends and Issues." In *Public Policy and Private Higher Education*, edited by David W. Breneman and Chester E. Finn, Jr., pp. 63-142. Washington, D.C.: The Brookings Institution.

Oates, Wallace E. 1972. *Fiscal Federalism.* New York: Harcourt Brace Jovanovich.

O'Neill, June A., and Margaret C. Simms. 1983. "Education." In *The Reagan Experiment*, edited by John L. Palmer and Isabel V. Sawhill, pp. 329-59. Washington, D.C.: The Urban Institute Press.

Palmer, Stacy E. 1986. "Students May Lose $244 Million under Deficit Law." *Chronicle of Higher Education* 31 (January 22): 1, 16-17.

Sunley, Emil M., J. 1978. "Federal and State Tax Policies." In *Public Policy and Private Higher Education*, edited by David W. Breneman and Chester E. Finn, Jr., pp. 281-319. Washington, D.C.: The Brookings Institution.

4 FUNDING FORMULAS

Mary P. McKeown

Since the state of Texas began to use mathematical formulas as the basis for allocating funds to institutions of higher education about forty years ago, controversy has surrounded the use of state funding formulas. The capacity of funding formulas to distribute adequate state funds to public colleges and universities in an equitable manner has prompted debates among state legislators, educators, and others concerned with the public funding of higher education. The increasing competition from other social services for state resources and demands for economy, wise use of scarce state resources, and accountability have prompted much of the debate. In the 1980s the debate appears to center on the provision of educational quality in a formula environment and the availability of adequate resources when enrollments decline or remain constant.

Recently, the federal courts also have become involved in the debate over the use of funding formulas in the equitable distribution of state resources to institutions of higher education. (In this context, the term *equity* or *equitable* refer to equal treatment of equals under equal circumstances.) States are required to submit to the federal government a statewide plan that indicates the state's efforts to racially integrate the public institutions of higher education. The federal government, through the Department of Education's Office of Civil Rights (OCR), has rejected plans in several states and asked the Justice Department to initiate litigation in the federal courts. In fact, all but one of the states against which the federal government has initiated higher education racial discrimination litigation was a formula state.

Formulas are used in almost every state in the allocation of state funds to elementary and secondary school districts. The stated public policy goal has been to attain equity in the distribution of funds through improvements in the funding formulas. Federal and state courts have rendered many decisions on the equity of the various elementary and secondary funding formulas. The accepted goal of equality of educational opportunity through equalized funding for elementary and secondary education has not been an accepted goal in higher education. In the funding of elementary and secondary schools, the public policy goal has been to provide equal protection for students. In related discussions about funding higher education, some persons appear to be advocating that equal protection be accorded to institutions, granting to institutions the same qualities that have been granted to students under the fourteenth amendment. This is in contrast to the civil rights litigation in elementary and secondary education in which institutional maintenance was considered to be of lesser importance than equality of educational opportunity for students.

Several witnesses for the federal government in the higher education court cases have questioned the ability of state funding formulas to distribute funds equitably and have maintained that funding formulas are not "zero-based" and continue past inequities by relying on historical data (Leslie 1985; Sullivan 1985). The positions taken in the federal court cases by "expert" witnesses for the original plaintiffs are not unlike the arguments that have been used by opponents of funding formulas in debates since the 1960s.

The use of funding formulas or funding guidelines for public institutions of higher education in the resource allocation or budgeting process varies from state to state. In certain states, the higher education coordinating board may use formulas as the method of recommending to the legislature and governor the resources for each public campus. In other states, the legislative or executive budget offices may use formulas to determine their recommended level of funding for each institution. Some states utilize formulas to determine the allocation of resources to each campus, given available funding. Although the latter use has been defined elsewhere to be the only "true" formula funding, for purposes of this chapter states will be defined to use formulas if a formula or guideline is used at any point in the resource allocation process.

Even though formulas for funding public higher education institutions are enrollment driven because they are based on credit hours, students, or faculty members, development of the optimal formula is made more complex by differences in institutional mission and differences in the current capacities of institutions to perform their missions. However, these differences do not negate the value of formulas but suggest that formulas can be used to provide the fiscal base. If additional funds are justified, supplemental funding can be used for special purposes, which avoids the need to rely on a "zero-based" budget and to subject all public funds for complex institutions to the vagaries of uninformed budget analysts and legislators who lack objective information to undergird their recommendations.

The debate over the equitable distribution of resources to public institutions of higher education has caused several states to examine critically the methods used to recommend or distribute funding to the public colleges and universities. When enrollments decline or remain constant, new methods are sought that will provide additional resources to institutions. Development of new programs and services to meet the varied needs of a changing clientele may require different configurations of resources in addition to different programs. The student of the 1990s may have not only different noninstructional needs but also different preferences for instructional programs. The trend in this area has already developed: Students appear to be seeking occupation-related training. Some disciplines, like business administration and computer science, enroll more students, and traditional disciplines, like classical languages, enroll fewer students. Additionally, as indicated in the recent reports calling for reforms of the nation's high schools, many college students may have needs for compensatory education to alleviate the impact of disadvantaged backgrounds or inadequate elementary and secondary education.

To accomplish the purpose of equitable distribution of available state funds, a majority of the states have used funding formulas in the development of budgets or in the allocation of resources to public institutions of higher education. A formula is a mathematical representation of the amount of resources or expenditures for an institution as a whole or for a program at the institution (Boutwell 1973). Programs in this context refer to those categories into which expenditures are placed, as defined by the National Association of and University Business Officers (NACUBO). The programs, nal categories, or budget areas that are commonly used are llowing (NACUBO 1982):

ˌnstruction	Institutional support
Research	Operation and maintenance of plant
Public service	Scholarships and fellowships
Academic support	Auxiliary enterprises
Student services	Hospitals

Many states provide funding for higher education based on these functional or budget programs, with the exception of auxiliary enterprises and hospitals. These two areas usually are not funded by the state and are not included in what are called educational and general expenditures (E&G). E&G expenditures are those that result from expenditures for the three basic missions of colleges and universities: instruction, research, and public service. Funding for the remaining categories may be based on formulas in the determination of the total resource allocation to the institution.

In most states, however, total institutional needs are not determined by a formula mechanism. Additions are made to the formula amounts to recognize special needs or special missions. Similarly, given the political structure and the competition for funds from other state agencies, the amount determined by a formula calculation may be reduced to conform to total resources available.

FORMULA DEVELOPMENT

Formulas have been considered the offspring of necessity (Gross 1979). The development of an objective, systematic method of dealing with the funding of many diverse institutions that served differing constituencies prompted many states to investigate and subsequently to begin using formulas (Miller 1964). Prior to 1946 institutions of higher education served a limited clientele. After World War II enrollments jumped, and each state had a variety of liberal arts colleges, land-grant colleges, teacher training colleges, and technical schools to meet the needs of its citizens. As the scope and mission of the campuses increased and changed (teachers colleges becoming regional universities, for example), so did the complexity of equitably distributing resources among the competing campuses. Unfortunately, state resources did not keep pace with expanding enrollments, and the competition for state funds became greater. Because no two campuses are ever alike, methods were sought to allocate available funds in an objective manner, to provide sufficient justification for additional resources to satisfy state legislators, and to facilitate interinstitutional comparisons.

The desire for equity was a prime factor in the development of funding formulas, but other factors served as catalysts: the desire to determine an adequate level of funding, institutional needs to gain stability and predictability in funding levels, and increased professionalism among college and university business officers (Miller 1964). The objective of equity in the distribution of state resources was to provide state appropriations to each of the campuses according to its needs. To achieve an equitable distribution of funds required a distribution formula that recognized differences in size, clientele, location, and the purposes of the colleges (Millett 1974).

The concept of adequacy was more difficult to operationalize in the distribution of resources. What might have been considered to be adequate for the basic operations of one campus would be considered inadequate for a campus offering similar programs but having a different clientele. Indeed, the concept of adequacy has created operational problems in the distribution of funds to elementary and secondary education and was one of the factors in the development of state foundation programs.

Texas was the first state to utilize funding formulas. By 1950 California, Indiana, and Oklahoma also were using funding formulas or cost analysis procedures in the budgeting or resource allocation process (Gross 1979). In 1964 sixteen states—Alabama, California, Colorado, Florida, Georgia, Indiana, Kentucky, Mississippi, New Mexico, New York, North Carolina, Ohio, Oregon, Tennessee, Washington, and Wisconsin—were identified as using formulas at some point in the allocation process (Miller 1964). By 1973 the number had increased to twenty-five states (Gross 1973).

Formulas have evolved over a long period of time and have contributed to a series of compromises between institutions, state coordinating agencies, and state budget officials. For example, institutions have sought autonomy, while state coordinating boards and budget officials have sought adequate information to enable control over resources. The development of the Texas formulas is an example of the tradeoffs and compromises that must be made between accountability and autonomy.

When sudden enrollment increases following World War II caused confusion in the amounts to be appropriated to Texas public colleges, each institution began to lobby the legislature for additional funds. Texas legislators felt that the institutional requests were excessive and that the division of resources among institutions was inequitable. Consequently, the legislature asked for some sort of rational mechanism to distribute funds. In 1951 a teaching salary formula based on workload factors was developed; this formula did not recognize differences among the campuses in roles and missions. By 1957 a series of budget formulas developed by institutions, citizens, and the new Commission on Higher Education was presented to the legislature. These formulas were developed only after completion of a major study of the role and scope of the institutions. The study included an inventory of program offerings and attempted to measure costs by program. After 1958 a Cost Study Committee was established that recommended adoption of five formulas, covering teaching salaries, general administration, library, building maintenance, and custodial services. In 1961 two formulas for organized research and departmental operating costs were added (Miller 1964). By 1982 Texas was using fourteen separate formula calculations that were based on complex cost studies of each of the program offerings at the campuses in the public system of higher education. At each stage of development, compromises were reached between the desire for additional data for increased accuracy and the cost of providing the data.

The trend in formula development in other states has been similar and has included the refinement of procedures, greater detail and reliability in the collection and analysis of information, and improvement in the differentiation between programs and activities. Different states appear to have used different methods to develop formulas. Some states, like Alabama, adapted the formulas used by Texas to the particular circumstances of their own state. Adaptation rather than development was the preferred method apparently because of the cost and time required to perform a program inventory and cost study. Accounting procedures may not have been refined enough to permit the calculation or assignment of costs differentiated by academic discipline and level of student. States continue to adapt formulas and formula components from other states. Methods that have worked in one state may work equally well in another or can be adapted with a saving of time and resources.

Many formulas have been based on simple least-squares regression analysis or the determination of an "average cost" for the provision of a particular type of service. Others have been based on staffing ratios and external determinations of "standard costs." The key to the process has been the isolation of variables or factors that were directly related to actual program costs (Anderes 1985b). Isolation of variables that are detailed, reliable, not susceptible to manipulation by a campus, and sufficiently differentiated to recognize different roles and missions has required collections of massive amounts of data. Data must be collected and analyzed in an unbiased manner that does not raise questions of preferential treatment for one campus or sector. For this reason, statewide coordinating boards or other state agencies have been given the responsibility for formula development.

For a formula to be effective, several criteria should be met (Miller 1964):

1. Formula development should be flexible.
2. Formulas should be used for budget development, not budget control.
3. Formulas should be related to quantifiable factors.
4. Data should be consistent among institutions.
5. Normative data should reflect local and national trends.
6. The formula should be useful to institutions, coordinating boards, other state agencies, and the legislature.

Formula Advantages and Disadvantages

The advantages of funding formulas are generally recognized:

1. Formulas provide an objective method for determining institutional needs on an equitable basis.
2. Formulas reduce political competition among and lobbying by state institutions.
3. Formulas provide state officials with a reasonably simple and understandable basis for measuring expenditures and revenue needs of campuses and determining the adequacy of support.

4. Formulas enable institutions to project needs on a timely basis.
5. Formulas represent a reasonable compromise between public accountability and institutional autonomy (Millett 1974).
6. Formulas facilitate comparisons between institutions and activities.
7. Formulas enable policymakers to focus attention on basic policy questions.
8. Formulas promote efficiency in institutional operation.

Although there is general acceptance of the advantages of formulas, heated debates have been held over the question of whether the disadvantages of formulas outweigh any advantages in their use. Formulas do have shortcomings, but these deficiencies can be recognized and then minimized. Some disadvantages of formula use include the following:

1. Formulas may not be based on an adequate estimate of the cost requirements for programs and may not recognize the varying quality of programs at different campuses; thus, formulas may be used to reduce all academic programs to a common level of mediocrity by funding each one the same.

2. Formulas may lead to a deduction of institutional income received from sources other than state appropriations. That is, formulas may reduce the incentives for institutions to seek outside funding or research support.

3. Formulas may, through their reliance on current or historical information, perpetuate inequities in funding among institutions that existed before the advent of the formula (Millett 1974; Gillis and Anderes 1984).

4. Enrollment-driven formulas may be inadequate to meet the needs of changing clienteles or circumstances and may be insensitive to new program initiatives (Halstead 1974).

5. Formulas cannot serve as substitutes for public policy decisions (Miller 1964).

6. Formulas involve the projection rather than prediction of budgetary needs and are only as accurate as the data on which the formulas are based (Miller 1964).

7. Formulas may not provide adequate recognition for differences among institutional roles and missions (Gross 1979).

8. Formulas are linear in nature and may not recognize sudden shifts in enrollments and costs (Boutwell 1973).

Methods of Dealing with Enrollment Decline

To overcome some of the disadvantages, states have attempted to consider the differences among institutions in the costs of providing educational programs and services by recognizing programmatic differences among institutions in the funding mechanism. Typically, funding formulas for institutions of higher education focus on productivity by estimating expenditures on some basis that varies by the types of instruction provided to students. Formulas provide similar funding for similar programs at different institutions so that each institution can be provided equitable treatment; however, formulas do consider differences in the types and levels of instructional programs offered by different institutions in a state. *Level*, in this case, refers to lower division undergraduates (freshman and sophomore), upper division undergraduates (junior and senior), masters, first professional, and doctoral courses, credit hours, or students.

Formulas can include factors that consider the size of the institution so that economies and diseconomies of scale may be recognized. (If an increase in the size of an institution results in reductions in the unit cost, or cost of a credit hour, the phenomenon is called an *economy of scale*. Similarly, if increases in institutional size result in increases in unit costs, the phenomenon is called a *diseconomy of scale*.) Formulas provide an equitable amount of funds to institutions in an equal manner for performing similar tasks.

As enrollments decline and shift among institutions in the 1980s and 1990s, and as colleges and universities review and revise their roles and missions, funding formulas afford the opportunity to recognize those changes, adjust resource allocations, and provide for the equitable allocation of resources among institutions that offer similar programs. Several methods of dealing with concomitant enrollment growth and decline have been used by the states. One method establishes ranges of enrollment change, within which both decline and growth are treated the same. Under this method, enrollment growth or decline below a specified percentage result in no change in the total dollar amount of funding.

A second method bases funding on close examination of how a changing number of students affects costs (Spence 1980). Enrollment-driven formulas provide additional funds in direct proportion to the number of credit hours, students, and so forth. As the number of hours increase, additional funding is generated. Conversely, as the number of hours decreases, proportionately fewer funds are generated. This method has provided a margin of safety to institutions with growing enrollments where state appropriations did not keep pace with enrollment increases and helped offset the impact of modification of the formula factors in relation to anticipated state revenues (Gross 1979).

However, this linear relationship between enrollment and resources can be devastating to institutional budgets when enrollment decreases, since only a marginal reduction in expenditures can be made. The amount of reduction depends on many factors including staffing requirements, tenure policies, and salary scales. To mitigate the impact, some states use formulas that have fixed cost, marginal cost, and variable cost components. Fixed costs are those that remain constant over the short run as volume changes. Some fixed costs may be altered by the administration of an institution and are termed *discretionary*. Others cannot be changed and are termed *nondiscretionary*. A marginal cost is one that is related to the increase or decrease in total cost attributable to the addition or subtraction of one unit. Another type of cost is termed *variable* and refers to costs that fluctuate in proportion to the volume. Semivariable costs are those that are fixed for a certain range of units but become variable when that range is exceeded. For example, the cost of the room space to offer a class is fixed until the room is full; however, once the capacity of the room is reached, another room will be needed. Identification of marginal costs requires additional data, more complex statistical procedures, and more time to identify adequately those costs that are fixed and those that vary with enrollments.

A third method has been called a *minimum staff approach* and has been used only by North Dakota (Rambo, Reich, and McFetridge 1985). Under this approach, a determination is made of the number of faculty positions needed for a certain level of academic program offerings at smaller campuses. These positions are funded at an average salary level regardless of enrollment fluctuations.

A fourth method of adapting funding formulas to deal with enrollment changes is to use factors that are unrelated to enrollment. The three major types of modifications to formulas that are responsive to enrollment and economic conditions can be classified as buffering, decoupling, and marginal costing (Spence 1980). Buffering retards or limits the rate at which institutions lose resources; decoupling refers to developing formulas that are based on factors or units of measure other than enrollment; marginal costing was described above. Each approach necessitates that tradeoffs be made among competing institutional roles and missions. However, each method can be perceived to be a way of recognizing and minimizing the disadvantages to formula use.

FORMULA USE BY THE STATES

Since 1980 at least thirty states have used funding formulas in the budget or resource allocation process. The number of states employing formulas is not fixed, since states continually adopt, modify, and drop formulas and since what one state may consider a formula may be called by another name in another state (Meissinger 1976). For example, Michigan typically is not identified as a formula state, although Michigan has used a formula in its appropriations process off and on for the last twenty years. States identified as having used funding formulas for higher education at some time since 1980 are listed in Table 5-1 and shown in Figure 4-1.

Only one southern state, North Carolina, has not used funding formulas in the budgeting or resource allocation process since 1980. Of the thirteen western states, six used formulas, while eight of the thirteen midwestern states and five of the ten northeastern states used formulas in at least one year since 1980.

Among the states there is great variety in the type and number of formulas and in the functional or budget areas for which formulas are used. The number of formulas used in each of the functional areas is included in Table 4-1. Of the thirty-four states identified as using formulas, only Arkansas had at least one formula in each functional area, but fifteen states had at least six formulas and Oregon had twenty-seven. Of the thirty-four states, twenty-two had only one formula in the instructional area, while Oregon had seven formulas, one for each of the identified cost areas related to instruction. The majority of the states applied formulas to all institutions; however, Minnesota excluded the University of Minnesota and New York applied its formulas to CUNY only.

Table 4–1. Formula Use among the States and Number of Formulas Applied to Each Functional Area.

	Instruction	Research	Public Service	Academic Support	Student Services	Institutional Support	Plant	Scholarships/Fellowships
Alabama	1	1	1	2	1	1	2	
Arkansas	1	1	1	2	1	1	1	1
California	1	a		1	b	b	6	
Colorado	2			1	1	1	1	
Connecticut	1			1	1		3	
Florida	2	1	1	3	1		5	
Georgia	3	a	1	1	b	b	2	
Kansas	1	1		2	1	1	5	
Kentucky	2	1		1	b	b	4	1
Louisiana	1	a		a	b	b	2	
Massachusetts	b			b	b	b	1	
Maryland	b			b	b	b	b	
Michigan	4			1	1	b	b	
Minnesota	1			b	b	b	b	
Mississippi	1	1		b	b	b	b	
Missouri	1			1	1	1	1	
Montana	1			b	b	b	b	1
Nevada	3							
New Jersey	1			b	b	b	5	b
New Mexico	1			b	b	b	b	
New York	1			1	1			
North Dakota	1			1	a	a	a	
Ohio	1	a		1	1	1	1	

Oklahoma	1	1		a	a	a	a
Oregon	7	1	1	6	3	3	7
Pennsylvania	1			1	1	1	1
South Carolina	1	1	1	2	1	1	4
South Dakota	1	a		3	a	a	a
Tennessee	3	1	1	2	1	1	1
Texas	3	1		2	1	1	5
Virginia	1			3	1	1	2
Washington	3			3	1		3
West Virginia	1			b	1	b	1
Wisconsin	1			1	1		1

a. Included with instruction.

b. Included in one formula.

Sources: Information supplied by each state's higher education coordinating or governing board; Missouri, Montana, and Pennsylvania from Gross (1982).

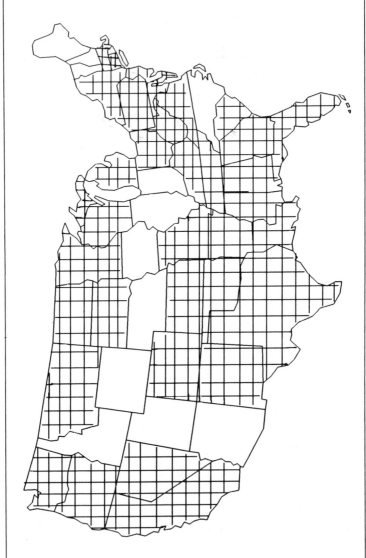

Figure 4–1.   States Using Formulas.

Source: State Coordinating Boards;   Gross (1982).

Formula Approaches

Formulas reflect one of two approaches: the all-inclusive approach, where the total entitlement or allocation for the program area is determined by one calculation; and the itemized approach, where more than one calculation or formula is used in each budget area. The second approach was used by the majority of the states.

Computational Methods

Three computational methods have been identified under which every formula calculation can be classified: (1) rate per base factor unit (RPBU), (2) percentage of base factor (PBF), and (3) base factor-position ratio with salary rates (BF-PR/SR) (Moss and Gaither 1976). The rate per base factor unit method starts with an estimate of a given base factor, such as credit hours or full-time equivalent students (FTES), and then multiplies that factor by a specific unit rate. The unit rates generally have been determined previously by cost studies and can be differentiated by discipline, level, and type of institution.

The PBF method assumes that there is a specific relationship between a certain base factor (for example, faculty salaries) and other areas (for example, departmental support services). The PBF method also can be differentiated (Miller 1964), but this is unusual. Reportedly, PBF was developed because of the perception that all support services were related to the primary mission of the university, instruction (Boling 1961).

The base factor-position ratio with salary rates method is based on a predetermined optimum ratio between a base factor and the number of personnel—for example, a student-per-faculty ratio or a credit-hour-per-faculty-member ratio. The resulting number of positions determined at each salary level then is multiplied by the salary rate for that level, and the amounts summed to give a total budgetary requirement. BF-PR/SR is the most complex of the computational methods.

Base Factors

Base factors used in most formulas can be classified into five categories: (1) head count, (2) number of positions, (3) square footage or acreage, (4) full-time-equivalent students (FTES), and (5) credit hours. Square footage or acreage is a factor used in operation and maintenance of plant, while credit hours, FTES, or positions are most prevalent in the areas of instruction, academic support, and institutional support. Head count is used most often in the areas of student services and scholarships and fellowships.

Differentiation

Formulas may differentiate among academic disciplines (such as social sciences, education, and agriculture), levels of enrollment (freshman and sophomore, junior and senior, masters, and doctoral), and types of institutions (community college, baccalaureate institution, and research university). States have found it necessary to introduce factors that differentiate among institutions in funding formulas because each institution, if closely scrutinized, is different. Differentiation has become more prevalent, and more complex, as reliable cost data have become available.

Differentiation is especially prevalent in the formulas used to calculate funds for Instruction. All of the thirty-four states using formulas provided differential amounts by discipline, institutional type, or level of enrollment. Only a few formulas in other functional areas varied by these three factors.

Formulas for Instruction

Each of the thirty-four states identified as using formulas in the budgeting or resource allocation process since 1980 explicitly or implicitly utilized at least one formula for instruction. This category includes all expenditures for credit and noncredit courses, for academic, vocational, technical, and remedial instruction, and for regular, special, and extension session. Excluded are expenditures for academic administration when the primary assignment is administra-

Table 4-2. Instruction Formula Use among the States.

	Number of States
Calculation method	
RPBU	15
PBF	6
BF-PR/SR	23
Approach	
Inclusive	23
Itemized	11
Base	
Credit hours	27
Positions	20
FTES or FTEF	10
Differentiation	
Discipline	34
Level	31
Institutional type	23
Fixed costs	10

tion (such as deans) (NACUBO 1982). Instruction is the most complex, and most expensive, component of an institution's expenditures. Because of its importance, identification of appropriate cost factors is critical to the validity of the formula development process. Summary information on the instruction formulas used by the states is displayed in Table 4-2.

Since the instruction program is the major component of expenditures at institutions of higher education, formulas for this activity were quite complex. Each state provided differential funding for activities within the instruction program to recognize differences in costs by level of instruction and among academic disciplines. Over time, formulas for instruction have become more complex because improvements in cost accounting procedures have resulted in more accurate data. A typical formula for the instruction area is shown as Table 4-3.

Calculation Methods. All three calculation methods were used to determine support for instruction—rate per base factor unit (RPBU), percentage of base factor (PBF), or base factor-position ratio with

Table 4-3. Sample Instruction Formula.

Discipline	Lower Division	Upper Division	Masters	Doctoral
Agriculture	$124	$146	$242	$1,072
Architecture and planning	27	154	450	507
Area Studies	43	323	120	886
Biological studies	68	109	160	1,137
Business	37	51	111	397
Communications	69	122	143	1,698
Computer science	194	101	162	1,093
Education	88	135	169	854
Engineering	83	102	187	1,459
Arts	98	185	412	981
Foreign languages	62	173	110	1,212
Health sciences	81	147	313	664
Home economics	113	160	547	2,491
Law	—	—	86	172
Letters	50	130	226	1,575
Library science	—	347	218	445
Mathematics	40	89	322	887
Military science	23	20	—	—
Physical science	68	135	435	1,692
Psychology	53	108	137	736
Public affairs	50	98	152	841
Social science	49	86	169	1,078
Interdisciplinary studies	44	90	137	—
Orientation; remedial studies	81	81	—	—

Note: Instruction funding = credit hours times the rates in this table.

salary rates (BF–PR/SR). As noted earlier, RPBU starts with an estimate of a given base factor, such as credit hours, or FTES, and multiplies the factor by a specific unit rate.

The percentage of base factor method assumes that there is a specific relationship between a base factor and other areas—for example, support services—while the BF–PR/SR method is formulated on a predetermined optimum ratio between the base factor and the number of personnel. The resulting number of positions at each salary level is multiplied by the salary rate at that level to give dollar requirements.

Approach. Instructional formulas were used that reflected either the all-inclusive approach, where the total for the budget area was determined by one calculation, or the itemized approach, where the amount for Instruction was the sum of two or more calculations. The all-inclusive approach was used by twenty-three states.

Base Unit. The base factors used by the states in the instruction budget area could be placed in three categories: credit hours, full-time equivalent students, or position count. Twenty-seven states used credit hours as the base for one or more instructional calculations, ten states used FTES, while twenty states used position count as the basis for calculations.

Differentiation. All of the states that used funding formulas differentiated instructional costs by discipline, level of enrollment, and type of institution. Since each formula provided varying amounts based on enrollments by level and discipline, each institution in a state received differing total amounts for instruction and different amounts per student. Differentiation has increased in many states. From a flat rate applied to a level of credit hours, FTES, or headcount enrollments, states have adopted rates by discipline by level.

All of the formula states differentiated by discipline and thirty-one identified differing costs by level. As many as thirty academic disciplines were identified by one state as having different costs in the instruction funding formula. Type of institution was implicitly or explicitly used as a factor in twenty-three states. Some states excluded certain professional schools from application of the formula while others provided separate formulas or sets of formulas for community colleges (see Table 4-2).

Research Formulas

This category includes expenditures for activities designed to produce research outcomes (NACUBO 1982). Funds for research were provided through funding formulas explicitly or implicitly in sixteen states. Six states provided a percentage of instructional costs for research, while two states funded research through the use of an institutional complexity factor that considered enrollments differentiated by levels of enrollment and program area. Five states considered research as an implicit component of instruction, while four states used ratios of faculty positions to research positions, differentiated by level of enrollment and discipline. A sample research area formula is given in equation (4.1).

$$\text{Research funding} = .02 \text{ times faculty salaries} + .20 \text{ times sponsored research funds of the previous year} \qquad (4.1)$$

Determination of factors that are clearly related to or associated with research is difficult. No basic factors have been found that are linked to this area with a high degree of correlation. Practices appear to indicate that developing a meaningful research formula based on multiple factors either is not feasible or not practical (Anderes 1985a).

Public Service Formulas

This category includes funds for activities that primarily provide noninstructional services to individuals and groups external to the institution (NACUBO 1982). Only seven states used a formula approach for the provision of state support for public service activities. Four of these states provided funding as a percentage of instruction, instruction and academic support, or as a percentage of sponsored or nonstate funded public service expenditures of the prior year. In two states, the BF–PR/SR method was used, while the other state allocated funds based on the number of continuing education units produced. Formulas seldom are used for public service because this area, by definition, is unrelated to instructional activities. A sample formula for the public service area is shown as equation (4.2).

$$\text{Public service funding} = .02 \text{ times funding for instruction} \qquad (4.2)$$

Academic Support

Table 4–4 displays summary information on the academic support formulas used by the states. The academic support category includes funds expended to provide support services to institutions in the missions of instruction, research, and public service, including libraries, academic computing support, academic administration, and media

Table 4-4. Support Formula Use among the States.

| | Number of States | | | |
	Academic Support	Student Services	Physical Plant	Institutional Support
Calculation method				
RPBU	19	15	19	13
PBF	12	8	6	9
BF-PR/SR	10	8	14	7
Base				
Credit hours	16	12	6	11
Positions	10	9	15	10
Headcount	1	9	7	4
GSF or acreage	—	—	22	2
FTES	15	6	7	6
Fixed costs	10	9	8	11

services. Costs associated with the offices of deans are included in this functional area; however, funds for the office of the chief academic officer of the campus are included in the institutional support category (NACUBO 1982).

To fund the library component of the academic support category, at least twenty-six states have used a formula or formulas. Six of these states included library support within a formula for all academic support activities or for institutional support activities. Several states use several formulas to fund only the library component.

All three methods were used to calculate formula amounts for academic support. Credit hours, full-time equivalent students, and number of volumes were used as base factors. The majority of the states that used formulas in this category differentiated the resources required by level of student enrollment, discipline, or institutional type.

Standards on the size of library collections, number of support personnel, and other factors have been developed by the American Library Association and the Association of Research Libraries. Formulas to apply these standards, like the Voight formula and the Clapp-Jordan formula, have been developed so that institutions may determine if their library holdings meet the minimum requirements established by professional librarians. For library maintenance, the formula approaches used by two states meet the Association of Research Libraries' criteria (McKeown 1982). Sample formulas for academic support and for the library subcomponent are displayed as equations (4.3) and (4.4).

Academic support = .05 times instruction   (4.3)

Library = $5.30 (undergraduate credit hours) + $10.30 (masters credit
hours) + $38.70 (law credit hours) + $45.83 (doctoral credit
hours) + $100,000   (4.4)

Institutional Support Formulas

This category includes expenditures for the central executive-level management of the campus, fiscal operations, administrative data processing, employee personnel services, and support services (NACUBO 1982). Table 4–4 displays data on the institutional support formulas used by the states since 1980. At least twenty-six states have used a formula for the functional area. Only one state used more than one formula in determining allocations in this area. However, formulas for this area have become more sophisticated and detailed to attempt to capture the relationships between all of the subactivities in the program. A sample formula for institutional support is shown as equation (4.5).

Institutional support = $1.50 (first 200,000 credit hours) +
$1.65 (next 200,000 credit hours) +
$1.79 (next 200,000 credit hours) +
$1.95 (all remaining credit hours)   (4.5)

Among the states that use a formula to determine allocations for the institutional support area, half employed the RPBU method. Full-time equivalent students, head count, credit hours, and all other E&G expenditures were used as the base in the calculations of institutional support costs. Another eleven states explicitly recognized fixed costs in the determination of resources for this category by including a cost factor that decreased as enrollment increased.

Student Services Formulas

This expenditure category includes funds expended to contribute to a student's emotional and physical well-being and intellectual, social, and cultural development outside of the formal instruction process. Included are expenditures for student activities, student organizations, counseling, the registrar's and admissions offices, and student aid administration (NACUBO 1982). Table 4–4 displays information on the student services formulas used by the states since 1980, and equation (4.6) displays a typical student services formula.

$$\text{Student services} = \$200 \text{ times headcount students} \qquad (4.6)$$

Since 1980 at least twenty-eight states used a funding formula for the student services category; ten of these states considered student services as a component of the general administrative formula and did not provide separate funding for the area. All three methods— RPBU, PBF, and BF–PR/SR—were used to calculate amounts allocated for student services, and some states used two or more methods in combination. RPBU was the method used by fifteen states; PBF was used by eight states, and eight states used BF–PR/SR. Economies of scale were recognized by nine states in the formula calculations.

Operation and Maintenance of Plant Formulas

Table 4–4 displays information on the plant formulas used by the states. The plant category includes all expenditures for current operations and maintenance of the physical plant, including building maintenance, custodial services, utilities, landscape and grounds maintenance, and building repairs (NACUBO 1982). Formulas used for funding of the plant category are among the most complex and diverse formulas in use for funding the different areas of higher education institutions. These formulas range from one calculation to complex sets of calculations to fund each of the cost centers in the plant program. Historically, formulas for plant have become increasingly complex since Texas's use of one formula in 1961. Apparently, this increase in complexity is the result of changes in the complexity of the physical plant and the desire to include a rational recognition of increased costs. Thirty-one states used formulas to allocate resources to this area.

Several types of formulas were used to calculate allocations for plant, including a workload standard formula that used estimates of work time and unit costs to develop the total budget; unit size estimates based on the theory that as physical plants increase in size, as measured by school size, costs increase; and the Weber formula that incorporates unit size estimates with personnel needs. In the terms used to classify the formula methods in the discussions of other categories of expenditure, unit size estimates correspond to the RPBU method, and workload standards and the Weber formula correspond to BF-PR/SR.

Gross square footage or acreage was used as the base for calculations in twenty-two states, while credit hours or FTES were used in six states. Factors unrelated to the campus were used in several states and included the size of the surrounding area, as measured by population. Costs of maintenance of building as determined by industry guides and based on type of construction and presence or absence of air conditioning were used by four states. Factors were included for high property values, perimeters of buildings, inflation, building replacement costs, and intensity of use in three states. A sample plant formula is shown as equation (4.7).

$$\text{Plant} = \$180,000 + \$2.80 \text{ times gross square feet} \qquad (4.7)$$

Scholarships and Fellowships Formulas

This category encompasses all expenditures for scholarships and fellowships, including prizes, awards, federal grants, and tuition and fee waivers awarded to students for which services to the institution are not required (NACUBO 1982). Only five states have formulas for the allocation of funds for this area. In each state, the amount was computed as a dollar value times the number of enrolled students, FTES, or credit hours. Derivation of scholarships and fellowships formula is extremely difficult because factors are highly correlated and the determination of factors is elusive.

TRENDS IN THE USE OF FUNDING FORMULAS

Trends in formula budgeting include a hybridization of data into various combinations to meet the unique needs of each state (Anderes 1985b). Differentiation among institutional roles, missions, size, and philosophy likely will increase, as states struggle to cope effectively with changing economic environments, economic circumstances, and student needs. Compromises will have to be made between the desire for more accurate and complex data and the difficulties and costs inherent in collection, analysis, and interpretation.

One way in which the hybridization of data is occurring is through the use of a combination of cost analyses of specific factors, like instructional costs, combined with a "marketbasket" analysis. For example, Washington and Kentucky conduct salary studies of colleges and universities in surrounding states. These institutions are perceived to compete in the same marketplace for faculty.

Inclusion of fixed and marginal cost factors has increased as states have sought to overcome difficulties with declining or steady enrollments. However, the calculation of marginal costs is difficult and requires tradeoffs to be made in data collection and analysis. Because of this, other methods, like enrollment averaging, buffering, and decoupling are being used to mitigate the impact of declining enrollments on institutional budgets.

One of the most interesting developments in the modification of formulas to meet changing needs is the inclusion of "quality" factors. Tennessee was the first state to include a "quality" component in its formula; up to 5 percent of educational and general expenditures is awarded to Tennessee institutions based on numerical ratings of output measures. In addition, Tennessee has established a 10 percent enrollment range within which institutional appropriations are not adjusted. Institutions may raise standards or limit or reduce enrollments within the 10 percent range without penalty. Those institutions below a specified level of support per student may negotiate enrollment reductions and thus receive more support per student.

Florida also has a multifaceted plan for "quality." Included in the components is a new budget system that will link allocation of resources to the evaluation of academic programs. Output measures like faculty productivity and student learning will be coupled with measures like expenditure per student, faculty degrees, and faculty salaries to evaluate the quality and effectiveness of each institution. Ohio, Georgia, Idaho, Kentucky, Louisiana, Maryland, Minnesota, Missouri, New Jersey, Virginia, and Washington are other states that have initiated efforts to measure and reward "quality" in the allocation of resources.

The trend has been for more states to use funding formulas that are more complex, involve more factors, and are based on very refined cost data. The concern and challenge appears to be to find the most flexible and productive combination of factors that will represent adequately the needs of the different institutions in the state. States likely will continue to use funding formulas as a means for rational, objective, and equitable resource allocation. The ability of formulas to achieve these goals is dependent on the capacity of the various institutions, coordinating or governing boards, and legislators to compromise and negotiate. Issues of program quality and enrollment management will continue to require flexibility in funding arrangements.

Formulas, however, will not solve all the resource allocation problems in higher education. Formulas cannot recognize the full range of objective and subjective differences among institutions, and they cannot anticipate changes in the mission of institutions. However, formulas can provide an objective allocation mechanism that is more equitable than independent funding of each institution with the inevitable power plays and patronage that characterize such allocation decisions. Methods for funding higher education will continue to be a political issue that involves the art of compromise to accommodate the changing condition of education in the 1990s and to preserve the quality of public higher education.

NOTES

1. The author thanks the staffs of the state agencies for higher education for their cooperation in providing information concerning higher education funding in their states and especially appreciates the help of staff members who forwarded information concerning the funding formulas used in their states.

REFERENCES

Allen, Richard H., and James R. Topping. 1979. *Cost Information and Formula Funding: New Approaches*. Boulder, Colo.: National Center for Higher Education Management Systems.

Anderes, Thomas. 1985a. "Formula Budgeting in Higher Education: An Examination of Past and Present Factors Used in Formula Development." Ph.D. dissertation, University of Connecticut.

_____. 1985b. "Formula Budgeting in Higher Education." *NACUBO Business Officer* 19 (November): 33–36.

Boling, Edward. 1961. "Methods of Objectifying the Allocation of Tax Funds to Tennessee State Colleges." Ph.D. dissertation, George Peabody College, Tennessee.

Boutwell, W. K. 1973. "Formula Budgeting on the Down Side." In *Strategies in Budgeting*, edited by G. Kaludis, pp. 41–50. San Francisco: Jossey-Bass.

Brinkman, Paul T. 1984. *State Funding of Public Higher Education: Improving the Practice*. Boulder, Colo.: National Center for Higher Education Management Systems.

Gillis, Arthur, and Thomas Anderes. 1984. "Formula Budgeting in Higher Education." Paper presented at the Annual Meeting of the American Education Finance Association, Orlando, Florida, March 15–17.

Gross, Francis M. 1973. "A Comparative Analysis of the Existing Budget Formulas Used for Justifying Budget Requests or Allocating Funds for the Operating Expenses of State Supported Colleges and Universities." Ph.D. dissertation, University of Tennessee.

_____. 1979. "Formula Budgeting and the Financing of Public Higher Education: Panacea or Nemesis for the 1980s?" *AIR Professional File* 3 (Fall).

_____. 1982. *Formula Budgeting for Higher Education: State Practices in 1979-80*. Boulder, Colo.: National Center for Higher Education Management Systems.

Halstead, D. K. 1974. *State Budgeting in Higher Education: Statewide Planning for Higher Education*. Washington, D.C.: U.S. Government Printing Office.

Leslie, Larry L. 1985. *United States v. State of Alabama*, 10 F.2d 1528 (N.D. Ala. 1985) (trial transcript, Civil Action No. CV-83-C-1676s).

McKeown, Mary P. 1982. "The Use of Formulas for State Funding of Higher Education." *Journal of Education Finance* 7 (Winter): 277–300.

Meissinger, Richard J., Jr. 1976. *State Budgeting for Higher Education: The Use of Formulas*. Berkeley: University of California.

Miller, James L., Jr. 1964. *State Budgeting for Higher Education: The Use of Formulas and Cost Analysis*. Ann Arbor: University of Michigan.

Millett, John D. 1974. *The Budget Formula as the Basis for State Appropriations in Support of Higher Education*. Indianapolis: Academy for Educational Development.

Moss, Charles E., and Gerald H. Gaither. 1976. "Formula Budgeting: Requiem or Renaissance?" *Journal of Higher Education* 47 (5) (September/October): 550–76.

National Association of College and University Business Officers. 1982. *College and University Business Administration.* Washington, D.C.: NACUBO.

Rambo, W., F. Reich, and J. McFetridge. 1985. "A Survey of Formula Funding in the United States: Strategies for Dealing with Declining Enrollments." Montana State University. Mimeo.

Spence, David S. 1980. *Funding for Higher Education Enrollment Shifts in the '80s.* Atlanta: Southern Regional Education Board.

Sullivan, Daniel. 1985. *United States v. State of Alabama*, 18 F.2d 2776 (N.D. Ala. 1985) (trial transcript, Civil Action No. CV-83-C-1676s).

5 STATE SUPPORT TO PRIVATE HIGHER EDUCATION

Lucie Lapovsky and Sandra Allard

An individual seeking higher education in the United States may select from a range of institutions unmatched in the world. This country's diverse system of higher education includes major research universities and community colleges, regional state universities and proprietary vocational schools, liberal arts colleges and technical training schools, residential campuses and commuter schools, and institutions with highly competitive admissions standards and with open admissions. Add to these church-related institutions, institutions for men or women only, military academies, and predominantly black institutions and it becomes apparent that the possible combinations of characteristics are virtually endless. This richness of alternatives clearly reflects the pluralistic society from which this system of higher education emerged (Gardner, Atwell, and Berdahl 1985). Much of this diversity is provided by the private higher education institutions. A private institution of higher education is a degree-granting college or university that is not publicly controlled.

There are more than 3,000 higher education institutions in the United States, and more than 50 percent of these are private (see Table 5-1). There is considerable variation in the number of private institutions in each state, varying from no private institutions in Wyoming to 174 in New York. More than half the private institutions are located in just eight states: New York, California, Pennsylvania, Illinois, Massachusetts, Ohio, Missouri, and Texas.

Table 5-1. Geographic Distribution of Public and Private Institutions of
Higher Education, Academic Year 1985–86.

State	Number Total	Public (percentage)	Private (percentage)
Alabama	56	64%	36%
Alaska	15	80	20
Arizona	25	72	28
Arkansas	31	61	39
California	294	45	55
Colorado	40	70	30
Connecticut	46	52	48
Delaware	8	63	37
District of Columbia	17	12	88
Florida	74	50	50
Georgia	71	48	52
Hawaii	14	64	36
Idaho	11	64	36
Illinois	155	40	60
Indiana	67	42	58
Iowa	58	36	64
Kansas	51	57	43
Kentucky	46	46	54
Louisiana	28	64	36
Maine	26	50	50
Maryland	53	58	42
Massachusetts	121	26	74
Michigan	92	48	52
Minnesota	62	44	56
Mississippi	41	66	34
Missouri	85	33	67
Montana	14	71	29
Nebraska	28	46	54
Nevada	7	86	14
New Hampshire	26	46	54
New Jersey	56	54	46
New Mexico	20	80	20
New York	258	33	67
North Carolina	117	63	37
North Dakota	19	58	42

Table 5-1. continued

State	Number Total	Public (percentage)	Private (percentage)
Ohio	125	47	53
Oklahoma	44	66	34
Oregon	45	47	53
Pennsylvania	184	34	66
Rhode Island	12	33	67
South Carolina	57	58	42
South Dakota	18	44	56
Tennessee	72	33	67
Texas	153	64	36
Utah	12	75	25
Vermont	22	27	73
Virginia	76	56	44
Washington	50	66	34
West Virginia	27	59	41
Wisconsin	60	50	50
Wyoming	8	100	0
Total	3,091	48	52

Source: Higher Education Publications (1985).

Private institutions serve 23 percent of enrolled students (see Table 5-2). Again, the distribution of these students by state varies significantly. More than 50 percent of the students enrolled in private institutions are in just six states: New York, Massachusetts, Pennsylvania, California, Illinois, and Ohio. On a state-by-state basis, the proportion that private enrollment is of total enrollment ranges from less than 1 percent in Nevada and Wyoming to more than 50 percent in Massachusetts, Rhode Island, and the District of Columbia.

As these data indicate, based on size alone, private institutions represent a significant component of the total system of higher education. Moreover, private higher education institutions contribute disproportionately to diversity with their broad array of institutional types and affiliations. These institutions serve a public purpose both by educating large numbers of students and by offering students choices not always available in the public sector. This chapter reviews

Table 5–2. Fall 1984 Enrollment by State in Public and Private Higher Education Institutions.

	Public Institutions	Private Institutions	Total	Private as Percentage of Total
Alabama	149,579	22,052	171,631	13
Alaska	26,005	986	26,991	4
Arizona	196,537	13,492	210,029	6
Arkansas	66,753	12,024	78,777	15
California	1,441,801	223,354	1,665,155	13
Colorado	144,885	19,509	164,394	12
Connecticut	100,754	60,822	161,576	38
Delaware	27,422	4,450	31,872	14
District of Columbia	13,450	66,300	79,750	83
Florida	354,156	89,906	444,062	20
Georgia	150,035	46,834	196,869	24
Hawaii	43,806	6,175	49,981	12
Idaho	34,918	8,385	43,303	19
Illinois	504,549	156,565	661,114	24
Indiana	192,618	57,339	249,957	23
Iowa	109,800	43,269	153,069	28
Kansas	127,211	14,705	141,916	10
Kentucky	112,702	30,853	143,555	21
Louisiana	154,846	25,142	179,988	14
Maine	33,436	19,278	52,714	37
Maryland	201,894	32,408	234,302	14
Massachusetts	183,084	235,882	418,966	56
Michigan	433,134	72,200	505,334	14
Minnesota	168,726	46,840	215,566	22
Mississippi	92,641	11,698	104,339	11
Missouri	170,092	70,828	240,920	29
Montana	32,716	4,345	37,061	12
Nebraska	80,221	17,201	97,422	18
Nevada	42,700	307	43,007	1
New Hampshire	27,323	25,726	53,049	48
New Jersey	243,388	61,942	305,330	20
New Mexico	64,261	2,246	66,507	3
New York	567,151	440,619	1,007,770	44
North Carolina	249,417	59,832	309,249	19
North Dakota	34,441	3,144	37,585	8

Table 5-2. continued

	Public Institutions	Private Institutions	Total	Private as Percentage of Total
Ohio	381,610	136,825	518,435	26
Oklahoma	145,822	22,212	168,034	13
Oregon	123,231	18,579	141,810	13
Pennsylvania	301,172	227,497	528,669	43
Rhode Island	34,507	34,638	69,145	50
South Carolina	105,213	26,266	131,479	20
South Dakota	24,023	8,450	32,473	26
Tennessee	152,797	48,140	200,937	24
Texas	703,717	91,620	795,337	12
Utah	67,215	34,648	101,863	34
Vermont	18,192	12,594	30,786	41
Virginia	245,104	38,005	283,109	13
Washington	200,857	29,810	230,667	13
West Virginia	68,384	10,625	79,009	13
Wisconsin	235,084	35,781	270,865	13
Wyoming	23,424	0	23,424	0
U.S. Service Schools	52,788	0	52,788	—
Total	9,459,592	2,782,348	12,241,940	23

Source: "Fact File: Fall 1984 Enrollment" (1986).

the history of public support for private higher education, examines the constitutional issues related to support, and describes current programs. The chapter concludes with a discussion of the challenges of the next decade.

HISTORY OF PUBLIC SUPPORT FOR PRIVATE HIGHER EDUCATION

The history of public support for private higher education has been outlined in *The States and Private Higher Education* (Carnegie 1977). In the United States, public support has been provided since colonial times to private institutions. Beginning in 1636 the General Court of Massachusetts provided the first funds for Harvard and con-

Table 5-3. State Support of Private Institutions (in millions of dollars).

	Scholarships and Grant Programs to Undergraduate Students in Private Institutions from Programs Available to		Direct Aid to Institutions				
			Unrestricted	Restricted			Total
				Financial Aid	Health and Other Contracts	Other	
	All Students	Students in Private Institutions Only					
Alabama	$ 1.623	$ 3.500	$ 2.900				$ 8.023
Alaska	.054						.054
Arizona	.077						.077
Arkansas	.993						.993
California	72.005						72.005
Colorado	.400						.400
Connecticut	2.330			$ 6.105	$ .047		8.482
Delaware	.170						.170
District of Columbia	.550						.550
Florida	9.634	13.300			.424		23.358
Georgia	1.555	10.900					12.455
Hawaii	.197						.197
Idaho	.102						.102
Illinois	77.000		12.900		17.500	$ 6.000	113.400
Indiana	9.459	8.942					18.401
Iowa	.341	20.733					21.074
Kansas	.218	4.350					4.568

State							
Kentucky	1.100	4.852					5.952
Louisiana	.362						.362
Maine	.259						.259
Maryland	2.683		14.721			4.955	22.359
Massachusetts	26.340		a		7.875		34.215
Michigan	5.000	39.990	4.190			3.200	52.380
Minnesota	23.232		3.115				26.347
Mississippi	.576						.576
Missouri	8.102						8.102
Montana	.037						.037
Nebraska	.294						.294
Nevada							
New Hampshire	.128						.128
New Jersey	23.528		16.100		4.441		44.069
New Mexico	.412						.412
New York	246.790		112.983	16.083	17.157		393.013
North Carolina	1.274	19.800		9.800			30.874
North Dakota	.034	.255					.289
Ohio	24.313			9.800	6.211		40.324
Oklahoma	2.391						2.391
Oregon	1.560				1.506		3.066
Pennsylvania	53.633		55.796	17.888			127.317
Rhode Island	1.801						1.801

(Table 5–3. continued overleaf)

Table 5-3. continued

	Scholarships and Grant Programs to Undergraduate Students in Private Institutions from Programs Available to		Direct Aid to Institutions				
			Unrestricted	Restricted			
					Health and		
				Financial	Other		
	All Students	Students in Private Institutions Only		Aid	Contracts	Other	Total
South Carolina	.142	14.600					14.742
South Dakota		.200					.200
Tennessee	6.609						6.609
Texas		18.806			39.561		58.367
Utah	.032						.032
Vermont	3.082						3.082
Virginia	1.074	12.540					13.614
Washington	1.562						1.562
West Virginia	1.338						1.338
Wisconsin	1.558	11.644			10.343		23.545
Wyoming							
Total	$615.954	$184.412	$222.705	$67.551	$100.390	$10.955	$1,201.967

a. Zero-funded in FY 1986, $3.6 million in FY 1985.

Sources: Balz (1983), Marks (1985), Reeher and Davis (1986), telephone surveys, Gardner, Atwell, and Berdahl (1985).

Note: Includes only funds spent by a state at in-state private institutions. Excludes funds provided as financial aid that students took out-of-state and excludes expenditures for contracts outside the state. Also excludes expenditures of state funds at private institutions attributable to competitive grant programs.

tinued to appropriate funds for the next hundred years. It has been estimated that colleges during the colonial period depended on public support for one-third to one-half of their income. In the post-Revolutionary period, publicly owned colleges were founded in increasing numbers, but the distinction between public and private institutions as recipients of public financial support remained blurred throughout the mid-nineteenth century.

Because of increasing public support for state institutions, the competing demands for public funds, the emergence of church/state issues concerning aid to private institutions, and the increase in total numbers of institutions, public support for private institutions gradually diminished during the last half of the nineteenth century. However, the primary source of operating funds for all public and private institutions during the last half of the nineteenth century was private funds. Direct state support for private institutions never was totally eliminated, but by the mid-twentieth century, most states were concentrating their financial support on public institutions.

In the 1960s the trend began to reverse, and states began initiating new programs of state support to private institutions. Much of the new support came in the form of need-based student financial aid programs, but programs of nonneed financial aid and direct institutional aid were started (Carnegie 1977). By 1986 all states except Nevada and Wyoming were providing financial support to private institutions either directly or through student financial aid programs (see Table 5–3). A new consensus appears to have emerged regarding the need for public support for private institutions. However, the form of this support varied considerably from state to state.

CONSTITUTIONAL ISSUES IN PUBLIC SUPPORT OF PRIVATE HIGHER EDUCATION

Much of the variation in funding methods used by states to finance private institutions is the result of constitutional requirements. The first amendment to the U.S. Constitution includes the establishment clause—which states that "the Congress shall make no law respecting an establishment of religion." While this clause applies only to the Congress, the U.S. Supreme Court has interpreted the establishment clause to be applicable to the states under the due process clause of the fourteenth amendment (McFarlane and Wheeler 1971). Because nearly 50 percent of the private higher education institutions are church-related to some degree (Breneman and Finn 1978), the establishment clause has been the basis of court challenges to state support. Some individuals have held the view that the establishment clause constitutes a "wall of separation" between church and state and that, consequently, no tax support is legitimate. However, the federal courts have held a more flexible point of view (McFarlane and Wheeler 1971).

Much of the litigation on church/state separation has involved elementary and secondary schools, but several key Supreme Court decisions were handed down in the 1970s regarding support to private higher education. *Tilton v. Richardson* (1971) upheld the Federal Higher Education Facilities Act of 1963, which provided federal construction grants for college and university facilities to use for nonsectarian purposes. In 1973, in *Hunt v. McNair*, the Court upheld the creation in South Carolina of an authority to issue revenue bonds to assist private higher education institutions in constructing capital facilities. In *Roemer v. Board of Public Works* (1975), the Court upheld a program of direct unrestricted grants to independent institutions, including some church-related colleges, in Maryland (Howard 1977).

In arriving at these decisions, the Court applied a three-part test that evolved from prior church/state decisions: (1) The program must have a secular legislative purpose; (2) the primary effect of the program can neither advance nor inhibit religion; and (3) the administration of the program cannot involve excessive government entanglement with religion (*Lemon v. Kurtzman* 1971). The Supreme Court generally has taken the position that the primary purpose of private higher education institutions is to provide their students with a secular education and that an institution must be "pervasively sectarian" before aid to the institution would have the primary effect of advancing religion (Howard 1977).

Given the existing case law and precedent, states have encountered little difficulty in devising programs to aid private higher education institutions that meet constitutionality tests with regard to the U.S. Constitution. State constitutions, however, may prove more significant constraints. State constitutions tend to be considerably more detailed and more restrictive concerning state power than the federal constitution (Howard 1977). Regarding state support for private higher education institutions, many state constitutions have clauses more restrictive than the first amendment to the U.S. Constitution (ECS 1977). Beyond the church/state issues, aid to private institutions may be limited by a state's debt, credit, or other finance clause provisions (Howard 1977). Some state constitutions explicitly prohibit aid to all nonpublic institutions (ECS 1977). In this complex legal environment, it is not surprising that state efforts to provide financial support to private institutions have resulted in a wide array of program combinations.

CURRENT PRACTICES IN STATE FINANCIAL SUPPORT FOR PRIVATE HIGHER EDUCATION

In FY 1986 all states except Nevada and Wyoming provided some aid to private institutions. States have various motivations for providing support to private institutions. This discussion focuses on access, choice, diversity, and efficiency. To provide access to a variety of institutions, both public and private, many states provide financial aid to students attending private institutions to narrow the "tuition gap"—that is, the difference between the average cost of attendance at private and public colleges as a percentage of the cost at public colleges. In 1976-77 the average cost of attendance at private colleges was $3,714 compared with $1,828 at public institutions (Table 5-4). In 1983-84 the average cost was $7,244 at private colleges, an increase of 95.1 percent since 1976-77, compared with $3,285 at the public colleges, an increase of 79.7 percent since 1976-77. The tuition gap had widened somewhat from 103 percent in 1976-77 to 120.5 percent in 1983-84.

Several states provide support for private institutions to ensure their viability and their diversity. States provide support both on a regular basis to private institutions as well as on an irregular basis to a specific institution that is having financial difficulty. States frequently contract with private institutions for instruction in expensive program areas so that the programs do not have to be duplicated in the public sector. In addition to the above rationale for state support for private higher education, private institutions make significant contributions to the economic development of state and local areas.

State support has been provided in three ways: financial aid to students attending private institutions, direct aid to private institutions, and indirect aid. Rather than providing direct assistance to

Table 5-4. Average Cost of Attendance at Independent and Public
Institutions, 1976-84.

Year	Independent Colleges	Public Colleges	Gap	
			Dollars	Percentage
1976-77	$3,714	$1,828	$1,886	103.0%
1977-78	3,968	1,932	2,036	105.4
1978-79	4,326	2,027	2,299	113.4
1979-80	4,699	2,198	2,501	113.8
1980-81	5,249	2,420	2,829	116.9
1981-82	5,949	2,701	3,248	120.3
1982-83	6,646	3,032	3,614	119.2
1983-84	7,244	3,285	3,959	120.5
Percentage Increase	95.1%	79.7%		

Source: The University of the State of New York (1986).
Note: Average cost of attendance includes tuition, fees, and room and board charges.

private institutions or their students, perhaps the most significant
assistance is in the form of indirect aid through public policy. Nelson
(1978: 68) has summarized the policy as follows:

> Among states, the amount of support for private higher education is un-
> related to the subsidies provided for public students. The states that support
> their private sectors most generously are those with high public tuition, a high
> budget priority for higher education, or a large percentage of their students
> enrolled in private institutions.

Aid to Students Attending Private Institutions

Table 5-3 displays the amount of aid by type provided by the states
in FY 1986. The most common mechanism used by states to support private institutions was financial aid to students. In FY 1986
states spent $800.4 million on financial aid to students attending
private institutions. These expenditures for students at private institutions represent more than 50 percent of the total financial aid
expenditures by the states (Reeher and Davis 1986). State financial
aid received by students accounted for almost 70 percent of all the
state funds at private institutions.

The states provided $184.4 million in financial aid through programs available only to students at private institutions. Fifteen states had such programs with the largest programs being in Michigan ($40.0 million), Iowa ($20.7 million), North Carolina ($19.8 million), and Texas ($18.8 million). Programs in five states (Alabama, Florida, Georgia, North Carolina, and Virginia) were not based on need; rather, a fixed dollar amount was provided to each undergraduate resident student who attends a private institution in the state; these programs generally are known as tuition equalization programs. The programs in the other ten states were need-based, and awards varied based on the cost of the private institution attended and the student's ability to pay.

The majority of student aid available to students attending private institutions, $616 million, was provided through programs available to students attending both public and private institutions. All states that aid private institutions except South Dakota and Texas had programs of this type.

Among these financial aid programs, the majority of the funds were in need-based programs. Some programs made awards based on academic achievement or merit, and there were numerous small special-purpose programs. The states with the largest programs were New York ($246.8 million), Illinois ($77.0 million), and California ($72.0 million). Generally, the average award to students attending private institutions was higher than to students at public institutions because of the significantly higher tuition and fees at the private institutions. Aid programs that benefit students at private institutions more are those that have high maximum awards. For example, in California, the Cal Grant A program had a maximum award of $4,110, and 77.5 percent of the total funds in the program were awarded to students at in-state private institutions. The majority of programs have maximum award levels between $1,000 and $2,000.

Direct State Aid to Institutions

A second major form of providing financial support to private institutions is direct state aid; sixteen states used this form of aid. Direct aid to institutions may be categorized as restricted or unrestricted. Unrestricted aid is money appropriated directly to private institutions with minimal conditions for its use by the institution; the funds may not be used for religious or sectarian purposes but may be used to support any other activity at the institution. Restricted aid includes funds appropriated to institutions for particular purposes only, such as financial assistance to students, medical education, purchase of contracts, or facilities.

Eight states provided $222.7 million in unrestricted aid in FY 1986. In six of these states aid was provided through a formula to the private institutions. Maryland and New Jersey had formulas that are based on state appropriations at the public four-year institutions. In Maryland, aid per student was equal to 16 percent of the per student appropriations at Maryland public institutions; in New Jersey the formula was based on 25 percent of appropriations at the state colleges, but this formula has never been fully funded. New Jersey considered only resident students in calculating the formula, whereas Maryland based its calculation on all students. In Maryland the state funds were distributed based on the institutional enrollment; in New Jersey the total pool of funds was allocated as follows: 10 percent across-the-board; 35 percent for students receiving $1,000 or more in aid; and 55 percent on the basis of New Jersey students enrolled.

The formulas in Illinois and Minnesota were based on a dollar amount per resident undergraduate student. In Michigan and New York, state aid was based on the number of degrees produced. The dollars provided increased with the level of the degree. For example, in New York the rates were $600 per associate degree (only paid at two-year institutions), $1,500 per bachelor's degree, $950 per master's degree, and $4,550 per doctorate. In New York, 97 private institutions participated in this program, known as the Bundy program.

Pennsylvania had twelve state-aided institutions, which received $55.8 million in FY 1986. Over half of these funds went to the University of Pennsylvania. Alabama provided $2.9 million in unrestricted state funds to four private institutions. Tuskegee received more than 50 percent of the state funds. Maryland also provided $900,000 in unrestricted aid to one private institution predicated only on the institution's raising $1 million for its endowment.

The states spent $178.9 million in restricted, direct aid to private institutions in FY 1986. Six states spent $67.6 million on aid to private institutions that can be used only for financial aid. Connecticut and Ohio had formulas based on state aid to public institutions. In Connecticut the private independent institutions received 8.5 percent of the per student appropriations at Connecticut State and the University of Connecticut for each resident student; in Ohio the private institutions received 25 percent of the state subsidy for all undergraduates at the public institutions. Massachusetts provided $7.9 million to its private institutions based on the institutions' expenditures on financial aid for needy resident full-time undergraduate students. New York provided $5 million for the institutional match for Federal College Work Study dollars and $11.083 million for the Higher Education Opportunity Program. Funds in this program were allocated to private institutions as a subsidy for providing special educational opportunities for financially and/or educationally disadvantaged students. The institutions must match these funds and more than half of the money must be used for financial aid. North Carolina provided a fixed dollar amount per resident undergraduate student. Pennsylvania provided $17.9 million in Institutional Assistance Grants to the seventy-four private institutions that are not state aided.

Ten states spent $100.4 million to purchase spaces for students in health and other fields. Almost $100 million of these funds were used to support medical and dental education either through the purchase of student spaces or direct appropriations to the schools. Texas spent almost $40 million on the medical and dental schools at Baylor, and Illinois and New York each spent more than $17 million to support health education. Not reflected in these data were student spaces purchased by states for medical, dental, and other specialized education at private institutions in other states. For example, many states purchased spaces for medical students at Meharry Medical School in Nashville. Two states contracted with in-state private institutions for non–health education programs. Connecticut spent $47,000 for engineering student spaces, and Florida purchased some student spaces in social work from private institutions.

The remaining $11 million supported capital funding in Illinois and Maryland. In Illinois $1 million was allocated to Elmhurst College to build a resource center; $5 million was allocated to the Build Illinois program, under which the state was to sell bonds for renovation and repair of laboratory facilities at private institutions. In 1986 Maryland provided $5 million as matching funds for capital facilities at four private institutions. Maryland provided up to 50 percent of the cost of selected nonauxiliary facilities at private institutions.

Indirect Assistance to Private Higher
Education Institutions

The third major form of aid to private institutions is indirect assistance. States provided indirect assistance to private higher education in several ways. Many states have established facilities authorities that allow the private institutions to issue tax-free bonds. New York and South Carolina allowed private institutions to use state contracts when purchasing goods.

Among the most important indirect forms of state aid are the exemption from property taxes of most land and facilities of private institutions and the sales tax exemptions. Sunley estimated the loss in property tax revenues exceeded $200 million in 1976 (Breneman and Finn 1978). In most states, private institutions are exempt from paying sales taxes on the goods and services they purchase. In addition, sales taxes are not levied on tuition and room and board charges. Most states allow deduction of contributions to private institutions from state income taxes. Idaho, Indiana, Michigan, and North Dakota permit a tax credit for contributions to private institutions (Balz 1983). New York and North Carolina allow deductions on the personal income tax for dependents attending college. New York also has a college IRA fund; under this program taxpayers may save pretax dollars for their dependent's college education.

New Initiatives

Several states have developed programs to foster economic development and quality improvement in specific areas. Most of these programs are competitive, and many states allow private institutions to compete along with public institutions. Funds for these purposes are not included in Table 5–4, since these funds usually are awarded through competitive proposals or require matching funds and therefore cannot be considered as basic institutional support. In general these programs were not designed specifically to provide aid to private institutions.

Illinois began a program of engineering equipment grants in FY 1986. This is a matching grant program for institutions with accredited engineering programs. The private institutions received $316,000 in the first year of the program.

Minnesota recently started a Job Skills Partnership program, which makes awards to public and private institutions to develop and provide training programs to Minnesota companies. New Jersey has initiated several new programs including the Fund for Improvement of Collegiate Institutions, the Innovation Partnership Grants Program to support and promote graduate level research, and several other programs focusing on specific disciplines. In FY 1984 New Jersey appropriated more than $9 million for these programs.

New York has several competitive programs. In FY 1986, four out of ten endowed chairs funded by the state were at private institutions. The research and development grants program funded research projects that have commercial potential at academic institutions and not-for-profit laboratories in New York. In 1984 New York established the Empire State Mathematics and Science Teacher Fellowships program under which 400 fellowships are awarded to students on the basis of a statewide competition. The fellowships may be used at any public or private institution in New York (Breslin 1986).

North Carolina established a Microelectronics Center (MCNC), which is a consortium of the five major universities in North Carolina and the Research Triangle Institute. More than $82 million in state funds were invested in the center for construction equipment and operating expenses.

Pennsylvania has funded the Ben Franklin program with several components. The Partnership Challenge Grant Program, established in 1983, has four Advanced Technology Centers, each one made up of a consortium of public and private institutions. The state matched the funds raised by the centers from industry and other sources. In 1986 the state contributed $21.3 million, and this amount was matched by $80.9 million from industry. Another of the Ben Franklin programs, the engineering school equipment grants, provided a total of $3 million in state funds and required a three-to-one match of private funds. These funds were distributed according to a formula to the fifteen colleges that offered engineering programs.

Ohio has enacted a competitive research program that provides that up to 20 percent of the state funds in the program may go to private institutions. Rhode Island has funded the Rhode Island Partnership, a consortium between the University of Rhode Island and Brown University that provides technical advice to companies. Several other states have established programs of this type, and many more are considering them. These partnerships between the state, industry, and higher education are emerging primarily as a catalyst to economic development.

THE CHALLENGE FOR THE NEXT DECADE

As noted earlier, much of the growth that resulted in the current programs of support for private higher education occurred during the 1960s and 1970s when the entire system of higher education in this country was growing at an extraordinary rate (see Table 5-5). Between 1960 and 1980 enrollment in higher education in the United States more than tripled from 3.6 million to 12.1 million students. Most of this growth occurred in the public sector as existing colleges and universities expanded both in size and mission and new institutions, particularly community colleges, were created. However, enrollments in the private sector increased from 1.5 million to 2.6 million during the same period. While their share of total enrollment was declining, private institutions were nonetheless serving a large number of students. During this period subsidies for students attending private institutions or for the institutions themselves appeared to be a less expensive alternative to taxpayers than building additional capacity in the already overloaded public sector. Programs of aid to the private sector were not initiated without controversy in the states. However, most of the programs were small, and state higher

Table 5-5. Number and Percentage Distributions of Enrollments in Public and Private Institutions, Selected Years 1950 to 1984.

Year	Total Enrollment	Public Enrollment	Private Enrollment	Percentage Public	Percentage Private
1950	2,296,592	1,154,456	1,142,136	50%	50%
1955	2,678,623	1,498,510	1,180,113	56	44
1960	3,610,007	2,135,690	1,474,317	59	41
1965	5,570,271	3,654,578	1,915,693	66	34
1970	7,985,532	5,845,032	2,140,500	73	27
1975	9,830,224	7,480,524	2,349,700	76	24
1980	12,096,895	9,457,394	2,639,501	78	22
1984	12,241,940	9,459,592	2,782,348	77	23

Sources: Breneman and Finn (1978: 22); Broyles (1983: 86–88); "Fact File: Fall 1984 Enrollment" (1986: 26).

education appropriations were growing for all sectors; thus, most disputes were relatively minor (Berdahl 1978).

The circumstances under which the programs of aid to private institutions developed no longer exist. The anticipated decline in enrollments as a result of the decline in the 18- to 24-year-old population has begun in some sectors of higher education. The number of high school graduates is projected to drop 25 percent between 1979 and 1994, resulting in a 15 percent decline in college enrollments (Gardner, Atwell, and Berdahl 1985). With a declining population and with increased competition from other programs for limited state resources, higher education may have difficulty sustaining its current share of state resources, much less increasing that share. Inevitably some contraction of the system of higher education must occur during this period. The issue facing states is whether they will attempt to manage the reduction through planning and cooperation among the various sectors or whether they will simply let the market determine where the reduction occurs.

Private higher education institutions are potentially much more vulnerable to declines in enrollment because tuition and fee revenues are their primary source of income for operating purposes (Table 5-6). Institutions that experience significant enrollment declines may be forced to close because replacement revenues are simply not available. The University of Albuquerque, for example, announced that it will close as of August 1986. Enrollment had declined from 1,500 to 1,100 between the falls of 1983 and 1984. The resulting tuition income was inadequate to maintain operations and the institution had no endowment ("U. of Albuquerque to Close in August" 1986). Similar enrollment declines might not result in the closing of public institutions if the state increases its subsidy to keep institutions open.

Two recent situations provide another example of what may happen when a state experiences significant revenue shortfalls. In Louisiana, when revenues were not realized as a result of declining oil prices, funding for the program of aid to private colleges was eliminated as part of required retrenchments. This program had been in existence since the early 1970s and had appropriations of more than $3 million in FY 1985. In Mississippi, after several rounds of cuts in higher education appropriations, the statewide governing board recommended the closing of two public undergraduate institutions, a dental school, and a veterinary medicine school to help pre-

Table 5-6. Comparison of Percentage of Distribution of Institutional Expenditures and Revenues for Public and Independent Institutions in the United States, FY 1982.

	Public Institutions	Independent Institutions
Expenditures		
Instruction	44%	37%
Academic support	9	8
Research	11	11
Public service	5	2
Other E&G expenditures	31	42
Total	100	100
Revenues		
State and local appropriations	59	2
Tuition and fees	17	51
Private gifts, grants, endowments	4	19
Government grants and contracts	13	18
Other E&G revenue	7	7
Total	100	100

Source: McCoy and Halstead (1984).

serve the quality in the remaining public sector institutions ("Mississippi Board Recommends Closing" 1986). The proposal quickly died in the state legislature and cuts were taken at all institutions ("Bills to Close 2 Mississippi Universities" 1986). Closing public institutions in most states is very difficult.

The condition of the system of higher education varies significantly from state to state. The overall demographic trends will not affect all states equally; some may see continued increases in total enrollment during this period. However, as observed above, over half of the nation's private institutions are in eight states concentrated in the northeast and the midwest, areas with projected low growth or decline in college-age population. In addition, the fiscal condition of all private institutions varies: Financial conditions range from marginal to robust. Consequently, there is no single prescription that will ensure the continued viability of private higher education in each state. States, regardless, will be faced with both an educational and political dilemma of trying to cope with enrollment decline. As Breneman and Finn (1978: 51) pointed out:

the possibility must seriously be entertained that if substantial overall contraction does occur in a state's postsecondary system, and if the state does not forcefully intervene in that process, then (1) the "wrong" programs and institutions will survive through their skill at political manipulation, (2) the private sector will suffer a disproportionate and possibly undesirable retrenchment, and (3) randomized, piecemeal erosion will occur, resulting in a large number of crippled institutions rather than a smaller complement of healthy ones.

States are not responsible for the survival of all existing private institutions or all public institutions. Each state must determine the overall system of higher education that will best meet the needs of its citizens and foster policies that will ensure the success of that system.

REFERENCES

Balz, Frank J. 1983. *Sources of State Support for Independent Higher Education 1982–83.* Washington, D.C.: National Institute of Independent Colleges and Universities.

Berdahl, Robert O. 1978. "The Politics of State Aid." In *Public Policy and Private Higher Education*, edited by D. Breneman and C. Finn, Jr., pp. 321–52. Washington, D.C.: The Brookings Institution.

"Bills to Close 2 Mississippi Universities Die in Legislature." 1986c. *The Chronicle of Higher Education* 31 (22) (February 12): 9.

Breneman, David W., and Chester E. Finn, Jr., eds. 1978. *Public Policy and Private Higher Education.* Washington, D.C.: The Brookings Institution.

Breslin, Janice. 1986. *State Initiatives to Promote Technological Innovation and Economic Growth.* Annapolis, Md.: State Board for Higher Education.

Broyles, S.G. 1983. *Fall Enrollment In Colleges and Universities 1982.* Washington, D.C.: National Center for Education Statistics.

The Carnegie Council on Policy Studies in Higher Education. 1977. *The States and Private Higher Education.* San Francisco: Jossey-Bass.

Education Commission of the States. 1977. *Final Report and Recommendations: Task Force on State Policy and Independent Higher Education.* Denver, Colo.: ECS.

"Fact File: Fall 1984 Enrollment." 1986. *Chronicle of Higher Education* 31 (19) (January 22): 26.

Gardner, J.W., R.H. Atwell, and R.O. Berdahl. 1985. *Cooperation and Conflict.* Washington, D.C.: Association of Governing Boards of Universities and Colleges.

Higher Education Publications, Inc. 1985. *1985 Higher Education Directory.* Washington, D.C.: HEP.

Howard, A.E. Dick. 1977. *State Aid to Private Higher Education.* Charlottesville, Va.: Michie.

Hunt v. McNair, 413 U.S. 734 (1973).

Lemon v. Kurtzman, 403 U.S. 602, 608, 614 (1971).

Marks, Joseph. 1985. 'State Supported Programs for Private Higher Education." Atlanta, Ga.: Southern Regional Education Board. Mimeo.

McCoy, Marilyn, and D. Kent Halstead. 1984. *Higher Education Financing in the Fifty States, 4th Edition.* Boulder, Colo.: National Center for Higher Education Management Systems, Inc.

McFarlane, William H., and Charles L. Wheeler. 1971. *Legal and Political Issues of State Aid for Private Higher Education.* Atlanta: Southern Regional Education Board.

"Mississippi Board Recommends Closing 2 Universities and 2 Professional Schools." 1986. *Chronicle of Higher Education* 31 (20) (January 29): 11.

Nelson, Susan C. 1978. "Financial Trends and Issues." In *Public Policy and Private Higher Education,* edited by David W. Breneman and Chester E. Finn, Jr. pp. 63–142. Washington, D.C.: The Brookings Institution.

Reeher, Kenneth R., and Jerry S. Davis. 1986. *17th Annual Survey Report 1985-86 Academic Year.* Harrisburg, Pa.: National Association of State Scholarship and Grant Programs.

Roemer v. Board of Public Works, 387 F. Supp. 1282 (D. Md. 1974), prob. juris. noted, 420 U.S. 922 (1975).

Sloan Commission on Government and Higher Education. 1980. *A Program for Renewed Partnership.* Cambridge, Mass.: Ballinger.

Tilton v. Richardson, 403 U.S. 672 (1971).

The University of the State of New York. 1986. *Net Cost of Attendance at Postsecondary Institutions in New York State.* Albany, N.Y.: State Education Department.

"U. of Albuquerque to Close in August." 1986. *Chronicle of Higher Education* 32 (3) (March 19): 2.

6 TUITION AND FEES
Pricing Strategies

Richard A. Yanikoski

The process of setting tuition prices usually occasions more anxiety than comfort. Decisionmakers must balance complex and sometimes incompatible educational, economic, ideological, political, and market considerations. Needs for additional revenue to maintain or improve quality butt against a desire to keep prices competitively low. Concerns about access, choice, and market share give pause to even the most aggressive price setters. Uncertainty about financial aid funding further complicates deliberations about pricing. In these circumstances year-to-year changes in tuition prices typically take the form of incremental adjustments.

During the past ten years, however, many colleges and universities have adopted price strategies that challenge some traditional assumptions. An increasing number of institutions are indexing tuition to costs, adopting differential pricing, adding new service fees, or imposing large course surcharges. Other institutions are offering guaranteed four-year prices to incoming freshmen or reduced rates to special categories of students.

This chapter examines selected pricing principles, outlines five basic price-setting approaches, and reviews several types of price variation currently in use. Three caveats are in order. First, this chapter focuses on issues pertinent to pricing decisions, not on the processes by which decisions are made. The latter, though of critical importance, are beyond the scope of this work. Second, the exam-

113

ples and accompanying analysis in this chapter are drawn predominantly from universities and senior colleges rather than from two-year colleges or special purpose institutions. Although many of the same issues apply with equal force to all institutions, the author's research has concentrated on baccalaureate and graduate institutions. Finally, this chapter examines only tuition and academic fees, not room and board charges or miscellaneous fees.

Two definitions also need to be noted. The term *price* in this chapter refers to charges listed in published recruitment literature. Any special discounts or surcharges published in college catalogs and offered to large groups of prospective students (for example, age-related discounts or out-of-state rates) are treated as price variations. All unpublished, individual discounts or waivers (for example, merit discounts or employee tuition waivers) are treated as forms of financial aid. The term *cost* in this chapter refers not to a student's expenditures but to the resources expended by an institution to educate one or more students.

SELECTED PRICING PRINCIPLES

Three aspects of tuition pricing stand out in bold relief to observers of U.S. higher education. First is the phenomenon of rapidly rising prices (Suttle 1983). A recent article in *Fortune* (Ross 1985) points out that in inflation-adjusted dollars average tuition prices were 43 percent lower a quarter-century ago than they are today. Much of the increase came in the late 1970s and early 1980s, when colleges battled to keep ahead of double-digit inflation. The National Center for Education Statistics (1985) reported that between 1973–74 and 1983–84 the average price of tuition at private four-year colleges and private universities rose 145.5 percent and 161.8 percent respectively, well above the 118.2 percent increase in the cost of living index adjusted to an academic calendar. At public four-year colleges and public universities average tuition prices increased 127.2 percent and 121.0 percent, still above the CPI but within proximate range.

No end to steep annual increases is in sight. Figures provided by the College Board (1985) show that average tuition prices continue to rise more than twice as fast as the consumer price index, which at the time of this writing is increasing at a rate below 3.5 percent per year. Average undergraduate tuition and fees in both public and private four-year institutions for 1985–86 were 8.5 percent above 1984–85 rates. In public and private two-year institutions increases averaged 7.3 percent and 8.1 percent respectively. Many colleges and universities are imposing price increases significantly higher than these national averages ("Tuition and Fees at 2,600 Colleges and Universities, 1985–86" 1985). During 1985–86 the University of Scranton raised prices 16.8 percent, Alaska Pacific University 18.7, Elmhurst College 19.3, and Bethel College 19.6. Perhaps the leader in 1985–86 was Eureka College, the president's alma mater, which increased tuition and mandatory fees 29.1. The prior year it raised rates 12.7. Graduate and professional programs, despite already higher charges, are not immune to large annual increases. In Illinois, for instance, 1985–86 tuition increases in six private and three public law schools ranged from 5.3 to 21.0 percent, with an average increase of 9.9 (McHugh 1985).

The total price of higher education for most students includes a variety of charges in addition to tuition and mandatory fees. Room and board, books and supplies, transportation, special fees, and other essential expenses add approximately $3,000 per year. In the public sector these charges frequently comprise three-quarters of an undergraduate's total college expenses. These figures reflect list prices, not actual student payments after financial aid or parental support.

A second obvious feature of tuition pricing in the United States is the wide and in some places widening gap between low-cost and high-cost institutions. Most readily observed are price differences between public and private institutions. In 1985–86 the average "gap" in annual undergraduate tuition and mandatory fees between the sectors nationally was $4,176. The current private-to-public price ratio of 4.4 to 1 is only slightly higher than the average ratio of the past two decades but is up markedly from 3.3 to 1 thirty years ago and 2.4 to 1 a half-century ago (McPherson 1978: 160). Similar disparities affect graduate and professional programs. In the law schools in Illinois, private tuition rates for 1985–86 averaged $6,749 more per year than charges in public institutions, resulting in a price ratio of 4.8:1 (McHugh 1985).

Arguments for and against a two-sector approach to tuition pricing have roots planted deep in U.S. educational practice (Van Alstyne 1974; Hearn and Longanecker 1985). This is not the place to reopen an old debate, but a summary of main points may help to clarify the current context for setting tuition prices in the public sector. The rationale for low-price public higher education rests chiefly on four premises: (1) Social benefits of higher education, like those of elementary and secondary schooling, justify generous tax support; (2) low tuition encourages a maximum number and variety of qualified students to try higher education, especially in states with few private institutions; (3) direct state funding provides a more stable planning environment for public institutions than portable scholarships would permit; and (4) over the long term, low tuition is easier to defend politically than inflation-driven increases in scholarship funds.

Three major counterarguments support the point of view that tuition in the public sector should cover an increasing portion of educational and general expenses: (1) Low tuition heavily benefits middle- and upper-middle-income families, who generally can afford to pay a significant fraction of educational costs and who attend with greater regularity than poorer families; (2) the social benefits of higher education are no longer as dominant as they once were judged to be, hence students should pay a major portion of college costs; and (3) partial removal of tax subsidies for senior public universities might foster healthier competition among public and private institutions and provide students with a fairer choice among options, provided states channel funds into portable need-based scholarships.

Notwithstanding several decades of federal hearings and state studies on these conflicting points of view, no fully satisfying resolution has been reached. Ideological preferences generally favor low tuition in the public sector and moderate tuition in the private sector, but in actual practice a majority of institutions appear to be seeking ways to enlarge the share of operational costs borne by students through tuition and fees. Moreover, recent shifts in federal financial aid policy seem destined to ensure that students, families, and employers will assume the greatest share of all forthcoming price increases.

The much-publicized tuition gap between private and public sectors has obscured the fact that within the private sector alone there is an extraordinary range of prices, from less than $2,200 per year to more than $12,800. At the high end are eighteen private colleges and fifteen universities that charge in excess of $10,000 annually for tuition and mandatory fees. These institutions and the hundred or so four-year institutions that trail immediately behind them are, as a set, moving away from the bottom half of the private price spectrum faster than the latter group is moving away from the public sector. The causes and effects of this trend bear close watching.

Pricing strategies based on regional or national indexes of inflation are in large part responsible for this phenomenon. Whenever institutions (or sectors) with widely differing base rates impose a similar annual percentage increase in prices, the absolute difference between them will grow with each succeeding adjustment. Any given rate of increase will bring approximately twice as much gross new revenue per student to institutions in the top quarter of the price range as it will to institutions near or below the median. A "price leader" effect helps some middle-price institutions justify percentage price increases well above the mean, but few colleges can afford to impose price increases that run greatly ahead of the well-publicized percentage adjustments of elite colleges and universities. It remains to be seen how long present trends can continue before serious questions arise about the rationality of tuition prices at the ends of the spectrum.

The third major feature of tuition pricing is of recent vintage. It is the already noted increase in attention to pricing *strategy*, as distinct from the simpler matter of setting annual rates within a relatively fixed price structure. Many state coordinating boards, consortia, and individual institutions are taking bolder, more analytical approaches to tuition pricing than was previously in evidence (Litten 1984). Greater sophistication in costing and budgeting techniques, ever-rising financial pressures, uncertainty about protection of market shares, improvements in pricing research, and a sense of limited flexibility with traditional approaches are leading more and more colleges and universities to rethink their price strategies. A recent unpublished survey of undergraduate tuition policies found that 228 of 662 responding senior institutions (34 percent) had adopted some form of special or experimental pricing by 1984–85, and another 94 institutions (14 percent) considered doing so, mostly since 1980 (Yanikoski 1985). Approximately half of these price variations reflect relatively new price strategies; examples will be mentioned later in this chapter.

Accompanying the surge of attention to price strategy is renewed respect for the difficulty of determining what is a fair price. The concept of "fair price" is elusive because many conflicting social objectives bear on pricing decisions: low cost and low price versus higher quality at higher cost; concentrated excellence versus dispersed opportunity; maintenance of low prices to ensure access versus provision of financial aid to improve student choice or to ensure high institutional recruitment yields; maximization of social benefits versus furtherance of personal choice. Such tensions do not always pull in opposite directions, but they seldom pull in identical directions. As a consequence, those who set tuition rates must make prudent judgments based on compromised premises.

Traditional supply and demand rules offer little help. Student demand seldom is predictable with precision, and a market's sensitivity to price varies by type of student, locale, institutional prestige, availability of financial aid, and a host of other factors hard to assess as far in advance as pricing decisions must be made. Institutions with deep prospect pools can risk bold price changes, but most other colleges and universities feel a need to proceed cautiously, usually by adjusting rates incrementally without tampering with traditional price structures. Flat hourly rates or full-time package prices still predominate. Even when institutions detect unusually weak or strong student demand, they are hard pressed to alter prices accordingly over the short term. In times of strong demand social norms prevent the educational equivalent of profit-taking. In circumstances of declining demand, which now are common, short-term price cutting is effectively precluded by inflexible fixed costs on campus and by a reluctance to reduce prices for students in curricula that are not suffering slack demand.

This last point addresses two types of market segmentation, each of which has become increasingly important during the past decade. One type acknowledges the relative growth in enrollment of adult, working, part-time students. At a time when full-time, traditional-age undergraduate and graduate students are in dwindling supply, most institutions are welcoming to campus ever-larger numbers of so-called nontraditional students. Although market research on these students lags far behind market research on high school seniors, enough is known to realize that adult students are less homogeneous as a group than younger students. Adult students vary greatly in their sensitivity to published prices, and for many of them scheduling is more important than price. Adults less often benefit from governmental or institutional aid but frequently receive reimbursement from employers. The challenge facing each institution is to select one or more price structures attractive to both traditional and nontraditional students without simultaneously establishing rates that somehow seem disproportional to the services actually rendered to one or the other group.

The other form of market segmentation is by discipline, which at the undergraduate level is a fairly recent development. From the earliest decades of American higher education it was customary to charge undergraduates a single price regardless of field of study. This approach made sense from several points of view. There were no significant variations in instructional costs when most curricula consisted of lectures, perhaps augmented by simple laboratory experiments. When most students were residential, campus officials could count on a steady flow of revenue from nontuition bills. And before the era of transportable financial aid, there was a strong desire to protect students' freedom to select curricular specializations on a given campus. Circumstances are different today. First, institutions facing explosive enrollment in costly scientific and technical curricula, coupled with declining enrollment in less costly humanities or social sciences, are finding it increasingly difficult to rely on price averaging to balance budgets. Second, since most students today are part-time and nonresidential, tuition prices carry a larger portion of most institutions' budgets than was formerly the case. Finally, because it is becoming more common for institutions to actively recruit students for specific fields of study, often with tailored aid packages, there is mounting pressure in some areas to use price as a competitive marketing tool. The more segmented student recruiting becomes in the future, the more likely will be price segmentation.

Evidence for these conclusions comes from the survey previously mentioned (Yanikoski 1985). Respondents from institutions that presently have a variable or atypical price structure at the undergraduate level were asked to name the specific considerations that led them to adopt their price policy. The three leading reasons were a "desire to maximize enrollment, institution-wide or in selected programs," a "desire to make the price structure more equitable," and a "desire to recover the higher-than-average unit costs of certain academic programs." Satisfaction with price initiatives is reported to be high: Only 8 percent of the responding financial officers reported any displeasure among campus colleagues with current experiments, and 21 percent anticipated adopting additional price variations within three years. Student reactions were said to be favorable or neutral in all but 4 percent of the institutions.

PRICE-SETTING APPROACHES

An institution has five major options when selecting a basis for pricing its educational offerings. Used alone or in combination, these five alternatives are inflation indexing, cost-recovery indexing, peer pricing, assessment of what the market will bear, and budget balancing.

Inflation-indexing, either in a strict sense or by loose approximation, is one of the most commonly used methods for setting tuition prices. Tuition prices are set to mirror some externally determined index, typically the Consumer Price Index, the Producer Price Index, some measure of per capita disposable income, or the Higher Education Price Index. The last named index, available since 1971, tracks actual price changes of a mix of goods and services normally purchased by colleges and universities. Included are professional and nonprofessional salaries, benefits, contracted services, supplies, equipment, books and periodicals, and utilities. During the past four fiscal years this index has risen progressively faster than the CPI (Research Associates 1985) and is therefore an attractive index for institutions wishing to raise prices above prevailing rates of consumer inflation. Other external indexes that may be used for more specialized purposes include the Research and Development Price Index and the Boeckh Construction Index.

Institutions that use the second approach—indexing tuition prices to their own anticipated costs—still must keep a close watch on external inflationary trends. In addition, when estimating educational and general costs for a forthcoming year, an institution's officers must project expense requirements for the particular mix of programs, services, and students at that college or university. If cost study data have been gathered regularly and reliably in prior years, the projection process can proceed through extrapolation of known trends, adjusted for planned interventions. In the absence of detailed data, those who set tuition rates may be reduced to indexing future prices to aggregate educational and general expenditures, as revealed in an institution's audited year-end statements.

If an institution's officers wish to index prices to costs on a program-by-program basis, by student level, by course type or course level, or in some other disaggregated fashion, accurate historical data to support such distinctions are highly desirable. At a minimum an institution or state system must reach consensus concerning appropriate future indicators of program costs or resource requirements. Experience has shown either approach to be difficult and expensive. Joint costs are hard to assign. Program-specific capital investments tend to be treated awkwardly. Accidental cost differences and marginal costs are exceedingly hard to calculate in a manner that supports educational quality. The mere process of gathering and analyzing data can become a major administrative burden.

Fewer than one-fourth of the nation's colleges and universities presently have both the data and procedures necessary to project full costs or resource requirements on a program-by-program basis. In light of this fact, it is not surprising that most institutions that index tuition prices to internal costs do so on an institutionwide or systemwide basis, rather than program by program. One noteworthy trend is that the number of states using cost of education as a basis for price deliberations tripled during the past decade, which is consistent with predictions made in a national survey in the late 1970s (Adams et al. 1978) that by 1995 three-quarters of all senior colleges and universities would use cost information in determining prices.

Peer pricing is a third approach to setting tuition rates. A given institution first determines its perceived and actual competitors, which are not always identical. The institution then strives to keep its own prices within the range of these competitors. Whether by accident or design, this often leads to a form of information sharing that borders on collusion, as a set of institutions year after year maintains positional parity. On occasion one institution will adjust its prices radically upward or downward in order to position itself within a new set of competitors. Of late a number of midrange institutions have raised prices well above their immediate competition, partly to signal qualitative superiority. It remains to be seen whether this gambit will work, though there is some evidence to suggest that in the private sector higher tuition prices are associated with perceptions of higher quality.

A fourth basis for setting tuition prices is to assess what the market will bear—that is, what prices prospective students and their families are willing to pay. This approach assumes a great deal of information about an institution's actual and potential market. In this era of generally declining demand and heightened attention to enrollment management, market information is more readily available than it was in decades past. At the same time, however, the marketplace is changing so quickly and in such unprecedented ways that most collegiate officers have only modest confidence in their ability to assess what their market will pay beyond current rates. Part of the challenge is to distinguish the effects of prices on an institution's current market, as defined by its matriculated students; its prospective market, as defined by its current or reasonably anticipated applicant pool; and its desired market, as defined by institutional objectives. Another part of the challenge is to project accurately the actions of third-party providers of financial aid.

An institution that overestimates its market's ability or willingness to pay soon will find itself in an undesirable recruitment position. On the other hand, underestimation of market strength can lead to foregone revenue. Because of these risks and the paucity of reliable information, this pricing approach seldom is used at the undergraduate level except in combination with other approaches.

One version that has found favor in a few universities is to link prices of select graduate and professional programs to the expected future earnings of graduates. The logic behind this is that students who anticipate significantly above-average career earnings because of their matriculation in a given program or institution will, in a spirit of investment, be willing to pay an above-average proportion of the costs of their education. This pricing technique has worked tolerably well for many schools of business, law, and medicine—among others—but it has some notable shortcomings. One is that it places extraordinary financial burdens on individuals who fail to complete the program or who do so but later fail to earn an income as high as that anticipated. This pricing method also places the program's recruitment efforts in jeopardy when demand begins to slacken across the board, unless there is a clear qualitative difference to support price differentials between programs or institutions.

The final pricing approach, budget balancing, is the least sensitive to external competitive pressures. It is akin to the cost-recovery method except that it does not index prices to programmatic costs by any predetermined algorithm. In the budget-balancing mode an institution first projects its gross expenditures for the forthcoming fiscal year, then deducts all other anticipated sources of revenue, and finally assigns the remaining balance to tuition and fees. This approach works particularly well for small private institutions that depend heavily on gifts, endowment income, or in-kind support from a sponsoring church or other agency. A modified version of this approach also has served many public institutions well. One factor that must be considered here, perhaps more than in other approaches, is the relationship between volume and price. An institution that sets its prices primarily to achieve a stated revenue objective must, of necessity, make accurate enrollment projections or else cushion its budget against shortfalls, perhaps through a tuition set-aside or by controlling marginal costs tightly.

One attractive feature of the budget-balancing approach is its emphasis on resource requirements. Unlike externally indexed pricing, which tends to focus on tuition revenue somewhat in isolation from expense requirements, the budget-balancing approach encourages an institution's academic and fiscal officers to concentrate first on programmatic objectives and their cumulative cost. This technique also places an early burden on other components of the revenue picture, which in alternative approaches sometimes receive insufficient attention.

PRICE VARIATIONS

Since none of the preceding five approaches is free of risk, few institutions base their tuition prices on a single foundation. The dynamic nature of the typical budgeting process helps to ensure this: When conservative pricing ideology mixes with galloping resource requirements, it is almost inevitable that institutions across the broad spectrum will search for innovative pricing strategies to serve their immediate needs. If there are natural limits to how high tuition rates can be taken within traditional pricing structures, then it stands to reason that new or hybrid price models will be developed by institutions with special needs. Close inspection of current pricing practices reveals a number of interesting approaches at the undergraduate level (Yanikoski and Wilson 1984).

Off-Peak Discounts

Off-peak prices probably are the oldest and most often used form of price variation. An institution offers a lower price for instruction provided at times when either demand is slack relative to capacity or institutional costs are relatively low per credit hour of instruction. Reduced summer rates, offered by nearly one-fifth of all colleges, are a common form of off-peak pricing. Sometimes these discounts are quite substantial. For example, summer rates at Wilmington College of Ohio are only 60 percent of regular-year prices, and at Texas Lutheran College they are half-priced. Special evening prices, offered by about 9 percent of all senior colleges, are another form of off-peak pricing. Evening rates are set lower than day rates for several reasons: Evening students usually use fewer services and facilities; evening students have access to fewer forms of financial aid; costs of instruction generally are lower in the evening due to extensive use of part-time or overload faculty; evening instruction may be treated as a form of public service and therefore be subsidized. Such rationales are losing some of their force as adult clienteles become a more significant component of an institution's total market, but evening discounts continue to be popular. Furman University and Drury College, among others, offer evening instruction at rates less than half of day prices. Many other institutions offer evening discounts of 20 to 40 percent.

The key to making off-peak prices work is to confine their use to intended audiences. If a college or university allows its regular students to take unintended advantage of deep price discounts, the institution will forgo income that it may ill afford to lose. And there may be adverse academic consequences. One urban university that offered large evening discounts to law students found that its day program suffered dwindling demand, while its evening division grew to the point of overcrowding academic facilities. Colleges that cater primarily to their own regular-year students during summer terms may find deep discounts to be similarly counterproductive.

Geographically Sensitive Prices

Geographically sensitive tuition rates are another longstanding form of price variation. Community colleges typically have out-of-district rates, and senior public institutions usually charge out-of-state students higher prices. The logic is straightforward: Those who do not subsidize the institution through taxes should not benefit from low tuition prices, unless reciprocal agreements are in effect. One private institution that employs a geographically sensitive price structure is

Wesleyan College in Georgia. Students who graduate from a high school in a local ten-county area and maintain a residence there are entitled to a price discount of approximately 11 percent.

Another form of geographical price variation takes into account site considerations, such as local differences in facility costs or variations in ability to pay. Students at off-campus sites often benefit from lower prices. For example, at Methodist College in North Carolina off-campus students pay only 41 percent of regular credit-hour rates, and at Doane College in Nebraska students at a remote campus pay only about half of normal rates. Courses offered at military bases often carry lower prices. As in the case of off-peak pricing, it is important for institutions offering site discounts to control who benefits. One college that opened a branch campus found that it had to prohibit students on the main campus from taking advantage of its off-campus discounts.

Pricing by Level

It has long been customary to charge more for graduate and professional instruction than for undergraduate instruction. By extension, a few institutions, including the University of Michigan, Michigan State University, and the University of Illinois, have experimented with lower- and upper-division price differentials. For full-time students such differentials typically range from $60 to $130 per semester. Wayne State University employs lower- and upper-division price differentials only for its nonresident students. The University of Oklahoma and the Florida State University system, instead of varying prices by student level, vary prices by course level. Upper-division courses carry a price 12 to 14 percent higher than lower-division offerings.

Several reasons support lower- and upper-division differentials: holding the line on lower-division prices helps to promote access and curricular choice; upper-division courses tend to be smaller, more specialized, and hence more costly than introductory instruction and so warrant higher prices; upper-division students possess greater earnings potential and thus can afford to carry a greater portion of their instructional costs; juniors and seniors are institutionally loyal and thus are not likely to transfer elsewhere because of marginally higher upper-division prices.

One minor variation of this approach might be termed "introductory" pricing. Several institutions offer special reduced prices to first-time students. For example, incoming part-time students who have never been enrolled for credit in any college program are entitled to six credits of instruction at Seton Hill College at half price, though they must pay full fees. A similar arrangement is available at St. Mary College, Kansas, for first-semester students.

Guaranteed Prices

A handful of institutions guarantee that entry prices for incoming freshmen will remain flat for four years. The College of New Rochelle has been using this approach for six years, and the strategy recently has been adopted by Lakeland College and Concordia College, both in Wisconsin. The common aim is to gain an edge in recruiting and to improve retention of continuing students. One obvious shortcoming of guaranteed prices, from a college's vantage point, is that it removes budgetary flexibility. In times of unusually high or low inflation this could cripple an institution. One college that is phasing out guaranteed prices is Quinnipiac College in Connecticut. In the past it had allowed one price adjustment, at the beginning of a student's junior year.

Governor James Blanchard of Michigan recently proposed a novel approach to guaranteeing prices ("Novel Tuition-Paying Method Proposed by Mich. Governor" 1986). If his plan is enacted, parents will be permitted to pay fixed weekly or monthly installments into a state trust fund until a child is age 18, at which time the child will receive a certificate redeemable for four years' full tuition at any of Michigan's fifteen public universities. The tax status of this and other prepayment plans remains unclear.

Program Differentials

Ever since George Brakeley's (1931) pioneering cost-study research, it has been evident that certain fields of study entail far greater institutional expense than other fields. Brakeley found that the University of Pennsylvania spent more than four times as much to educate an undergraduate mechanical engineer as it did an undergraduate economist. Similar differences persist today, with scientific, technical, and medical curricula usually heading the list of high-cost programs. Some institutions have chosen to pass along a portion of such cost differences to students. At the graduate level it is common for universities to charge higher rates for study in law, medicine, business, and select other fields. At the undergraduate level most price variation occurs through imposition of course fees. Private institutions have been especially prone to add special charges for laboratory courses, musical instruction, student teaching, and health field externships. One-fifth of all institutions responding to a recent survey had at least one course charge or other academic fee in excess of $100 per term (Yanikoski 1985).

Approximately fifty senior institutions employ a pricing strategy that differentiates base prices according to students' majors. Valparaiso University has used such an approach on and off for over thirty years. In 1985–86 Valparaiso had four different full-time undergraduate rates, one each for nursing, engineering, business administration, and arts and sciences. Similar pricing schemes were in place at Marquette University, Columbia University, Florida Institute of Technology, the University of Detroit, and Madonna College. Other institutions, including Virginia Commonwealth University, George Washington University, Evansville University, Rutgers University, Alverno College, and Baldwin-Wallace College, charge a single price to all students except those in one particular program, usually engineering, music, or a health discipline. Russell Sage College charges higher prices only to seniors majoring in physical therapy or medical technology. At the other end of the spectrum is the University of Minnesota, which has distinct tuition prices, undergraduate and graduate, for each of its numerous colleges and schools. Minnesota indexes prices to institutional costs.

A few universities not only charge different gross prices for different majors but also employ different methods of pricing. For example, DePaul University uses package pricing (one rate for twelve to twenty credit hours) for theater students. Majors in commerce, liberal arts and sciences, and education pays a flat hourly rate for twelve hours of day instruction, then receive a discount of about 17 percent on any additional hours. Music students are billed in a similar fashion but with higher rates applicable in each category. Finally, a straight hourly rate applies to undergraduate students in the university's nontraditional college. The thinking behind these variations is that theater students need a package rate because of their intense performance schedule, while adult students will benefit from a flat hourly rate that encourages flexible scheduling of credit-hour loads. Volume discounts in other programs assist full-time students to take additional courses when desired, without unduly shifting a financial burden to or from part-time students.

Differential pricing can be difficult to administer, particularly if students attempt to "game the system." Enrollment and revenue are harder to project with differential pricing than with uniform prices. Accounts receivable operations can become hopelessly complicated unless an institution prepares properly, usually through efficient computerization. Admissions staff sometimes find differential pricing hard to explain to prospective students, and financial aid computations can be made more burdensome by use of multiple budget bases. Institutions that presently have differential prices seem to have found workable solutions to such difficulties, but they pay a price for their labors. Less clear is the impact, if any, that differential pricing may have on the sense of community within a university, or on the money-consciousness of program directors and deans.

Course Differentials

An alternative to varying prices by students' majors is to vary prices by type of instruction. For example, an institution could routinely charge more for laboratory courses—all laboratory courses regardless of field of study—than it does for lecture courses. One institution that has such a pricing policy is Saint Peter's College in New Jersey. All laboratory courses, computer courses, film courses, and nursing courses are priced approximately 7 percent higher than the standard hourly rate. Certain chemistry courses carry a still higher price. These prices are charged regardless of what major any given student in a course may have selected. Other institutions use a modified version of this approach by charging special rates for only select courses. Our Lady of Holy Cross College, for instance, charges a premium price for nursing clinical courses but otherwise charges nursing students the prevailing hourly rate. The University of Alabama handles engineering courses in a similar manner. In most respects this approach is indistinguishable from the traditional method of adding supplementary fees to selected courses.

Clientele Differentials

Institutions that serve or wish to serve distinctive clienteles some-times find it advantageous to offer special prices. Seton Hill College offers half-price undergraduate rates to its own alumnae and to grad-uates of any other senior college. Defiance College provides more than a 70 percent price discount to students age 60 or older. John Brown University offers a 50 percent price break to any student age 50 or older. Alverno College extends a price reduction of $100 to any family that has two or more students enrolled concurrently. Bard College, in a recently announced move, will offer a major price break to students whose grades place them among the top ten stu-dents in their high-school graduating classes ("Bard Offers Top Students Public-Tuition Rates" 1986). Instead of paying Bard's normal yearly charge of $14,450, these top students will be billed only for the equivalent of the comprehensive tuition and fee charge at New York's public universities. The common element of almost all such pricing options is that they are intended to attract a special-ized clientele without negatively affecting the revenue base provided by an institution's main market.

CONCLUDING COMMENTS

Given the great variety of pricing options already tried or readily conceived, it is fair to ask why more institutions have not yet modi-fied their traditional price policies. The main reason, as revealed in the author's 1985 survey, is that a great many colleges and universi-ties are satisfied with present arrangements. Other frequently men-tioned considerations, listed in decreasing order of importance, in-clude "insufficient diversity of programs and/or students to warrant differential prices"; "fear of negative impacts on enrollment"; "gen-eral reluctance to change longstanding policies"; "lack of adequate information about program costs"; and "lack of information about pricing options."

No matter what pricing strategy an institution chooses, its main consideration usually is revenue. Revenue from tuition and aca-demic fees provides a significant and mounting proportion of oper-ating budgets at most colleges and universities. Data for fiscal years 1979 through 1982 (Minter et al. 1982) show that tuition and fees provided a slowly rising portion of educational and general expenditures in all categories of senior institutions except small public campuses. In 1982 one-fourth of all private colleges and universities paid more than 80 percent of their educational and general expenses from tuition and fee revenue. A more recent survey by the American Council on Education (Anderson 1985) confirms that this trend is continuing.

When business officers recently were asked to indicate what proportion of unrestricted educational and general revenue they derived from tuition and academic fees, public institutions reported an average of 26 percent, church-related institutions 67 percent, and independent institutions 69 percent. More than one-fourth of all private institutions reported being at least 80 percent tuition-dependent. This suggests that higher education institutions must continue to be attentive to new developments in price strategy. It also suggests that further research on alternative pricing strategies is much needed.

REFERENCES

Adams, Carl R.; Russell L. Hankins; Gordon W. Kingston; and Roger G. Schroeder. 1978. *A Study of Cost Analysis in Higher Education.* Washington, D.C.: American Council on Education.

Anderson, Charles J. 1985. *Conditions Affecting College and University Financial Strength.* Higher Education Panel Survey No. 63. Washington, D.C.: American Council on Education.

"Bard Offers Top Students Public-Tuition Rates." 1986. *Chronicle of Higher Education* 31 (January 29): 2.

Brakeley, George A. 1931. "Tuition and the Student's Share of the Cost of Education." *Educational Record* 12 (July): 312–21.

College Board. 1985. "Total Annual College Costs Increase by 7 Percent." *College Board News* 14 (Fall): 1, 5.

Hearn, James C., and David Longanecker. 1985. "Enrollment Effects of Alternative Postsecondary Pricing Policies." *Journal of Higher Education* 56 (September/October): 485–508.

Litten, Larry H., ed. 1984. *Issues in Pricing Undergraduate Education.* New Directions for Institutional Research No. 42. San Francisco: Jossey-Bass.

McHugh, Carol. 1985. "Tuition Increases Certain as Death, Taxes." *Chicago Law Bulletin* 131 (September 6): 3, supp.

McPherson, Michael S. 1978. "The Demand for Higher Education." In *Public Policy and Private Higher Education*, edited by David W. Breneman and Chester E. Finn, Jr., pp. 143–96. Washington, D.C.: Brookings Institution.

Minter, John; K. Scott Hughes; Daniel D. Robinson; Frederick J. Turk; and Fredric J. Prager. 1982. *Ratio Analysis in Higher Education*, 2d ed. New York: Peat, Marwick, Mitchell and Co.

National Center for Education Statistics. 1985. *The Condition of Education, 1985 Edition.* Washington, D.C.: U.S. Government Printing Office.

"Novel Tuition-Paying Method Proposed by Mich. Governor." 1986. *Chronicle of Higher Education* 31 (February 5): 17.

Research Associates of Washington. 1985. "Higher Education Prices and Price Indexes: 1985 Update." Washington, D.C.: RAW.

Ross, Irwin. 1985. "Why College Bills Don't Level Off." *Fortune* 112 (September 30): 67-71.

Suttle, J. Lloyd. 1983. "The Rising Cost of Private Higher Education." *Research in Higher Education* 18 (May): 253-70.

"Tuition and Fees at 2,600 Colleges and Universities, 1985-86." 1985. *Chronicle of Higher Education* 30 (August 14): 13-18.

Van Alstyne, Carol. 1974. "Tuition: Analysis of Recent Policy Recommendations." *Hearings before the House Special Subcommittee on Education*, 93d Cong., 2d sess.: pt. 7, 136-85.

Yanikoski, Richard A. "Undergraduate Tuition Prices: Results of a Survey." 1985. Unpublished paper, DePaul University.

Yanikoski, Richard A., and Richard F. Wilson. 1984. "Differential Pricing of Undergraduate Education." *Journal of Higher Education* 55 (November/December): 735-50.

7 FEDERAL PROGRAMS
A View of the Higher Education Act

Terry W. Hartle and James B. Stedman

The federal role in higher education is multifaceted and can appear to be insignificant, supportive, intrusive, or dominant depending on the observer, the issues in question, and the institutions involved. A long history of statutory development fashioned that role, ranging from legislation in which higher education was a clear focus, such as the First and Second Morrill Acts in 1862 and 1890, the Serviceman's Readjustment Act in 1944, the National Defense Education Act of 1958, and the Higher Education Act of 1965, to legislation in other domains that directly affects higher education, such as the Civil Rights Act of 1964, the National Science Foundation Act of 1950, and the National Foundation on the Arts and the Humanities Act of 1965.

The contours and objectives of the federal role are periodically debated and redefined, most often when the Higher Education Act (HEA) must be reauthorized. On some occasions the federal action is monumental, as it was when the Higher Education Act was created in 1965. More recently, the Congress approved "landmark" amendments to the HEA in 1972 that established "a basic charter for federal higher education policy . . . , one that would have enduring significance" (Gladieux and Wolanin 1976: 223). In other cases the

The views expressed in this chapter are those of the authors and not necessarily those of their employing organizations, the American Enterprise Institute for Public Policy Research and the Congressional Research Service of the Library of Congress.

amendments are an attempt to consolidate and integrate policy without altering the shape or focus of the federal role.

This chapter reviews the evolution and current status of the federal government's role in higher education by looking at the development of federal policy since the 1972 amendments. It outlines the major elements of the federal role as expressed through the HEA, identifies the salient issues that influenced congressional and executive branch action, and examines how the basic charter has fared since 1972. The following sections of the chapter examine the federal role in higher education and the creation of the Higher Education Act; the 1972 amendments to the HEA; the higher education issues that engaged the legislative and executive policymakers; the legislative action on HEA in 1976, 1978, 1980, and 1981; and some of the issues that will shape the debate on the federal role in higher education in the coming years. The final section presents some concluding observations about the evolution of federal policy and its future direction.

FEDERAL ROLE IN HIGHER EDUCATION

One looks in vain for an enunciated, formal higher education policy behind the federal presence. Nevertheless, the federal role is largely characterized by concern for equal opportunity, advancement of knowledge, and institutional development (Carnegie Council on Policy Studies in Higher Education 1975; Congressional Budget Office 1977; Special Task Force to the Secretary of Health, Education, and Welfare 1973).

The concern for equal opportunity is seen in enforcement on college campuses of Title VI of the Civil Rights Act of 1964 (prohibiting discrimination on the basis of race, color, and national origin in federally funded programs or activities) and Executive Order 11246 (requiring affirmative action with regard to employment from certain employers with federal contracts), and provision of large amounts of federal student assistance to low-income students. The federal government furthers the advancement of knowledge by supporting research and development and graduate education, among other activities. Support for institutional development includes aid for developing colleges under the HEA and programs to upgrade research equipment and facilities.

Table 7-1. Current-Fund Revenues for Higher Education by Source, 1970-71 and 1981-82 (*in millions of dollars*).

	1970-71	1981-82	1983-84
Total (in dollars)	$23,879	$72,191	$86,537
Government	12,106	33,378	37,802
Federal	4,601	9,592	10,903
State	6,595	21,849	24,707
Local	910	1,938	2,192
Private gifts and grants	1,227	3,564	4,415
Students (tuition and fees)	8,146	23,896	29,171
Institutional	2,401	11,353	15,149
Total (in percentages)	100.0%	100.0%	100.0%
Government	50.7	46.2	43.7
Federal	19.3	13.3	12.6
State	27.6	30.3	28.6
Local	3.8	2.7	2.5
Private gifts and grants	5.1	4.9	5.1
Students (tuition and fees)	34.1	33.1	33.7
Institutional	10.1	15.7	17.5

Source: U.S. Department of Education, Center for Statistics, unpublished data. See also Plisko and Stern (1985: 114) (notes in original omitted in this table).

The amount of federal dollars going to higher education institutions is important, and perhaps crucial, for some institutions and activities. Despite this, federal aid represents only a small portion of total support for higher education. Table 7-1 shows that the federal share of higher education revenues was 12.6 percent in 1983-84, down from 19.3 percent in 1970-71. The contribution by state governments, which grew slightly over the period from 27.6 percent to 28.6 percent, is now more than twice as large as the federal investment. The most rapidly growing source of revenue comes from institutional sources (such as endowment, sales and services of educational activities, hospitals, and so forth), which increased from 10.1 percent of the total to 17.5 percent.

At the heart of federal funding for higher education are the student aid programs authorized by the HEA. These programs use a wide range of mechanisms to help ensure that financial need will not prove an insurmountable barrier to college attendance. Over the last

Table 7-2. Appropriations for Selected Higher Education Act Programs, Selected Years (*in thousands of dollars*).

	FY 1975	FY 1985	FY 1986[a]
Pell grants	$840,200	$3,612,000	$3,588,000
Supplemental Educational Opportunity Grants	240,300	412,500	412,500
College work-study	420,000	592,500	592,500
National Direct Student Loans	329,449	217,482	218,000
Guaranteed student loans	580,000	3,798,323	3,300,000
Institutional aid	110,000	141,208	141,208

a. These are the appropriated amounts prior to any reductions under the Balanced Budget and Emergency Deficit Control Act of 1985 (Gramm-Rudman-Hollings).

Source: U.S. Department of Education, unpublished statistics; and *Congressional Record* (1985: H10936).

twenty years, the size, complexity, and cost of these programs have increased dramatically. Brief descriptions of these programs are in order. A much more comprehensive analysis of HEA programs can be found in a recent U.S. Senate Committee print (U.S. Senate 1985) (see Table 7-2). The following descriptions do *not* reflect any changes to the programs resulting from congressional action to reauthorize the Higher Education Act in 1986.

Under the Guaranteed Student Loan program, the federal government insures (against student borrowers' default) loans made principally by private lenders. In 1985 students could borrow up to $2,500 a year as undergraduates and $5,000 annually as graduate or professional students; cumulative loan limits were $12,000 and $25,000, respectively. The interest rate for borrowers was 8 percent, and borrowers were charged a loan origination fee of 5 percent when the loan was made. Federal costs for the program are incurred primarily through the payment of interest while the borrowers are in school and in a six-month grace period following graduation; payments on defaulted loans; and "special allowance" payments designed to ensure lenders a specified rate of return (in 1985, 3.5 percent) above the average ninety-one-day Treasury bill rate. In 1985 the program was available to students whose families' adjusted gross income was $30,000 or less or those who could prove financial need by virtue of a needs test.

The federal government also provides a related program (Auxiliary Loans to Assist Students) of loans open only to independent students and parents of students. This program charges higher interest rates with less federal subsidization but is federally guaranteed against default.

The Pell grant program is aimed at the financially neediest students. In 1985 it provided grants to undergraduates based on a needs test in amounts ranging from $200 to $2,100. No grant could exceed 60 percent of the cost of attendance at students' colleges.

The Supplemental Educational Opportunity Grant, College Work-Study, and National Direct Student Loan programs are collectively known as the "campus-based" programs because they are administered by financial aid officers at colleges and universities across the country. Like the Pell grants, all three programs are need-tested. The Supplemental Grant program provides grants, which (in 1985–86) ranged from $200 to $2,000. The College Work-Study program helps students work their way through college by providing up to 80 percent of the compensation from an on-campus job or employment in the nonprofit sector. The National Direct Student Loan program provides low-interest (5 percent in 1985) loans to low-income students. Federal grants to these institutions are matched ($1 of non-federal contribution for every $9 of federal capital contribution) by the colleges, who lend the money and collect it. In 1985 National Direct loans had annual $3,000 limits and cumulative loan limits of $6,000 and $12,000 for undergraduate and graduate students, respectively.

The Institutional Aid program, Title III of the HEA, is the principal non-student aid source of HEA spending. Under this title, institutions can receive assistance for such activities as planning, curriculum development, faculty improvement, and acquisition of equipment. In general, eligible institutions have a high percentage of students receiving large average amounts of federal need-based student aid and relatively low amounts of per student expenditures.

THE BASIC CHARTER OF 1972

Federal need-based student aid dates from the National Defense Education Act of 1958, which authorized the National Defense (now

Direct) Student Loan program. In 1965 the Congress enacted the Higher Education Act, a landmark piece of social legislation that was somewhat obscured at the time by the passage earlier that year of the Elementary and Secondary Education Act. The HEA created two new programs—Guaranteed Student Loans and Educational Opportunity Grants (later Supplemental Grants)—and gave the Office of Education responsibility for the College Work-Study Program, a program actually created by the Economic Opportunity Act of 1964.

Congress took another major step to support higher education when it enacted the Education Amendments of 1972. Among its most visible legacies, the act created the Basic Educational Opportunity Grants and established that program as the centerpiece of federal student aid policy. But more important was that the law established higher education as a national priority in its own right. In the past, federal policy had used higher education as a means to an end—such as protecting national security or alleviating the effects of poverty.

At the time, the 1972 amendments were called the most significant federal higher education legislation since the Morrill Act. The principles or charter for federal higher education activity outlined in this law became the focus of federal policy during the 1970s.

The charter, according to Gladieux and Wolanin (1976), set forth eight basic positions:

1. Equal opportunity underlies all federal higher education activities;
2. Student needs come before institutional needs;
3. Federal involvement has national objectives, while state governments are responsible for the basic support of higher education;
4. The federal and state governments have a partnership for action;
5. The focus of federal efforts includes nontraditional students and institutions;
6. The federal government will encourage reform and innovation in the higher education system;
7. The federal government will support the collection and analysis of new information about higher education; and
8. The charter reaffirms previous legislative efforts by building on the existing programs.

Two of these goals—primacy of student needs and equal opportunity—merit closer examination because they were at the heart of the

1972 action and have been central to all higher education policy debates since then.

Among the most important outcomes of the 1972 congressional action was the nearly complete rejection of institutional aid in favor of student aid as a vehicle for federal policy. The choice between institutional and student aid was actually a decision about who would receive the money. Colleges and universities had campaigned for direct federal aid that they could parcel out to students. Opponents of institutional aid argued that money should flow directly to students to create a marketplace that would enable them to choose the postsecondary program that best met their needs. The resulting competition, it was assumed, would be healthy for students, institutions, and the federal government.

At the same time, the Congress voted to target student aid on the poorest students. Since the mid-1960s both the rhetoric and the federal efforts aimed at low-income and disadvantaged students had increased dramatically. By the early 1970s, however, there was mounting evidence that too much of this money was diverted to other, less needy populations. The Basic Grant program was designed to solve this problem. With this program, the Congress sought to remove the financial barriers facing low-income students and, in the process, made equal educational opportunity "the central commitment of federal higher education policy," a commitment to be met largely by need-based student aid (Gladieux and Wolanin 1976).

The conventional wisdom holds that this basic focus of federal student aid policy has changed very little in the intervening years. One higher education reform report (Newman 1985: 18–19) issued a decade later noted that a thorough reexamination of basic policy questions was overdue:

> A review of national policy toward higher education is urgently needed. More than a decade has passed since the United States Congress and educational leaders last engaged in a major debate about the purposes of higher education and the best means to achieve them.

Clearly there have been no landmark pieces of higher education legislation equal to the 1972 amendments in the intervening years. Nonetheless, analysis shows that the charter did not lie unchanged.

ISSUES OF THE 1970s AND EARLY 1980s

Five major issues have shaped the post-1972 development of the federal role in higher education:

1. A continuing debate between institutional aid and student aid;
2. Efforts to strike the proper balance between access and choice as objectives of federal aid;
3. Continual concern with waste, fraud, and abuse;
4. Efforts by middle-income families to get a bigger share of federal student assistance; and
5. Steadily increasing federal program costs.

Despite the clear focus on student aid, the 1972 amendments did not immediately close the door on institutional aid. The 1972 law did include a cost of instruction allowance that authorized some direct aid to institutions. However, this provision was never funded. The HEA also provided financial help to developing institutions, and the annual appropriation for this title has increased from $52 million in FY 1972 to $141 million in FY 1985.

Private colleges and universities continued to press for institutional aid after the 1972 amendments. The initial argument was that financial pressures would force many schools to close their doors (Jellema 1973; Cheit 1971). When the doors did not close despite the absence of substantial federal institutional aid, private higher education shifted ground, acknowledging its likely survival but questioning whether financial constraints did not threaten the sector's contribution to the diversity of U.S. higher education (Gladieux and Wolanin 1978). At this point, given the apparent ascendance of student aid as the principal form of federal aid, the private sector began trying to protect those aspects of the student aid programs that favored private institutions, such as the Pell grant half-cost limitation. Under this rule, Pell grants could not exceed half the cost of attendance at a recipient's college. In essence, even where the maximum Pell grant could have covered all or nearly all of a student's cost of attendance at low-tuition public institutions, it was prohibited from doing so (1985–86 award year grants can cover 60 percent of students' cost).

"Access and choice" became a shorthand way of referring to the complex issues surrounding the targets of federal student aid. The Education Amendments of 1972 took a substantial step toward providing students with both aid to attend higher education (access) and to choose among institutions (choice). When the true cost of making these goals a reality became apparent, *access* and *choice* became code words: *Access* meant aid programs that would primarily help public institutions, while *choice* referred to programs that help private colleges. Getting students into a low-cost public college was much less expensive than ensuring that they could meet the sharply higher costs at private colleges. As a result, ultimately the question was whether the federal government would continue to expand student aid sufficiently to make the choice goal a reality. While higher education spokesmen continue to pay homage to both goals, fiscal constraints in recent years have meant that these seemingly complementary objectives have become competing priorities.

Waste, abuse, and fraud have also been a problem. For example, the default rates in the federal loan programs—Guaranteed Student Loans and National Direct Student Loans—climbed dramatically during the 1970s. By mid-decade, estimates of the default rates for the Guaranteed Student Loan program were as high as 18 percent (U.S. House of Representatives 1976). Steps have been taken to address this problem, and indeed the default rate has fallen considerably in recent years. Still, the default rate now hovers at about 10 percent, and the annual cost to the federal Treasury of defaults is about $1 billion. Some misuse of funds also occurs in the Pell grant program. Recent studies by Advanced Technology (1984) and the U.S. General Accounting Office (1985) both concluded that a substantial proportion of the Pell grant awards involve over or under awards to students. The U.S. Office of Management and Budget (1985) maintains that the Pell program has a higher error rate than any other federal social program.

Extending the benefits of federal aid to other populations has also been a visible and contentious issue. Throughout the 1970s, middle-class families increasingly sought to obtain a share of federal largesse in many social areas; higher education was no exception. For student aid, the calls were justified by rising college costs, which were allegedly outstripping the families' ability to pay. Whatever the reality of those claims, the pressure was real, and the legislative and executive branches responded to it.

The costs of federal student aid programs emerged as an issue early in the post-1972 period. The expansive nature of the 1972 amendments raised quite naturally the question of costs. Authorizing committees of the Congress fashioned the 1972 charter; appropriations committees confronted most directly the issue of paying for it. Gladieux and Wolanin (1976: 245) asked whether "by not exercising greater discipline . . . the authorizing committees of Congress [are not] in effect abdicating power to the Administration and the Appropriations Committees, which determine which legislation and parts of legislation will be funded and which will not." Compounding the problem was the establishment of the congressional budget process under the Congressional Budget and Impoundment Control Act of 1974. The budget process, through which the Congress attempted to set overall spending limits and thus force tradeoffs among financial commitments to meet spending ceilings, intruded increasingly into the legislative consideration of higher education in the late 1970s and early 1980s.

LEGISLATIVE ACTIONS IN THE 1970s AND EARLY 1980s

The HEA underwent major amendments four times between 1972 and 1985. As funding authorities were set to expire, the Ninety-fourth Congress (in session in 1975 and 1976) gave the HEA the first comprehensive look following the 1972 amendments. The Ninety-fifth Congress (1977 and 1978) amended the HEA to address the perceived plight of middle-income families. The Ninety-sixth Congress (1979 and 1980) addressed the expiration of funding authorities in the act. A year later, the Ninety-seventh Congress (1981 and 1982) amended many HEA programs as part of the budget cutting effort that accompanied the Reagan administration's first year in office. This section briefly reviews these four legislative actions, highlighting the issues Congress faced and the changes it made.

Education Amendments of 1976

When the 1972 amendments came up for review in 1975 and 1976, there was no shortage of issues that needed attention. The most visible controversy surrounded the skyrocketing default rates in the Guaranteed Student Loan program, a problem that could not be avoided. Other issues that attracted attention included the financial health of private colleges; the federal role in damaging and strengthening that sector; the inequities and inefficiencies of low tuition policies in the public sector; the federal role in helping to maintain low tuition levels or meet the costs of increased levels; the adequacy of the student aid programs for ensuring that all low-income students have access to higher education; and the extent to which the choice goal should be underwritten by the federal government.

Substantial amendments to the HEA addressing these and other issues were considered, but they sparked considerable controversy and generated very little consensus. For example, Representative James O'Hara (D-Mich.), chair of the House subcommittee handling the legislation, sought to target the Pell grants more specifically on low-cost institutions and to introduce student merit as a factor to be considered in awards under the Supplemental Educational Opportunity Grant program (U.S. House 1975). In the process, O'Hara generated vehement opposition from the private colleges concerned that these changes would make low-cost public institutions irresistible to students. A legislative stalemate created by the O'Hara proposals was broken by a House-approved compromise that amounted to little more than a one year extension of HEA programs.

The Senate was less willing to contemplate major reforms than the House of Representatives. Senator Claiborne Pell (D-R.I.) chair of the Senate subcommittee responsible for higher education, asserted that the HEA programs, with the obvious exception of Guaranteed Student Loans, were in need only of some fine tuning and that a long reauthorization period was in order to allow these programs some stability and continuity (U.S. Senate 1975). Pell's position ultimately prevailed, although the Congress accepted a four-year authorization instead of his seven-year proposal.

This reauthorization did, however, result in major changes in the Guaranteed Student Loan program. These amendments sought to return the program more fully to its original vision of active state involvement backed by federal guarantees. Based on testimony and research, the Congress came to view the direct federal administration of the loan program as a root cause of the high default rate plaguing the program (U.S. House 1976). State guarantee agencies, it was argued, had low default rates because they were closer to the action and thus were able to work more closely with lenders and to track defaulters more carefully. Through a series of financial incentives, the Education Amendments of 1976 sought to induce states to establish guarantee agencies.

Middle-Income Student Assistance Act

A principal tenet of the 1972 amendments was the emphasis on equal opportunity for students from low-income families. Five years later, groups advancing middle-income families' interests petitioned Congress for aid to meet rising college costs. Over 100 bills were introduced during 1977 and 1978 to address this concern ("Controversy in Congress" 1979). By the end of 1978 the emphasis on low-income students in the 1972 charter had been seriously challenged, if not substantially weakened.

Although college costs rose rapidly in the 1970s, it was not clear from available analyses that middle-income families had indeed failed to keep pace with their children's higher education expenses (Van Alstyne 1979; Congressional Budget Office 1978). Nevertheless, the popular perception was that they had, and the Congress considered two competing proposals to extend federal assistance to middle-income families—federal income tax credits equal to a portion of college-level costs paid by a taxpayer and amendments to allow higher-income families to participate in student aid programs ("Almanac" 1978).

Proponents of the tax credit approach nearly prevailed at least twice during the Ninety-fifth Congress. In 1977 a vital social security refinancing bill was held up when the conference committee deadlocked over a higher education tax credit. Eventually the credit was deleted, but the controversy called considerable attention to the issue and increased the demand for action. A year later, a higher education tax credit proposal was reported from conference committee to both houses of Congress only to be recommitted by a House vote because the proposal did not include tax credits for private elementary and secondary education expenses. A second report from the same conference following the recommittal was rejected on a voice vote by the Senate.

The executive branch and the education community steadfastly opposed tax credit proposals. President Carter threatened to veto any tuition tax credit proposal, in part because of the revenue losses associated with this approach, and early in 1978 his administration offered legislation to amend student aid programs in lieu of tax credits. The Carter proposals were immediately endorsed by the higher education community.

Ultimately, the Congress approved the Middle-Income Student Assistance Act (MISAA), a package of amendments to the existing student aid programs. MISAA adjusted the needs analysis calculations of the Pell grant program to require families to contribute less discretionary income toward higher education expenses. The net effect was to make families earning $25,000 a year eligible for these grants. Perhaps more important, MISAA removed any consideration of family income level from determining a student's eligibility for Guaranteed Student Loans. All students, regardless of family income or assets, were henceforth to be eligible for subsidized loans.

MISAA succeeded beyond all expectations. Although reliable figures on the income characteristics of Guaranteed Student Loan borrowers are not available, MISAA triggered an explosion in borrowing. In 1977–78 students borrowed a total of $1.7 billion; by 1979–80 the annual borrowing reached $3.9 billion, a 129 percent increase. This was a rise unlike prior growth rates; between 1975–76 and 1977–78, for example, borrowing rose only 31 percent, from $1.3 to $1.7 billion. The MISAA borrowing explosion carried into the 1980s. In 1980–81 students secured $6.2 billion in loans. Federal costs associated with this program, not surprisingly, also shot up, from $480 million in 1978 to $1.6 billion by 1980, and still further to $2.5 billion by 1981 (Gillespie and Carlson 1983).

Data on the Pell grant program show a sharp realignment of aid to families with higher incomes in the immediate post-MISAA period. Students from families with incomes at or below $15,000 a year (constant 1982 dollars) declined as a percentage of all Pell grant recipients from 63 percent in 1977–78 to 38 percent in 1979–80. Meanwhile, the percentage of recipients with family incomes above $25,000 increased from 7.4 percent to 34 percent (Gillespie and Carlson 1983).

A federally funded study of MISAA (Applied Management Sciences 1980: 3.6) found that

> while the Federal student support programs remain primarily directed toward those most economically disadvantaged, the effect of MISAA has been to greatly broaden the eligible income spectrum.

MISAA was both consonant with and divergent from the 1972 charter. On the one hand, needs-based student aid remained the primary vehicle for providing federal higher education assistance, but on the other hand, the low-income focus had been clearly diluted.

Education Amendments of 1980

Work by the Ninety-sixth Congress to reauthorize the HEA nearly came to naught as a result of growing concern over the federal budget deficit and the costs of federal college aid, particularly the student aid programs. The Education Amendments of 1980 emerged from congressional deliberations that saw forces seeking to further the 1978 expansion of federal student aid opposed by forces seeking to constrain federal expenditures (The College Board 1980; "Almanac" 1980).

In general, the House of Representatives sought to expand student aid programs even further. Among the House-initiated changes were an increase in the maximum size of the Pell grant from $1,800 to $2,520 and a lifting of the half-cost limit to 70 percent of cost. The House rejected efforts to curb student loan costs. In the Senate budgetary concerns received more attention, but the emphasis was still on program expansion. The Senate bill raised the interest rates charged to students under the federal student loan programs; tied the federal subsidy of guaranteed loan interest to family income; moved the National Direct Student Loan program's costs off budget; increased the Pell grant maximum awards; authorized a new program of parental borrowing under the Guaranteed Loan program at higher interest rates than the new program proposed by the House; and amended the Institutional Aid program to curb misuse of program funds (U.S. House of Representatives 1980).

Eventually, House and Senate conferees, seeking a compromise between the bills, reported out legislation that did little to curb the expansion of benefits. Even general commentary was critical: A Jane Bryant Quinn story on CBS news noted the incredible generosity of the higher education package before the Congress passed it (*Congressional Record* 1980: 24103–24105). But the attention emboldened the critics: The Senate Budget Committee informed the Senate conferees that the agreement they had reached was "unacceptable from a budgetary point of view" and successfully held that position in the Senate as that body rejected the conference report, a very uncommon legislative step ("Almanac" 1980: 425).

A second conference committee approved a bill that was estimated to cost some $1.4 billion less than the measure originally reported ("Almanac" 1980). Both houses quickly approved the second conference report, and President Carter signed the legislation into law just before the 1980 election.

As finally enacted, the amendments raised the maximum level of Pell grants from $1,800 to $2,600 by 1985–86 and permitted the cost of attendance limitation to rise from 50 percent to 70 percent by 1985–86 (subsequent congressional action kept the maximum grant below that level); tied the expansion of Pell grants to specific appropriation levels for the campus-based programs; increased the Guaranteed Loan interest rates for new loans from 7 to 9 percent and for National Direct Loans from 3 to 4 percent; raised the annual and cumulative loan limits for students under the Guaranteed Loan program; authorized a program of unsubsidized but guaranteed loans to parents; and amended the Institutional Aid program by creating a three-part program of grants to institutions with eligibility dependent on a comparative analysis of institutions' education expenditures per student and enrollment of students with federal need-based aid.

Despite the battles fought over the cost of the new law, the legislation did not retreat from the 1978 expansion. A number of technical changes in the HEA were explicitly designed to increase student participation in the federal programs. One analyst (Gladieux 1980: 26) noted this and commented:

> In 1980 Congress cannot fairly be accused of doing too little for higher education. The question is whether by trying to do *too much* the most recent legislation may blunt the effectiveness of federal efforts to equalize educational opportunity, the overriding objective of federal higher education policy for more than a decade. There is a real danger that federal benefits will drift increasingly toward the relatively well-off at the expense of the poor and the neediest.

Perhaps one of the primary effects of the Education Amendments of 1980 was that by failing to rein in student aid costs, the legislation set the stage for major cost-cutting amendments to be adopted through the congressional budget process less than a year later.

Omnibus Budget Reconciliation Act of 1981

Between 1972 and 1980 federal education spending underwent a remarkable shift. In 1972 spending on elementary, secondary, and vocational education was two and a half times greater than direct spending on higher education (exclusive of research and development, and the Veterans and social security education benefits programs). Eight years later, elementary, secondary, and vocational education outlays were a mere 3 percent more than higher education spending. Even more significant, student aid, which contributed 19 percent of total education outlays in 1972, constituted some 34 percent of the total in 1980. Finally, between 1972 and 1980 higher education spending, driven largely by student aid costs, rose over three times faster than elementary, secondary, and vocational education spending.

With the emergence of higher education spending as a substantial component of total education spending, it was to be expected that any major budget cutting would look for savings from this part of domestic spending. Indeed, the explosive growth in student loans made it likely that the legislative and executive branches would take a careful look at student aid (see Table 7-3).

Ironically, the need to reduce the growth in student loans was not lost on the Carter administration. In submitting the fiscal 1981 budget, it proposed a handful of steps to tighten eligibility for guaranteed loans—proposals that were adopted by the Reagan administration. The new administration also requested eligibility changes for

Table 7-3. Federal Education Outlays for 1972, 1975, 1980, and 1984 (*dollars in millions*).

	Elementary, Secondary, Vocational	Higher Education	(Student Aid)[a]	Research and General Education Aids	Total Education Outlays
1972	$3,687	$1,447	$1,040	$ 319	$ 5,453
1975	4,351	2,190	1,493	780	7,321
1980	6,908	6,726	5,091	1,197	14,831
1984	6,520	7,383	6,988	1,210	15,113

a. Student Aid outlays included in Higher Education outlay column.
Source: Evans, Rimkunas, and Falk (1985: 17).

Pell grants and suggested eliminating social security benefits going to college students.

In the Omnibus Budget Reconciliation Act of 1981 the Congress made a number of changes that gave the Reagan administration some, but not all, of what it wanted. The Congress did limit GSLs to the amount needed to cover educational costs and established a needs test for applicants, but the test applied only to students with family incomes above $30,000, not to all students as the administration wanted. The proposal to eliminate the in-school interest subsidy for student loans was not seriously considered, but the Congress did impose a 5 percent origination fee on each new loan; a student who needed a $2,000 loan would have to pay a $100 fee.

Congress also placed appropriations limits on Pell grants. The Department of Education was authorized to modify the Pell regulations so that the annual appropriations ceilings would not be exceeded. Congress also terminated social security survivors benefits paid to college students. While not a need-based program, eliminating the benefit did reduce federal aid by nearly $2 billion.

The changes in the Department of Education programs further weakened the focus on low-income students. Enlarging the program in 1978 and 1980 was accomplished by making the programs available to more middle income students. But the 1981 budget cuts preserved the programs, at least in part, for the middle class at the same time it reduced aid for the neediest students. Federal generosity toward the middle class was reduced, but a wide range of student aid benefits remained in place.

ISSUES FOR THE LATE 1980s

Public policy debates change over time. The issues that dominate one era may fade in importance as others move to the forefront. Nevertheless, the basic issues that drove federal policy discussions in the 1970s remain unsettled. The most pressing issues driving the debate over federal higher education policy in the late 1980s are:

1. Costs to the federal government;
2. Education of minority students; and
3. The quality of the higher education enterprise.

Control of federal spending continues to be the Reagan administration's primary objective in higher education and, in light of the federal budget deficit, an inescapable fact of life. When Education Secretary William Bennett (1985: 1) submitted the administration's legislative package to implement its fiscal year 1986 budgetary proposals for higher education, he asserted:

> Over the last twenty-five years, the postsecondary student financial assistance programs now administered by the Education Department have grown dramatically in size, number, scope, and complexity, and share of individual postsecondary costs which they cover. The current student aid programs administered by the Department are poorly focused, overly complex and unnecessarily costly to the taxpayer.

Bennett outlined the "key principles" that the administration believed should form the basis of the HEA reauthorization—"reasonable objective limitations on amounts of aid per student, income eligibility limits, emphasis on aid for lower income persons, significant improvement in the integrity and efficiency of aid programs, and reduction of unnecessary subsidies to banks and states" (Bennett 1985: 8). Each of these "principles" focuses on cost reduction; most further challenge the expansion of aid instituted in the late 1970s.

Congress rejected the administration's proposals to cut student aid spending in the 1986 budget, as it did every year since 1981. This reluctance to reduce student assistance outlays resulted in a 37 percent increase in federal student aid outlays, between 1980 and 1984 (Table 7-3). It is important to note that this gain took place despite a sharp fall in the interest rates, which reduces federal costs in the Guaranteed Loan program. In short, regardless of which political party occupies the White House, it appears that the cost of federal student aid programs will remain a visible and controversial concern.

Policymakers also will be confronted by complex issues surrounding minority participation in higher education. For example, although the absolute number of blacks ages 18 to 24 who had graduated from high school rose 39 percent between 1975 and 1984, the rate at which these graduates enrolled in college fell by 15 percent. A similar pattern applies to Hispanic students. Among whites, however, the number of high school graduates and the percentage of these graduates going to college grew slightly from 1975 to 1984 (U.S. Bureau of the Census 1985).

There are no easy solutions to this dilemma. Nobody knows exactly why minority enrollment rates have fallen or how to reverse the trend. It is clear, however, that a host of factors are involved: relative levels of student aid, the growing reliance on loans to finance higher education, the availability of special programs to meet the needs of minority students, the adequacy of high school counseling, and the role of community colleges (which enroll a disproportionate share of minority students) in providing an adequate foundation for further education. Some educators have suggested that one possible solution to this dilemma is to expand the federal government's Institutional Aid program aimed at historically black colleges, thus strengthening a set of institutions that have traditionally educated a large number of minority students.

The concern for educational quality blossomed in the early 1980s, fueled in part by the National Commission on Excellence in Education's *A Nation at Risk* (1983). Higher education's role in fostering quality education at the elementary and secondary level was recognized from the start—a perceived inadequacy of the teaching force was blamed in part on the admissions requirements and the academic rigor (or lack thereof) in many colleges and universities.

Several study groups have now turned their attention to higher education. In 1984 the Department of Education sponsored a report on higher education, *Involvement in Learning*, which decried the lack of involvement in their education by students and the absence of concern for educational quality by colleges. Secretary of Education Bennett, in his previous position as chairman of the National Endowment for the Humanities, wrote *To Reclaim a Legacy: A Report on the Humanities in Higher Education* (1984), a sharply critical assessment of the state of the humanities in colleges and universities.

Still another study came from the Carnegie Foundation for the Advancement of Teaching (Newman 1985), which found that the nation's higher education system had not responded well to the new forces, such as technology and the internationalization of the economy, that placed new demands on the institutions. The report emphasized that concern over access to higher education alone is not enough; attention must be paid to what students learn—that is, to educational outcomes. The emphasis on the quality of higher education has found a receptive audience. Many states have taken steps to ensure that college graduates have achieved a level of knowledge that might reasonably be expected to accompany a college degree. All signs suggest that in the next decade the concern will be not only who goes to college but what they learn as well.

CONCLUDING OBSERVATIONS

As this is being written, Congress is once again reauthorizing the Higher Education Act. The debate over this reauthorization has seen continued attention to the issues that have been at the heart of federal policy since the 1972 amendments: institutional aid; the balance between access and choice; waste, fraud, and abuse; aid to middle-income families; and program costs. Minority participation in higher education has always been a key issue in federal policy debates, and, in light of recent evidence, it has received considerable attention in this reauthorization.

It appears that the legislation will result in modest revision of federal programs and not a major restructuring. This is not surprising; policy usually changes incrementally, and, given budget pressures, reforms that preserve the current structure may be more acceptable than comprehensive action. Making this outcome even more likely are political differences: The various groups involved in reauthorization often find it hard to agree on incremental improvements, let alone any far-reaching changes.

The inability to agree on major revisions is in large part a function of uncertainty about the central purpose of federal student aid in an era of fiscal retrenchment. Public policy debates usually come down to a very basic question: Who benefits? Higher education policy is no different. Congress sought to answer this question in 1972 when it chose to emphasize the needs of financially disadvantaged students. Throughout the rest of the 1970s, however, the federal government gradually expanded access to student aid. As long as budget appropriations increased, it was relatively easy to accommodate the needs of all claimants. When the money became tight, it became impossible to meet the needs of all students seeking federal help.

The issues for the 1980s—cost, minority participation, and quality—are all related to the equal opportunity tenet of the 1972 charter. Only when the federal government decides whether to target aid on the financially neediest students (as it promised in the 1972 amendments) or on a wider range of students (as it sought in

1978 and 1980) will we know if the ambitious charter laid out in
1972 will be realized.

REFERENCES

Advanced Technology. 1984. *Quality in the Pell Grant Delivery System*, vol. 1,
   Findings. Prepared under contract with the U.S. Department of Education.
   Reston, Va.
"Almanac: 95th Congress, 2nd Session. . . . 1978." 1978. *Congressional Quar-
   terly*. Washington, D.C.: 248–56, 568–71.
"Almanac: 96th Congress, 2nd Session. . . . 1980." 1980. *Congressional Quar-
   terly*. Washington, D.C.: 420–27.
Applied Management Sciences. 1980. *Study of the Impact of the Middle Income
   Student Assistance Act (MISAA)*. Final Report. Prepared under contract with
   the U.S. Department of Health, Education, and Welfare. Silver Spring, Md.
Bennett, William J. 1984. *To Reclaim a Legacy: A Report on the Humanities
   in Higher Education*. Washington, D.C.: National Endowment for the Humanities.
_____. 1985. Letter to Honorable George Bush, President of the Senate (April
   15).
Carnegie Council on Policy Studies in Higher Education. 1975. *The Federal Role
   in Postsecondary Education: Unfinished Business, 1975–1980*. San Francisco,
   Calif.: Jossey-Bass.
Cheit, Earl. 1971. *The New Depression in Higher Education*. New York: Mc-
   Graw-Hill.
College Board. 1980. *Report from Washington on the 1980 Reauthorization of
   the Higher Education Act*. Washington, D.C.
_____. 1985. *Equality and Excellence: The Educational Status of Black Ameri-
   cans*. New York.
Congressional Budget Office. 1977. *Postsecondary Education: The Current Fed-
   eral Role and Alternative Approaches*. Washington, D.C.: U.S. Government
   Printing Office.
_____. 1978. *Federal Aid to Postsecondary Students: Tax Allowances and
   Alternative Subsidies*. Washington, D.C.: U.S. Government Printing Office.
Congressional Record. 1985. Daily ed. 131 (167) (December 5).
_____. 1980. Bound ed. 126, pt. 18 (September 4).
"Controversy in Congress over Federal Student-Aid Policy: Pro & Con." 1979.
   Congressional Digest. Washington, D.C.
Evans, Angela M., Richard V. Rimkunas, and Gene Falk. 1985. "Federal Spend-
   ing for Education." Congressional Research Service. Library of Congress.
   Mimeo.

154 VALUES IN CONFLICT

Gillespie, Donald A., and Nancy Carlson. 1983. *Trends in Student Aid: 1963 to 1983.* Washington, D.C.: College Board.

Gladieux, Lawrence E. 1980. "What Has Congress Wrought?" *Change* 12 (7) (October): 25–31.

Gladieux, Lawrence E., and Thomas R. Wolanin. 1976. *Congress and the Colleges: The National Politics of Higher Education.* Lexington, Mass.: Lexington Books.

_____. 1978. "Federal Politics." In *Public Policy and Private Higher Education,* edited by David W. Breneman and Chester E. Finn, Jr., with the assistance of Susan C. Nelson, pp. 197–230. Washington, D.C.: Brookings Institution.

Jellema, William W. 1973. *From Red to Black? The Financial Status of Private Colleges and Universities.* San Francisco, Calif.: Jossey-Bass.

National Commission on Excellence in Education. 1983. *A Nation at Risk: The Imperative for Education Reform.* Washington, D.C.: U.S. Government Printing Office.

Newman, Frank. 1985. *Higher Education and the American Resurgence.* Princeton, N.J.: Princeton University Press.

Plisko, Valena White, and Joyce D. Stern. 1985. *The Condition of Education, 1985 Edition.* National Center for Education Statistics. Washington, D.C.: U.S. Government Printing Office.

Special Task Force to the Secretary of Health, Education, and Welfare. 1973. *The Second Newman Report: National Policy and Higher Education.* Cambridge, Mass.: MIT Press.

Study Group on the Condition of Excellence in American Higher Education. 1984. *Involvement in Learning: Realizing the Potential of American Higher Education.* Sponsored by the National Institute of Education. Washington, D.C.: U.S. Government Printing Office.

U.S. Bureau of the Census. 1985. *School Enrollment—Social and Economic Characteristics of Students: October 1984 (Advance Report).* Series P–20, no. 404. Washington, D.C.: U.S. Government Printing Office.

U.S. General Accounting Office. 1985. *Pell Grant Validation Imposes Some Costs and Does Not Greatly Reduce Award Errors: New Strategies Are Needed.* Washington, D.C.: General Accounting Office. GAO/PEMD-85-10.

U.S. House of Representatives. 1975. *The Student Financial Aid Act of 1975.* Hearings before the Subcommittee on Postsecondary Education of the Committee on Education and Labor, 94th Cong., 1st Sess. Washington, D.C.: U.S. Government Printing Office.

_____. 1976. *Guaranteed Student Loan Amendments of 1976.* House Report 94-1232, Committee on Education and Labor, 94th Cong., 2d Sess. Washington, D.C.: U.S. Government Printing Office.

_____. 1980. *Higher Education Extension and Revision.* House Report 96-1337, Conference Report, 96th Cong., 2d Sess. Washington, D.C.: U.S. Government Printing Office.

_____. 1981. *Omnibus Budget Reconciliation Act of 1981*. House Report 97–208, Book 2, 97th Cong., 1st Sess. Washington, D.C.: U.S. Government Printing Office.

U.S. Office of Management and Budget. 1985. *Background on Major Spending Reforms and Reductions in the FY 1986 Budget*. Washington, D.C.: U.S. Government Printing Office.

U.S. Senate. 1975. *Higher Education Legislation, 1975*. Hearings before the Subcommittee on Education of the Committee on Labor and Public Welfare, 94th Cong., 1st Sess., pt. 1. Washington, D.C.: U.S. Government Printing Office.

_____. 1985. *Reauthorization of the Higher Education Act: Program Descriptions, Issues, and Options*. Senate Print 99–8. Committee on Labor and Human Resources, 99th Cong., 1st session. Prepared by the Congressional Research Service. Washington, D.C.: U.S. Government Printing Office.

Van Alstyne, Carol Frances. 1979. "Is There or Isn't There a Middle Income Crunch?" Washington, D.C.: American Council on Education. Mimeo.

8 STUDENT FINANCIAL AID IN THE 1980s

Alan P. Wagner

The growth of direct aid to students enrolled in postsecondary education has been well documented. By 1985–86 student aid provided by federal agencies, states, institutions, and other public and private sources amounted to some $21 billion. Even after adjusting for inflation, the available amounts have increased more than tenfold over the past two decades.

Current economic and demographic pressures have increased the importance of student aid beyond its share of postsecondary education expenditures (Wagner 1984). At the state and federal levels, revisions in student aid programs are among the favored policy options for trimming public spending through more emphasis on targeted aid to students as opposed to institutional subsidies and on loans instead of grants. Revisions also have been made for encouraging postsecondary educational institutions to improve quality in academic programs (through satisfactory progress requirements and merit awards), for meeting specific manpower interests (through cancellation provisions in loan programs), and for serving a potential student population that has become far more heterogeneous in terms of educational background, age, family status, racial/ethnic background, employment status, and attendance status (through modifications in need analysis and extending eligibility for part-time students). For postsecondary educational institutions, the growing pressures on budgets and student enrollments have raised new and important

157

issues in the use of student aid funds. With a growing competition for the shrinking college-age pool from the military, industry, and other schools and colleges, many institutions have sought to sustain enrollments by financing larger numbers and amounts of institutional grants through a general rise in tuition rates. Funds allocated to student aid potentially reduce the resources available to improve quality or to respond to shifts in student program enrollments across campus.

In highlighting the context in which student aid operates in the mid-1980s, this brief overview also reveals the surprisingly diverse set of purposes student aid is intended to serve. Finn (1985) identified ten such overlapping or competing purposes, ranging from broadly defined public access, choice, and manpower objectives to narrowly defined institutional enrollment and financial solvency concerns. The rationales have in common a belief that student aid incentives influence the enrollment (and related spending) decisions of students and their families and the pricing and resource allocation decisions of postsecondary educational institutions.

For whatever purposes it serves, student financial aid has become a critical and volatile element in state and federal intervention in postsecondary education and for program planning and financing at institutions. The purposes of this chapter are to describe the relative scope, types, and distribution of student financial aid, to review what is known about the impact of student financial aid on student/family, institutional, and donor behaviors, and to highlight emerging issues faced by public policymakers and institutional administrators.

THE DIMENSIONS OF STUDENT FINANCIAL AID

Today's postsecondary education students receive direct support from an array of sources. Conventional distinctions group aid into four *types:* (1) grants or scholarships; (2) educational benefits provided as part of broader programs (such as social security, Veterans Administration, state rehabilitation); (3) proceeds from student loans; and (4) earnings from a term-time job. Student financial aid may also be categorized by *source:* (1) federal programs (a public source); (2) state programs (also a public source); (3) institutional sources (generated through tuition, private gifts, or endowment income); and (4) noninstitutional programs (employer, corporate, professional association, or community group support). Although this is but one way to describe the mosaic of student aid programs, these distinctions help to emphasize important changes in the volume and distribution of direct aid to students, and the impact of these changes on the decisions of students, their families, and postsecondary institutions.

According to federal and state program statistics and information culled from postsecondary educational institutions, students received an estimated $21 billion in direct support in 1985-86. This figure likely understates the amount actually provided to students by 15 percent. Employers (including colleges and universities themselves) provided perhaps $1 billion in tuition aid. Other noninstitutional student aid donors generate as much as $750 million more. In addition, probably half of all student term-time employment is monitored by institutions; funds from other term-time jobs likely provide an additional $1 billion.

Trends in Direct Aid to Students

The volume, source, and composition of student financial aid has shifted over the past two decades, at times dramatically. For most of the history of higher education in North America, student aid has been financed largely by institutions through tuition revenues, private gifts, and income from endowments. The first state program appeared at the turn of this century. As recently as 1963-64 colleges and universities provided almost 60 percent of the financial aid available to students (Table 8-1). Following the establishment of the College Work-Study, Educational Opportunity Grant, and Guaranteed Student Loan programs in 1965, the federal share of student financial aid volume grew. By 1970-71 institutionally financed sources of aid provided about a quarter of the funds received by students. The state program share had fallen to 5 percent.

It may seem surprising that the federal stake in financial aid to students is such a relatively recent phenomenon. Most place the first significant federal involvement in college student financing with the GI bill for World War II veterans, enacted in 1944. In most respects, this program was enormously successful. In 1947-48, nearly 50 percent of the 2 million enrolled in college were veterans (Bowman,

Table 8-1. The Volume and Sources of Student Financial Aid, 1970-71 to 1985-86 (*dollars in millions*).

	1963-64		1970-71		1975-76		1981-82		1985-86[a]	
	Amount	Percentage	Amount	Percentage	Amount	Percentage	Amount	Percentage	Amount	Percentage
Total	$673	100.0%	$4,755	100.0%	$10,826	100.0%	$18,381	100.0%	$21,027	100.0%
Federal	232	34.5	3,294	69.3	8,561	79.1	14,704	80.0	15,781	75.0
Grants[b]	9	1.3	150	3.2	1,221	11.3	2,839	15.4	3,831	18.2
Benefits[c]	67	10.0	1,620	34.1	5,273	48.7	3,347	18.2	746	3.5
Loans	114	16.9	1,297	27.3	1,772	16.4	7,894	42.9	10,511	50.0
Work	42	6.2	227	4.8	295	2.7	624	3.4	693	3.3
State[d]	56	8.3	236	5.0	490	4.5	921	5.0	1,375	6.5
Institution[e]	385	57.2	1,225	25.8	1,775	16.4	2,756	15.0	4,032	19.2
Grants	300	44.6	965	20.3	1,435	13.2	2,323	12.6	3,426	16.3
Loans	35	5.2	40	.8	50	.5	65	.4	130	.6
Work	50	7.4	220	4.6	290	2.7	368	2.0	476	2.3

a. Institutional grant, loan, and work amounts for 1985-86 assume 5 percent annual real rate of growth from 1983-84. See Lanchantin (1986).

b. Federal grants include amounts provided through general and categorical student aid programs.

c. Federal benefits include amounts provided through the Veteran's Administration and the Social Security Administration.

d. Figures refer to state grant programs only. Grants to graduate students are excluded for the years between 1970-71 and 1980-81; these students receive less than 5 percent of state student aid funds. States provide additional direct support to students outside of the state grant programs. In 1985-86 the volume of this aid was about $70 million, $100 million, and $25 million for grant, loans, and work, respectively. The amounts of such aid have increased substantially in this decade. See National Association of State Scholarship and Grant Programs (1986).

e. Figures refer to aid generated and administered by the institution. Institutional share of the federal NDSL and CWS programs is included under those programs. Some federal and state student aid (for fellowships or tuition waivers) are included here.

Sources: Estimated from Gillespie and Carlson (1983: table A-1); Lanchantin (1986); National Association of State Scholarship and Grant Programs (1986: tables 1, 6, and 7); Thrift and Toppe (1986: table 2); Stampen (1985: table 3); Davis (1985: table 2); Sanders and Nelson (1970: table 2); College Entrance Examination Board (1975: App. B); Wagner (1977: table 6); U.S. Department of Health, Education and Welfare, Office of Education (1968: App. A).

Volkert, and Hahn 1973). By 1951, however, the proportion of students supported by the GI bill had fallen to 15 percent. No other student aid initiative since then (including subsequent versions of the GI bill, the Pell grant program, or the Guaranteed Student loan program) provided subsidies to as large a share of students.

Between 1970-71 and 1975-76 as the volume of direct aid to students doubled from $4.7 billion to $10.8 billion, the federal share of the volume increased to 80 percent. In fact, the growth in aid volume was fueled not so much by the phased increases in eligibility and funding for federal student aid programs as by a fourfold increase in GI bill educational benefits to $4.2 billion and a doubling of social security educational benefits to $1 billion. Further liberalization of need analysis and eligibility requirements in federal grant and loan programs gave rise to a 70 percent increase in student aid volume from 1975-76 to 1981-82. Although the amount of available aid had increased another 15 percent by 1985-86, the $15.8 billion provided through federal programs represented a somewhat smaller 75 percent share of the total. By 1985-86, aid from post-secondary institutions had grown to $3.4 billion (19.2 percent of the total), while state grant programs contributed $1.4 billion (6.5 percent of the total).

The composition of available student aid has also shifted significantly over the past two decades. Nonrepayable aid, in the form of grants, scholarships, and educational benefits, accounted for about three-fourths of available aid through the mid-1970s. By 1985-86 less than one-half (44.5 percent) of all available aid was provided as outright grants or benefits to students. Over the last ten years, grants and scholarships from all sources have increased as a share of all aid from 29 percent to 41 percent. However, support provided through educational benefits in the GI bill and social security program has declined from nearly half (48.7 percent) of all aid in 1975-76 to less than 5 percent in 1985-86.

Self-help aid through loans and work currently accounts for over half (55.5 percent) of all direct support to students. This share represents a substantial increase over the past two decades. The growth in self-help aid came largely from the increase in loan financing during the last ten years. Providing $1.7 billion (16.9 percent) of the aid volume in 1975-76, student loans from all sources accounted for more than $10 billion (50.6 percent) of the aid provided to post-secondary education students in 1985-86.

Table 8-2. Trends in College and University Enrollments, Tuition, Institutional Costs, and Direct Support for Students, 1963-64 to 1985-86.

	1963-64 to 1970-71	1970-71 to 1975-76	1975-76 to 1981-82	1981-82 to 1985-86
	Average Annual Change:			
FTE Enrollment	+14%	+5%	+1%	+0%
College Expenditures/FTE	+4	+5	+11	+10
Tuition	+6	+4	+14	+11
Student Aid Subsidies/FTE	+37	+23	+6	+2
Federal/FTE	+11	+31	+5	-2
State/FTE	+17	+14	+12	+11
Institution/FTE	+16	+3	+7	+12

Source: *Enrollments* — U.S. Department of Education (1985c: tables B-13, B-13A, B-13B); U.S. Department of Education (1985a: table 2.17). Projections adjusted by actual enrollments in 1985-86.

College expenditures — Gillespie and Carlson (1983: table 4); "Revenues and Expenditures of Colleges and Universities, 1983-84" (March 19, 1986: 20). The expenditure figures refer to education and general expenditures, net of grants and scholarships. Expenditures for 1985-86 assume a rate of growth from 1983 to 1985 equivalent to 1981 to 1983 rate of growth.

Tuition — U.S. Department of Education (1985a: table 2.16); Evangelauf (1986: 2); U.S. Department of Health, Education and Welfare (1974). The single tuition measure used here is an average of public and independent sector figures, weighted by FTE enrollments in each sector. This weighting has the effect of taking into account shifting enrollment patterns over the twenty-two-year period (with relatively larger numbers of students enrolling in public sector institutions and attending part-time).

Financial aid subsidies — Estimated from Table 8-1. The subsidies measure that proportion of student aid that directly offsets the full costs — direct and forgone earnings — of attending college. The subsidy measure for each year includes, for example, the full amount of student earnings and one half of federally subsidized loans (the latter reflecting an assumption that interest subsidies, cancellations, and defaults result in a direct subsidy of fifty cents for every dollar of NDSL and GSL advanced). For the comparisons shown here, the subsidy measure includes only aid provided to students enrolled in colleges and universities. In 1985-86 students in proprietary schools received perhaps $4 billion in aid.

Has the volume of student aid subsidies kept pace with the growth in postsecondary education enrollments and increases in costs over this twenty-two-year period? The question is difficult to answer, partly because the data required to take into account changes in the composition of postsecondary education enrollments and in the eligibility for aid are not easy to develop. Moreover, the answer to such a question would not indicate whether student aid subsidies are adequate to meet aid donor or institutional purposes (for example, that sufficient numbers from targeted subpopulations enroll or that sufficient numbers enroll in particular types of institutions or programs). Nonetheless, a comparison of relative changes in enrollments, costs, and aid do provide one indication of how closely these measures track each other. The relevant figures are presented in Table 8-2.

Through the mid-1970s, the rate of growth of student aid subsidies per FTE enrollment clearly exceeded the rate of growth in college expenditures per student or tuition. From 1970–71 to 1975–76, for example, expenditures per FTE and weighted average tuition increased at 5 and 4 percent average annual rates, respectively, while aid subsidies per student increased by 23 percent. Over the past ten years, however, increases in financial aid subsidies per student have lagged behind college expenditures and tuition increases. In the 1980s, as college spending per FTE and tuitions have increased by more than 10 percent per year, aid subsidies per FTE grew by 3 percent. In contrast to the 1963–64 to 1975–76 period, state and institutionally provided financial aid subsidies per student have increased at a more rapid rate than federal aid subsidies per student over the last ten years.

Student Aid Recipients

In 1983–84 about two-fifths of all postsecondary students used some type of nonfamily support to meet their costs of attendance. The proportions aided varied by sector. About 30 percent of students enrolled in public institutions received financial aid, while the aided share at independent colleges and universities approached 60 percent. The proportion of students attending proprietary postsecondary schools who received aid probably exceeded 60 percent, although precise numbers are not available.

As shown in Table 8-3, participation in major student aid programs differed by source. Federal student aid programs dominated: close to four of five aid recipients received support from at least one federal program, with proportions higher for self-supporting recipients and recipients attending public colleges and universities. State need-based aid (which accounted for some 85 percent of all state grant dollars) was awarded to about one in four recipients, with

Table 8-3. Participation in Major Student Aid Programs by Undergraduate Student Aid Recipients, 1983-84[a] (*percentage*).

	Total	Dependent Students	Independent Students	Public Colleges	Private Colleges
Pell grant	54%	51%	62%	65%	32%
SEOG	17	19	14	16	20
College Work-Study[b]	28	31	20	12	41
NDSL	21	23	17	20	25
GSL	42	45	37	35	58
State need-based	27	30	20	23	34
Institution need-based	16	20	6	4	39

a. Data refer to students receiving financial support administered or monitored by college or university financial aid offices. Perhaps 20 percent of total aid volume flows to students outside of financial aid offices. Of the sources examined, participation in the GSL program is most likely to be understated. The percent of undergraduate aid recipients receiving GSL's probably exceeds 47 percent (Congressional Budget Office 1985).

b. Includes federal and state work-study programs.

Source: Estimated from American Council on Education (1984: table 3); Thrift and Toppe (1986: table 2); Stampen (1985: tables 3 and 13).

dependent aid recipients and recipients at independent colleges more likely to have received this aid. Finally, institutionally provided need-based aid was packaged for about 16 percent of all aid recipients. Such aid was predominantly awarded to students attending independent colleges and universities.

Financial aid recipients are likely to be younger, to be drawn from minority backgrounds, and to have lower family income than the average college student (Table 8-4). However, the characteristics differ by dependency status. In 1983-84 somewhat less than a quarter (23 percent) of all dependent aid recipients were age 22 or older. More than four-fifths (83 percent) of recipients classified as self-supporting for student aid purposes fell into this older age group. An estimated 24 percent of all aid recipients came from minority backgrounds. Finally, about 23 percent of dependent aid recipients and 81 percent of self-supporting recipients had family incomes below $12,000. At the top end, 11 percent of aid recipients came from families with incomes above $36,000. Nearly all of these recipients were classified as dependent on their families for financial support.

Table 8-4. Characteristics of Student Financial Aid Recipients, 1983–84 (*in percentages*).

| | All Students | Aid Recipients[a] | | |
		Total	Dependent	Independent
Age	100%	100%	100%	100%
21 or less	46	57	77	17
22–25	20	25	21	32
26 or more	34	18	2	51
Percent minority	14	24	23	27
Family income	100	100	100	100
Under $6,000	9	26	11	56
$6,000–$12,000	11	18	12	25
$12,000–$24,000	23	26	31	16
$24,000–$36,000	22	18	25	3
Over $36,000	35	11	17	—

a. Data refer to students receiving financial support administered or monitored by college or university financial aid offices. Perhaps 20 percent of total aid volume flows to students outside of financial aid offices.

Source: Estimated from American Council on Education (1984: table 3); Thrift and Toppe (1986: table 2); Stampen (1985: tables 3 and 13); U.S. Bureau of the Census (1985: table 4); U.S. Department of Education (1985b: unpublished tabulations).

THE EFFECTS OF STUDENT FINANCIAL AID

Student financial aid awards and programs potentially influence the decisions of students and their families, institutions, and donors. Not surprisingly, the sizes of direct effects of student aid on student enrollment decisions have generated the greatest interest on the part of policymakers, institutional officials, and researchers. However, as McPherson (1985, 1986) argues, these direct effects may be partly offset by the potentially important indirect effects of student aid on the levels and sources of the family's contribution toward educational expenses, the tuitions and aid packages established at post-secondary institutions, and aid policies imposed by federal, state, institutional, and private student aid donors. Each of these is discussed in turn.

Enrollment Decisions

Since financial aid reduces the portion of student costs of attendance actually borne by potential students and their families, the size and composition of aid awards presumably affect decisions about whether to enroll, where to enroll, whether to continue in school for an additional year, and whether to choose a particular field of study. Relatively few studies actually provide direct estimates of the effect of student aid on these decisions. Student aid's likely effects on enrollment decisions are frequently inferred from the estimates of the effects of differences in tuition or associated costs (such as commuting expenses). The extant research has been criticized on conceptual and methodological grounds as well. As reviews by Jackson and Weathersby (1975), McPherson (1978), and Leslie and Brinkman (1985) indicate, the available studies employ quite different types of data and approaches. The studies exploit time-series or cross-section data, use aggregate measures or rely on sample data for individuals, and refer to single institutions or national populations. In spite of the flaws and the variety of approaches, however, several sets of reasonably consistent findings do emerge.

Whether to Enroll. The available research suggests that a $100 increase in aid (evaluated in 1982–83 dollars) should lead to an enrollment increase of about 1 to 2 percent (Leslie and Brinkman 1985). This estimate is inferred from studies examining the effects of any difference in price (through, for example, variations in tuition, other associated costs, or student aid awards). Although a number of the more detailed studies seem to indicate that enrollments are more responsive to tuition changes than to equivalent changes in student aid awards, several recent studies show potential students to be at least equally sensitive to differences in aid or in direct costs (Manski and Wise 1983; Schwartz 1985). Among types of aid, enrollments appear to be more responsive to grants than to equal dollar amounts of term-time earnings or loans. Carlson's (1974) estimates imply that enrollments are twice as responsive to grants.

How should these findings be interpreted? McPherson's (1978) observations seem appropriate. First, the enrollment response to student aid awards is significant, if not sizable. Second, however, providing financial aid subsidies to large groups of potential students represents a relatively expensive way to encourage enrollments because a large number of students who would have enrolled without aid receive subsidies under broadly based student aid schemes. So, for example, if aid subsidies are provided to *all* who enroll, some $3 billion would be required to generate a 5 percent increase in undergraduate FTE enrollment (or about $7,000 per *additional* student). Third, a more cost-effective strategy would call for directing aid subsidies toward those potential students least likely to enroll without the support, other things equal.

Differences in responsiveness to student aid incentives apparently do exist among groups of potential students identified by income, ability, age, and sex (Leslie and Brinkman 1985; Terkla and Jackson 1984). Indeed, the difference in responsiveness across income groups provides part of the rationale behind need-based student aid programs. According to Manski and Wise (1983), awards from the Basic Educational Opportunity Grant (now Pell grant) program increased 1979–80 enrollments of current year high school graduates over what would have taken place without the program by 21 percent, at a cost of $3,783 per additional enrollment.

Where to Enroll. Although the available research results differ, they imply an "order-of-magnitude" increase in public sector enrollments of 1 to 2 percent in response to a $100 increase in aid subsidies (evaluated in 1982–83 dollars) at public institutions. An equivalent change in aid subsidies at independent institutions might increase independent sector enrollments by something less than 1 percent (Leslie and Brinkman 1985; McPherson 1978). In each case, the increased enrollments are likely to be drawn, in about equal parts, from students not previously enrolled and from students previously enrolled in the other sector (McPherson 1978). The effects of increased aid awards on institutional choice decisions differ by student family income, racial/ethnic group, gender, academic ability, and parental alumni status (Leslie and Brinkman 1985; Tierney 1984; Tierney and Davis 1985; Corman and Davidson 1984; McPherson 1978; Ehrenberg and Sherman 1984).

Again, McPherson's (1978) comments help to place these general findings in perspective. First, the effects of student aid on the choice of institution are significant but not huge. The estimated effects suggest that relatively large numbers and amounts of aid awards would be required to shift enrollments from the public to the independent sector (or vice versa). Second, although low-income students generally seem to be relatively more responsive to differences in price (and, by inference, student aid subsidies) when making college choice decisions, students from higher-income families are also responsive. The implication is that increased aid subsidies provided to higher-income students at public (or independent) institutions will increase enrollments within the public (independent) sector at the expense, in large part, of enrollments in the other sector (McPherson 1978; Ehrenberg and Sherman 1984). Finally, the great variability in the estimated effect of financial aid subsidies on institutional choice decisions implies that broad sector results may not apply within more narrowly defined institutional types or at individual institutions (McPherson 1978; Ehrenberg and Sherman 1984; Corman and Davidson 1984; Leslie and Brinkman 1985).

Whether to Continue. With some important exceptions, financial aid subsidies appear to improve the likelihood that students will continue in college by 2 to 15 percent. Grants and scholarships increase the probability of persistence by an estimated 1 to 3 percent, with higher effects observed for males and low- to middle-income students. Loan financing, on the other hand, apparently increases the probability of dropping out. For freshmen, the use of loans *increases* attrition rates by 6 percent for males and 2 percent for females. Freshmen with on-campus employment are among the least likely to drop out, with persistence improved 4 percent for whites and 13 percent for blacks attending predominantly white institutions (Astin 1976). For full-time males, increased hours of work raised the probability of dropping out (Ehrenberg and Sherman 1985). Various combinations of aid types, when provided to freshmen from different backgrounds and attending different types of institutions, appear to be associated with widely varying changes in continuation rates (Astin 1976).

Although the effects seem to be large, most research studies suggest that other student and institutional factors account for most of the observed differences in student attrition (Noel 1985; Stampen and Cabrera 1985). Indeed, student aid subsidies generally appear to be less influential on decisions to persist than on decisions of whether and where to enroll. Finally, increases in the volume of student aid, shifts in the composition of financial aid subsidies, and changes in the composition of student enrollments may have altered student aid's overall effect on persistence beyond those revealed in Astin's follow-up study of largely young, full-time, dependent freshmen enrolled in 1968. Based on their review of available evidence, for example, Stampen and Cabrera (1985) believe that an apparent narrowing of differences in rates of attrition across income groups may have occurred, partly as a result of substantial increases in the volume of student aid subsidies. Student aid's effects on the continuation rates of self-supporting, older, and part-time students have yet to be fully examined (but see Pappas and Loring 1985).

Whether to Choose a Particular Field of Study.   The interest in student aid's effects on field of study (and career) choices has recently been heightened by a concern about whether increases in accumulated educational debt significantly influence these decisions. In addition, federal and state initiatives to encourage enrollments in particular fields (most particularly, education and health) are growing in number and scope. Although careful and current research on the effects of student aid on field of study choices is limited, the available research and data suggest that the effects are probably quite modest.

Increasing use of student loans, other things equal, should encourage students to choose fields leading to careers with higher, more immediate earnings potential. However, more recent trends in career preferences of entering freshmen indicate a movement away from such fields as engineering and allied health (Cooperative Institutional Research Program 1985). On employment, average accumulated debt does vary by occupation, with those in higher-pay occupations carrying larger amounts of educational debt than those in low-pay occupations. However, within occupations, those who do not borrow apparently earn as much as borrowers (Davis 1986). Together, these data provide no indication that accumulated educational debt, at least at current levels, has affected student borrower field or occupational choices.

Programs restricting aid to students majoring in particular fields also are not likely to greatly influence field of study choices. Currently, the most favored approach calls for student loans with a cancellation of principal for those who work in the particular field following graduation. For these programs, the monetary incentive implied in the loan forgiveness feature represents perhaps 4 to 7 percent of beginning salaries over a relatively few years (after which the benefit disappears). Given exising differences in earnings among fields, these amounts are not likely to greatly alter the relative financial attractiveness of careers (McMahon and Wagner 1982). Moreover, current student aid policies and practices generally require that aid received through programs with no provisions favoring enrollment in particular fields must be *reduced*, in part, by the amounts of aid offered through programs with such provisions. To the extent students qualify for substantial amounts of aid from other programs, this design feature likely reduces the effects of programs with subsidies linked to specific fields of study (Kemmerer and Wagner 1985).

Family Savings, Labor Supply, and Educational Spending Decisions

Financial aid subsidies potentially influence family savings and labor supply decisions as well as the amounts and distribution of the family's contribution toward postsecondary educational costs. These effects largely derive from the need-based criteria used to allocate most student aid. "Need" is defined as what it costs to attend a postsecondary institution *less* an "expected contribution." The "expected contribution" is the amount the family is required to contribute out of income and assets for college expenses. "Expected contribution" calculations, however, introduce incentives for a family to alter its accumulation of savings, its amount of work, and the student's dependency status in order to qualify for larger aid subsidies. Families also may adjust the amounts actually contributed in response to student aid subsidies. Although these potential effects have not been fully evaluated, several available studies and extant data permit some general comments about their nature and likely impact.

Savings and Labor Supply. In a recent attempt to evaluate the effects of student aid subsidies on the family's accumulation of assets, Case and McPherson (1985) estimated that precollege savings could be reduced by 2 to 50 percent for a family, depending on the assumptions employed. Similarly, the availability of student aid subsidies could reduce the parents' supply of labor by as much as 5 percent by the husband and 20 to 25 percent by the wife. Although these represent significant incentives, Case and McPherson go on to suggest that 20 percent or fewer families of financial aid filers confront incentives large enough to greatly alter their savings and labor supply decisions.

Dependency Status. The potential incentives in the definition for otherwise dependent students to claim financial independence appear to be considerable. Wagner and Carlson (1983) estimate that a family at the lowest income quartile would give up $1,000 in reduced tax liability (by forgoing the exemption for the student on the federal tax return), while gaining $2,000 to $3,000 more in Pell grants alone. For families at the highest income quartile, the net gain approaches $6,000. Given these potential incentives, it may seem surprising that dependent students establishing financial independence as a matter of convenience apparently account for, at most, 5 percent of all independent students (Hansen 1985). The low proportion may indicate that the net gain from establishing independence is not as large as previously estimated. Families choosing to establish the student's financial independence would lose the value of federal *and* state tax exemptions, the net savings in room costs provided when the student lives at the family's home beyond the six weeks permitted in the definition, and other aid subsidies directly by states and institutions primarily toward dependent students.

Parents' Contribution. Student aid subsidies apparently replace, in part, the contributions parents would have provided without aid. Based on a study of 1972–73 full-time first-year students, Wagner (1978) estimated that aid offset parental contributions at rate of $2 for every $10 in aid. For higher-income families, the estimated effect was twice as great. Since need-based financial aid is intended to enable students to enroll without imposing excessive financial burdens on their families, some substitution of aid for the family contribution might well be appropriate. Although Wagner's data imply that financial aid led to actual contributions below the "expected" amounts, findings from a more recent survey of families suggest the opposite. According to unpublished tabulations from the College

Scholarship Service's Family Financing Survey, families of 1984–85 financial aid applicants contributed about 10 percent more than expected through need analysis calculations (Doran, Wagner, and White 1985).

Institutional Pricing Decisions

The growth in the volume of student aid subsidies provided through federal, state, and noninstitutional sources may potentially encourage postsecondary institutions to raise tuitions in order to capture larger amounts from these external sources. Moreover, aid from federal and state entitlement programs (Pell, Guaranteed Student Loan, or most state grant programs) may encourage institutions to provide additional subsidies from institutionally allocated sources of aid. This would be the case if the remaining financial needs of students receiving entitlement-like aid were reduced to a level that could effectively be met through relatively small awards from institutionally allocated sources. The available research on these questions is, at this point, only suggestive.

Tuition Increases.   Although a link between aid volume and tuition has been suspected, there is very little indication that the growth in student aid volume has led to increases in tuition rates. Though the massive influx of GI bill beneficiaries into postsecondary education in the late 1940s clearly helped to fuel a nearly 50 percent rise in tuitions, the circumstances of the early post-World War II era were unique. Perhaps as much as 45 percent of student fees and 25 percent of educational and general income were derived from GI bill payments (Finn 1977). Moreover, existing postsecondary educational institutions lacked the capacity to accommodate the increased enrollments. Neither of these conditions has prevailed during the more recent growth in student aid volume.

Indeed, over the past two decades, there has been no clear association between tuition rates and increases in aid provided through federal and state programs. Over the 1970 to 1975 period, for example, tuitions increased by an average 4 percent a year in both public and private colleges and universities, while federal and state student aid subsidies jumped at average annual rates of 31 and 14 percent, respectively (Table 8–2). By contrast, as tuition rates grew at an 11 percent rate in the first half of the 1980s, total aid subsidies per student from federal and state sources held steady. McPherson (1986) believes the lack of any clear effect may be explained by formulas for allotment of federal campus-based aid program funds and by award criteria in the Pell, Guaranteed Student Loan, and state grant programs, which are relatively insensitive to tuition. Increases in funds from these sources may simply have helped to moderate tuition increases by enabling institutions to allocate relatively more resources to academic programs than for institutional scholarships and grants.

Aid Packaging. According to information culled from a number of surveys on financial aid packaging, students qualifying for aid in the entitlement-like programs do receive additional support from sources administered by institutions. Willie and Wagner (1984) found that more than two-fifths of all 1978–79 undergraduate aid recipients received both entitlement-like aid and institutionally awarded aid, with higher proportions of these combined packages at independent colleges and universities than at public or proprietary institutions. In 1983–84 an estimated two-thirds of all full-time dependent undergraduates receiving Pell grants also received campus-based federal aid (Miller and Hexter 1985a, 1985b). Although information on the packaging of institutionally financed aid is not readily available, it appears that at least a quarter of low income full-time dependent Pell grant recipients at independent colleges and universities also receive institutional grants.

Aid Donor Decisions

Given the large number of federal, state, institutional, and private aid sources, the interaction of funding, eligibility, and award criteria among aid programs have attracted considerable interest. Aid donors particularly fear that their funds will substitute for, rather than augment, funds provided through other aid sources. Efforts to limit this substitution have taken the form of explicit requirements for packaging or offsetting aid awards as well as provisions that seek to encourage additional funds from other sources through "matching"

requirements. As an example of the latter, the federal SSIG allotments to state grant programs must be matched on a dollar for dollar
basis. Institutions also are required to match federal allotments for
College Work-Study and NDSL awards at 20 and 10 percent shares,
respectively. According to assessments of these programs, the effects
of matching requirements in encouraging *additional* state and institutional allocations appear to be, at best, marginal. The SSIG program
likely encouraged twenty-three states to implement grant programs.
By 1983, however, all but one state had more than met the 50/50
federal matching requirement (Hansen 1983). When Gladieux (1975)
examined the distribution of federal campus-based aid, he concluded
that the programs' matching requirements accounted for little of the
observed differences across institutional sectors. The current "fair-
share" method for distributing campus-based aid to states and
institutions further reduces the potential effects of the matching
requirements.

Some association between federal and institutional student aid
subsidies, however, apparently does exist. In particular, the rate of
growth of institutionally financed aid subsidies per student seems
to vary inversely with relative changes in federal aid subsidies per
student. Institutional aid subsidies per student grew at an average
annual rate of 3 percent in the early 1970s while federal aid subsidies
jumped some 31 percent per year (see Table 8-2). During the early
1980s, as federal aid subsidies held steady, institutional aid subsidies
per student increased by 12 percent per year, Even without knowing
what the levels of institutional aid subsidies might have been in the
absence of such changes in federal aid, the pattern is suggestive
(McPherson 1986).

EMERGING ISSUES FOR STUDENT
FINANCIAL AID

The changing patterns in student aid funding, institutional finance,
and student enrollments raise new questions about financial aid programs, administration, and use. The changes renew interest in student
aid's effects on access and choice while directing new attention to
need analysis, recruitment, and financial aid packaging practices of
postsecondary educational institutions. These have become the most
controversial and relevant issues in financial aid today.

Access and Choice

Although potentially serving a wide range of purposes, student aid is chiefly expected to increase enrollments from subpopulations currently underrepresented in postsecondary education. Beyond access, student aid is intended to ensure that students may choose among postsecondary educational options unconstrained by a lack of money. Over the past two decades, student aid has contributed significantly to both of these objectives. However, recent reductions in federal aid subsidies during the 1980s place these gains in jeopardy. The existing enrollment data are strongly suggestive: From 1980 to 1984, the college enrollment rates of black and hispanic high school graduates ages 18 to 19 declined by 6 and 8 percentage points, respectively, while the enrollment rate for whites held steady (U.S. Department of Commerce 1985). Current enrollment and budget pressures, however, are likely to limit student aid's effectiveness in maintaining or increasing access and choice for underrepresented groups.

First, postsecondary education enrollments will be increasingly drawn from minority, older, and self-supporting populations. But existing student aid programs and award amounts are likely to be less effective in encouraging enrollments from these groups. The new potential students tend to be less informed about postsecondary educational opportunities and about their eligibility for financial aid. Even with greater information, potential students from these new populations are likely to be more sensitive to costs and to require more support once enrolled than their younger, dependent counterparts. The changing composition of potential and enrolled student pools, therefore, implies that enrollments from underrepresented groups will be maintained only through relatively larger allocations of resources per student for dissemination of information, counseling, and financial aid.

Second, the reductions in federal support have made it necessary for institutions to augment student aid budgets with support from private gifts and general revenues. But the potential for even further increases in the use of these resources to promote wider access and choice may be limited. The private student aid dollars often carry restrictions on who may receive the awards, and institutional awards increasingly are viewed as a means to attract enrollments, high-ability students, and high revenue-bearing students (that is, those who contribute more in tuition and institutional appropriations than it costs to provide them with instruction at the margin). As some of these students receive larger aid subsidies than they would financially require to enroll in the institution of their choice, other potential students might have fewer options due to a lack of available financing.

Institutional Aid Packaging and No-Need Awards

The need to maintain enrollments and increase institutional revenues in the face of a growing competition for students has already increased student aid's use as a strategic tool for recruitment. The most obvious approach is to set tuition rates, net of discounts, to differences in the elasticity of demand among potential student pools for the individual institution. The institution price discriminates, charging those with the lowest price elasticity relatively higher tuition rates, net of discounts, than those with high price elasticity. From the institution's perspective, the principal advantage of this approach is its potential for collecting additional revenues from students and families willing and able to pay more. There are also advantages to the public and to students. The relatively higher tuitions paid by some groups of students signal other providers who may be able to offer programs of comparable quality at the same, or a lower, price. This potential competition limits the scope of institutions to sustain inefficient programs.

These considerations, however, also raise the potential for damaging price competition among institutions. From the institution's point of view, potential students likely to be sensitive to costs should be offered price discounts. But this policy can be expected to produce results only in the short run. As competing institutions with resources match the discounts provided to students from the targeted populations, larger inducements will be required to hold their enrollments. A relatively modest responsiveness to student aid subsidies within pools of students highly desired by the institution (such as those with high ability) may compound the problem. An increasing proportion of resources will be devoted to price inducements that do nothing to increase access to higher education generally, let alone enrollments at individual institutions.

Indebtedness of Postsecondary Education Students

The dramatic increase in the volume of student loan financing introduces new questions about the capacity of students to meet repayment obligations following graduation. The scope of the potential problem is large: Outstanding federal loans amount to some $40 billion, while about one-fourth of all students borrow each year to meet postsecondary education expenses.

Although it is hard to generalize from the available data, some broad figures indicate what is known about the impact of current levels of indebtedness on repayment. Perhaps 5 to 10 percent of all borrowers default on their student loans, while another 10 percent have some difficulty handling their monthly loan payments (Hauptman 1983; Martin 1986). Borrowers in repayment in 1982 had educational debts in excess of $6,000 on average, with the indebtedness of those who borrowed at both the undergraduate and graduate levels averaging slightly more than $11,000 (Martin 1986). But for these borrowers, educational loan payments average 5.5 percent of gross income and 7.5 percent of after tax income (Martin 1986).

These data suggest that student loan repayment burdens do not appear to be greater than might be anticipated for loans of this type (Hauptman 1983). Although significant increases in accumulated debt *relative to income* could raise troubling repayment problems, the experience over the early 1980s seems to indicate that borrowers (as well as college administrators and lenders) may be very much aware of the amounts of debt they can handle. According to Davis (1986), average indebtedness appears to have increased less rapidly than the rate of growth of annual loan volume and about as rapidly as incomes. The more important question may be the extent to which large anticipated educational indebtedness discourages potential students from entering postsecondary education, enrolling in particular institutions or programs, or continuing through degree completion at the undergraduate or graduate levels. Updated answers to these questions have yet to be formulated.

CONCLUSIONS

Student financial aid clearly has become an important source of financing for students and for postsecondary educational institu-

tions. Although potentially useful as a way to influence the enrollment decisions of students, the pricing decisions of institutions, and
the funding decisions of aid donors, the nature, extent, and interaction of these direct and indirect effects have not been thoroughly
investigated. Further, the amount and distribution of student aid
must be evaluated in relation to an overall system of postsecondary
education financing that provides substantial public tax, student aid,
and institutional subsidies to some students, institutions, and programs but not to others. If postsecondary educational opportunities
are to be provided to all who may potentially benefit, public officials
and institutional administrators will need a better understanding of
student aid's direct and indirect effects as well as its role in the overall financing of postsecondary education.

REFERENCES

American Council on Education. 1983. "Who Gets Student Aid? Comparing
Data from Public, Independent, and Proprietary Institutions." Unpublished
paper. Washington, D.C.
_____. 1984. "Who Gets Student Aid? A 1983–84 Snapshot." Unpublished
paper. Washington, D.C.
Astin, Alexander W. 1976. *Preventing Students from Dropping Out.* San Fran-
cisco: Jossey-Bass.
Bowman, James L., J. Jay Volkert, and J. Victor Hahn. 1973. *Educational Assis-
tance to Veterans: A Comparative Study of Three G.I. Bills.* Princeton, N.J.:
Educational Testing Service.
Carlson, Daryl. 1974. "Student Price Response Coefficients for Grants, Loans,
Work-Study Aid, and Tuition Changes: An Analysis of Student Surveys."
Unpublished paper. Department of Agricultural Economics, University of
California at Davis.
College Entrance Examination Board. 1975. "Estimating the Unknown: Unmet
Financial Needs of 1975–76 College Students." Unpublished paper. Washing-
ton, D.C.
Congressional Budget Office. 1985. "Proposed Changes in Federal Student Aid."
Unpublished memorandum. Washington, D.C.
Cooperative Institutional Research Program. 1985. *Computer Careers Losing
Appeal.* Los Angeles, Calif.: American Council on Education/University of
California, Los Angeles.

Corman, Hope, and Patricia K. Davidson. 1984. "Economic Aspects of Postsecondary Schooling Decisions." *Economics of Education Review* 3 (2) (Fall): 131-39.

Davis, Jerry S. 1985. "State Supported Work-Study Programs." Unpublished paper. Pennsylvania Higher Education Assistance Authority.

_____ . 1986. "Long-Term Implications of Student Borrowing: A Commentary." In *Proceedings of College Scholarship Service Colloquium on Student Loan Counseling and Debt Management*, Denver, Colo., December 2-4.

Doran, Micheileen J., Alan P. Wagner, and Constance White. 1985. "Family Contributions toward Higher Education Expenses: Their Amounts, Sources, and Impacts." Paper presented at the College Board Annual Forum, San Francisco, Calif., October 23-25.

Ehrenberg, Ronald G., and Daniel R. Sherman. 1984. "Optimal Financial Aid Policies for a Selective University." *Journal of Human Resources* 19(2) (Spring): 202-30.

_____ . 1985. "Employment While in College, Academic Achievement, and Post-College Outcomes: A Summary of Results," Cambridge, Mass.: NBER Working Paper Series 1742.

Evangelauf, Jean. 1986. "College Costs Expected to Continue Rising, but 'Modestly.' " *Chronicle of Higher Education* 31 (23) (February 19): 2.

Finn, Jr., Chester E. 1977. *Scholars, Dollars, and Bureaucrats.* Washington, D.C.: The Brookings Institution.

_____ . 1985. "Why Do We Need Financial Aid? or, Desanctifying Student Assistance." In *An Agenda for the Year 2000*, edited by College Scholarship Service, pp. 1-23. New York: College Entrance Examination Board.

Gillespie, Donald A., and Nancy Carlson. 1983. *Trends in Student Aid: 1963 to 1983.* Washington, D.C.: College Entrance Examination Board.

Gladieux, Lawrence E. 1975. *The Distribution of Federal Student Aid: The Enigma of the Two-Year Colleges.* New York: College Entrance Examination Board.

Hansen, Janet. 1983. *Another Look at SSIG.* Unpublished paper. College Entrance Examination Board.

Hansen, W. Lee. 1985. "The Growth of Independent Students and the Incentive to Become Independent." *Program Report 85-12.* Madison: Wisconsin Center for Education Research, University of Wisconsin.

Hauptman, Arthur M. 1983. "Student Loan Default Rates in Perspective." *Policy Brief.* Washington, D.C.: American Council on Education.

Jackson, Gregory A., and George B. Weathersby. 1975. "Individual Demand for Higher Education: A Review and Analysis of Recent Empirical Studies." *Journal of Higher Education* 46 (6) (November/December): 623-52.

Kemmerer, Frances, and Alan P. Wagner. 1985. "The Economics of Educational Reform." *Economics of Education Review* 4 (2) (Winter): 111-22.

Lanchantin, Meg. 1986. *Trends in Student Aid: 1980-86*. Washington, D.C.: The College Board.

Leslie, Larry L., and Paul T. Brinkman. 1985. "Student Price Response in Higher Education." Unpublished paper. Center for the Study of Higher Education, University of Arizona.

Manski, Charles F., and David A. Wise. 1983. *College Choice in America*. Cambridge, Mass.: Harvard University Press.

Martin, Dennis J. 1986. "Long-Term Implications of Student Borrowing." In *Proceedings of College Scholarship Service Colloquium on Student Loan Counseling and Debt Management*, Denver, Colo., December 2-4.

McMahon, Walter W., and Alan P. Wagner. 1982. "Monetary Returns as Partial Social Efficiency Criteria." In *Financing Education: Overcoming Inefficiency and Inequity*, edited by W.W. McMahon and T.G. Geske, pp. 150-88. Urbana: University of Illinois Press.

McPherson, Michael S. 1978. "The Demand for Higher Education." In *Public Policy and Private Higher Education*, edited by D.W. Breneman and C.E. Finn, Jr., pp. 143-96. Washington, D.C.: The Brookings Institution.

_____. 1985. "On Assessing the Impact of Federal Student Aid." In *Reports and Papers of the NASSGP/NCHELP Research Conference*. Springfield: Illinois State Scholarship Commission.

_____. 1986. "Federal Student Aid Policy: Can We Learn From Experience?" In *Rockefeller Institute Conference Proceedings*. Albany, N.Y.: Nelson A. Rockefeller Institute of Government.

Miller, Scott E., and Holly Hexter. 1985a. *How Low-Income Families Pay for College*. Washington, D.C.: American Council on Education.

_____. 1985b. *How Middle-Income Families Pay for College*. Washington, D.C.: American Council on Education.

National Association of State Scholarship and Grant Programs. 1986. *17th Annual Survey Report*. Harrisburg, Pa.: Pennsylvania Higher Education Assistance Authority.

Noel, Lee. 1985. "Increasing Student Retention: New Challenges and Potential." In *Increasing Student Retention*, edited by L. Noel, R. Levitz, and D. Saluri, pp. 1-27. San Francisco: Jossey-Bass.

Pappas, James P., and Rosalind K. Loring. 1985. "Returning Learners." In *Increasing Student Retention*, edited by L. Noel, R. Levitz, and D. Saluri, pp. 138-61. San Francisco: Jossey-Bass.

"Revenues and Expenditures of Colleges and Universities, 1983-84." 1986. *Chronicle of Higher Education* 31 (March 19): 20.

Sanders, Edward, and James Nelson. 1970. "Financing of Undergraduates, 1969-70." Unpublished paper. Washington, D.C.: College Entrance Examination Board.

Schwartz, J. Brad. 1985. "Student Financial Aid the College Enrollment Decision." *Economics of Education Review* 4(2) (Fall): 129-44.

Stampen, Jacob O. 1985. *Student Aid and Public Higher Education.* Washington, D.C.: American Association of State Colleges and Universities.

Stampen, Jacob O., and Alberto F. Cabrera. 1985. "Is the Student Aid System Achieving Its Objectives?: Evidence on Targeting and Attrition." *Program Report 85–11.* Madison: Wisconsin Center for Education Research, University of Wisconsin.

Terkla, Dawn G., and Gregory A. Jackson. 1984. "State of Art in Student Choice Research." Cambridge, Mass.: Harvard University. Unpublished.

Tierney, Michael L. 1985. "Differential Pricing: The Implications for Student Recruitment." Paper presented at DePaul/Exxon Invitational Conference on Undergraduate Differential Tuition Pricing, Chicago, Ill., January 24–25.

Thrift, Julianne Still, and Christopher M. Toppe. 1986. *Paying for College.* Washington, D.C.: National Institute of Independent Colleges and Universities.

U.S. Bureau of the Census. 1985. "School Enrollment—Social and Economic Characteristics of Students, October 1984 (Advance Report)." *Current Population Reports,* No. 404. Washington, D.C.: U.S. Government Printing Office (and unpublished tabulations).

U.S. Department of Education. 1985a. *Condition of Education 1985.* Washington, D.C.: U.S. Government Printing Office.

_____. 1985b. *Participation in Adult Education, May 1984.* Unpublished tabulations. Washington, D.C.

_____. 1985c. *Projections of Education Statistics to 1992–93.* Washington, D.C.: U.S. Government Printing Office.

U.S. Department of Health, Education, and Welfare, Office of Education. 1974. *Digest of Educational Statistics.* Washington, D.C.: U.S. Government Printing Office.

_____. 1968. *Higher Education Finances: Selected Trend and Summary Data.* Washington, D.C.: U.S. Government Printing Office.

Wagner, Alan P. 1977. "Unmet Need, Revisited: Comparing the Costs of Attendance and Available Financial Resources of 1977–78 College Students." Unpublished paper. Purdue University.

_____. 1978. "Parental Investments in Children: Contributions Toward Postsecondary Eduation Expenses." Unpublished paper. Purdue University.

_____. 1984. "The Changing Role for Student Financial Aid." *Review of Education* 10(2) (Spring): 129–32.

Wagner, Alan P., and Nancy Carlson. 1983. *Financial Aid for Self-Supporting Students: Defining Independence.* Washington, D.C.: The College Board.

Willie, Nancy A., and Alan P. Wagner. 1984. "Institutionally Awarded Student Aid." Paper presented at the Northeast Association for Institutional Research Annual Meeting, Albany, N.Y., October 11–13.

9 BENEFIT–COST ANALYSIS OF INVESTMENT IN HIGHER EDUCATION

Elchanan Cohn and Terry G. Geske

Although even the early economists (Adam Smith, Heinrich Von Thünen, and Alfred Marshall) alluded to the notion of human capital, this concept did not receive much attention from the academic community until fairly recently. Theodore W. Schultz, in his presidential address to the American Economic Association (1961) and with the publication of *The Economic Value of Education* (1963), was one of the first scholars to stress the value of human capital and the significance of the benefits of education. In addition to the Schultz work, a major publication by Gary S. Becker (1964) and also early work by Jacob Mincer (1958, 1962) provided the framework that stimulated major research efforts into human capital formation. Recent advances in human capital theory and empirical research have provided the basis for examining and estimating the returns to investments in education.

From an economic perspective, investments in human capital formation, such as formal education, on-the-job training, and health care, can be evaluated on the basis of their ability to generate future returns in terms of additional lifetime income and greater personal satisfactions. Thus, when formal education is viewed as a form of capital, governmental and family allocation decisions with respect to schooling are treated as investment decisions. These investment decisions about education are influenced by some of the same factors that guide other investment decisions. In short, additional investment in education is encouraged if the return from investing a given amount in education equals or exceeds the return available from alternative sources (such as real estate, stocks, bonds, or saving certificates).

This chapter begins with a brief overview of benefit-cost analysis of investment in higher education (including the basic concepts of net present value and internal rate of return) and also mentions some of the difficult methodological problems involved. Next, the direct and indirect costs of higher education are examined, and the benefits of higher education are explored, particularly the monetary benefits such as increased lifetime earnings. The net present value of college education is estimated, and the findings of selected internal rate of return studies of higher education are summarized. Also examined are the returns to graduate education and the returns to specific groups in society. The chapter concludes with a summary of the implications of recent evaluations of investments in higher education.

BENEFIT-COST ANALYSIS IN EDUCATION

Measurement of the profitability of higher education involves the use of benefit-cost analysis techniques that are based on the "maximum social gain" principle. If it is assumed that decisionmakers (governments and individuals) seek to maximize social welfare or their own well-being, respectively, then the "maximum social gain" principle dictates that prospective benefits must exceed anticipated costs and, more important, that the excess of benefits over costs must be maximized. A popular method to appraise the value of public expenditure investment is the calculation of a ratio that represents the "present value" of the total benefits of the project or program to the total costs of the undertaking. The values specified in the benefit-cost ratio are economic benefits and costs expressed or measured in dollars. The theoretical underpinnings of optimal investment decisions and criteria that provide the basis for benefit-cost analysis have been discussed at length in numerous publications (such as Prest and Turvey 1965; Cohn 1979; Mishan 1983; Ray 1984), and it is not necessary to provide a detailed description of the technique here. Mention should be made, however, of two benefit-cost criteria that will be discussed in this chapter: (1) net present value (NPV) and (2) internal rate of return (IROR).

Net Present Value

The net present value (NPV) criterion states that a project is profit-able if the sum of its *discounted* benefits is at least as great as the sum of its *discounted* costs. For education projects the implication is that the lifetime earnings differentials due to education, properly discounted, exceed the sum of the discounted costs. Mathematically, if b_t and c_t are the expected benefits and costs in year t, if i is the discount rate, and if the project is expected to have an economic life of T years, then the net present value is given by:

$$NPV = \sum_{t=0}^{T} (b_t - c_t) / (1 + i)^t \qquad (9.1)$$

The equation may be rewritten as follows:

$$NPV = \sum_{t=0}^{T} b_t / (1 + i)^t - \sum_{t=0}^{T} c_t / (1 + i)^t = B_o - C_o \qquad (9.2)$$

where B_o and C_o are, respectively, the discounted sums of benefits and costs.

Internal Rate of Return

The internal rate of return (IROR) criterion states that a project is profitable if the calculated IROR exceeds the "appropriate" rate of discount i. To calculate the IROR, equation (9.3) must be solved by a process of sequential approximations:

$$\sum_{t=0}^{T} (b_t - c_t) / (1 + IROR)^t = 0 \qquad (9.3)$$

That is, the value of the discount rate that would make $NPV = 0$ is sought. If $IROR > i$, then the project is said to be worthwhile.

These NPV and IROR criteria also are used to assist in making a choice among projects (determining which of a set of projects is best) or to rank-order projects. The IROR has been preferred by many analysts over the NPV rule because it is not necessary to determine in advance an "appropriate" discount rate. Projects can be ranked on the basis of their respective IRORs, which are independent of i. At the same time, if there is a budgetary constraint, as there almost always is, then the NPV rule might break down for ranking projects. Although these are valid reasons for preferring the IROR rule, this criterion itself is subject to many problems (Cohn 1972a, 1972b), and alternative proposals have been made to rank projects under varying conditions (Sassone and Shaffer 1978).

Methodological Problems

A number of difficult conceptual and methodological problems must be confronted when using census and other survey data to estimate the returns to education. The relevant research issues have been explored in detail elsewhere (Becker 1964; Cohn 1979), but some mention of them should be made here to point out the complexity of this type of research. For the most part, research conducted on the economic value of education during the last decade has focused much more on addressing the inherent methodological problems than on providing actual rate of return estimates.

Supposing that it is possible to estimate lifetime income associated with different levels of education, can it also be argued that these income differentials are due to education? Is it not possible that a portion (or all) of the earnings differentials are due to differences in ability, motivation, socioeconomic, and environmental characteristics of individuals, and other nonschool factors—all of which happen to correlate with years of school completed? Although recent research has been based on the earnings function, which includes controls for work experience, socioeconomic status, and other nonschooling variables, it is not clear whether the controls are insufficient (as argued by Taubman 1976), or whether too many control variables are included that correlate with education (such as occupation, as argued by Becker 1964). In the former case, the implication is that the education-earnings relation is biased upward; in the latter case the opposite may be true.

Estimates of the bias resulting from omission of ability and other pertinent variables vary from 0 to 65 percent. The latter figure was obtained by Taubman (1976) in a study of male twins ages 45 to 55. He shows that the bias is only about 12 percent when the earnings functions include variables typically employed in income-education studies of the Mincer (1974) variety, but increases to 65 percent when environmental and genetic factors are removed through the use of identical twins. Several researchers have challenged this work, but the truth of the matter is that no one really knows what proportion of the observed education-income relationship is strictly due to education.

Another major research issue concerns the use of cross-sectional data versus life cycle data. Most studies on the economic returns to education are based on cross-sectional analysis. In essence, a snapshot of the income-age-education relationship for individuals or groups of people is taken for a given year, and then this cross-section is projected into the future. The life cycle (also known as cohort) approach, on the other hand, is based on longitudinal income data. Successive census or other survey data are used to estimate lifetime income differentials due to education, which are then projected into the future.

A basic shortcoming of the cross-sectional approach is that it presupposes a constant age-education-income relationship over time, which tends to underestimate lifetime earnings by education during periods of economic growth. Although longitudinal data are not readily available at this time for the construction of complete life cycle income-age profiles, the use of such data would involve significant conceptual problems as well, including controls for changes in price level, and for effects caused by recessions, wars, and domestic crises. Several recent studies have combined both cross-sectional and longitudinal approaches to calculate more reliable estimates of the returns to education.

There are several other methodological issues that must be addressed when calculating lifetime income differentials due to education. Nearly all studies focus on the effects of quantity of schooling (years completed) rather than on the effects of quality of schooling. The few studies that have considered the quality dimension have employed expenditures as a measure of quality and have found some impact of school quality on income, but the degree of impact varies from study to study and for different reasons (Johnson and Stafford 1973; Solmon 1973; Link and Ratledge 1975; Ribich and Murphy 1975). Another problem involves the choice of a discount rate for use in determining net present values. Additional lifetime income for any educational level becomes successively smaller as a higher rate of discount is applied. Even the selection of annual income or hourly wages as the dependent measure presents some difficulties. Several writers (Morgan and David 1963), for example, have argued that lifetime income estimates are not sensitive to individual choices regarding the amount of time allocated to work versus leisure. In addition to addressing these types of difficult methodological problems, the seemingly more straightforward task of identifying and measuring the relevant costs and benefits can also become a very complex procedure.

THE COSTS OF HIGHER EDUCATION

Students enrolled in institutions of higher education (IHEs) sustain a variety of costs, including fees and tuition, books and supplies, room and board, transportation costs, and, most important, earnings forgone. Since students (and their parents) are typically charged for only a fraction of the total educational costs (because of subsidies provided by governments and philanthropies), there are considerable differences between the costs of education assumed by the student (the "private" cost) and the total costs of education assumed by society (the "social" cost).

Measurement of private and social costs is an easier task than measuring the benefits of education, but the task is not simple. Complicating the analysis are factors such as the following:

Room and board charges reflect not merely costs due to education per se but costs that people would have to sustain in any event (subsistence). Only the *excess* of room and board charges over what one's costs of subsistence might have been otherwise is relevant, and this is not easy to determine.

Measurement of the social costs of education requires the inclusion of costs sustained by IHEs and other units in society that are not reflected in student private costs. It is extremely difficult, however, to separate institutional expenditures on *students* from those on research and public service because all such expenditures are interrelated.

Calculation of earnings that students forgo while in school is highly problematic, and estimates of earnings forgone are, at best, reasonable approximations.

Table 9-1. Costs of Higher Education in the United States, 1970, 1975, and 1980 (*in billions of current dollars*).

	Total Expenditures by IHEs	Earnings Forgone by Students	Property Tax Exemption	Implicit Rent and Depreciation	Books and Supplies	Total Costs
	1	*2*	*3*	*4*	*5*	*6*
1970	26.9	21.6	0.7	3.5	2.2	54.8
1975	42.6	37.4	1.2	5.0	3.7	89.9
1980	70.4	59.3	1.0	6.7	5.9	143.3

Sources: Column (1) from Frankel and Gerald (1982: table 26); column (2) is based on methodology explained in Cohn (1979: table 4–6) and data obtained from Frankel and Gerald (1982) and *Economic Report of the President* (1985: table B–39); columns (3) and (4) are based on methodology explained in Cohn (1979: 74–79), employing data from U.S. Bureau of the Census, *Census of Governments* (various editions) and Frankel and Gerald (1982); column (5) is 10 percent of column (2), and column (6) is the sum of columns (1) through (5).

Estimated Costs of Higher Education

Data on the costs of higher education in the United States for the years 1970, 1975, and 1980 are displayed in Table 9-1. Column 1 includes total expenditures by IHEs, as reported by the U.S. Department of Education (based on the Higher Education General Information Survey). Column 2 provides approximate estimates of the earnings forgone by students, based on the Schultz method, as explained in detail in Cohn (1979). Also included are estimates for the property tax forgone (column 3), implicit rent and depreciation (column 4), and books and supplies (column 5), which were calculated on the basis of the methodology also explained in detail in Cohn (1979). Total educational costs (column 6) represent the sum total of resources devoted to education.

Although it appears from the data in Table 9-1 that the total costs of higher education almost tripled between 1970 and 1980, the real value of these resources, in effect, increased by a much smaller mar-

Table 9-2. Costs of Higher Education in the United States per Full-Time-Equivalent (FTE) Pupil, 1970, 1975, and 1980 (*in current and 1972 prices*).

	Total Costs[a]	Total Costs Excluding Forgone Earnings[a]	FTE Pupils (000)	Costs per Pupil[b]	Costs per Pupil Excluding Forgone Earnings[b]
	1	2	3	4	5
1970	54.8 (61.9)	33.2 (37.5)	6,737	$8,134 (9,181)	$4,928 (5,562)
1975	89.9 (69.5)	52.5 (40.6)	8,481	10,600 (8,192)	6,190 (4,784)
1980	143.3 (74.8)	84.0 (43.9)	8,749	16,379 (8,553)	9,601 (5,014)

a. Top number is expressed in billions of current dollars, and bottom number in parentheses is expressed in billions of 1972 dollars.

b. Top number is in current dollars and bottom number in parentheses is in 1972 dollars.

Sources: Column (1) from column (6), Table 9-1; column (2) = column (1) – column (2), Table 9-1; column (3) from Frankel and Gerald (1982: table 14); column (4) = column (1) ÷ column (3); and column 5 = column (2) ÷ column (3).

gin. When measured in 1972 dollars (employing the Implicit Price Deflator for Gross National Product for state and local government purchases of good and services; see *Economic Report of the President* 1985: table B-3), total costs increased only moderately between 1970 and 1980. Moreover, when measured on a per-student basis, costs per FTE student in 1972 dollars decreased from 1970 to 1975; and even though there was a slight increase in per-student costs from 1975 to 1980, the figure for 1980 was still lower than that for 1970. Similar results are obtained when forgone earnings are eliminated from the calculations (compare columns 4 and 5 of Table 9-2).

BENEFITS OF HIGHER EDUCATION

Several scholars, including Schultz (1963) and more recently Bowen (1978), have provided taxonomies of educational benefits. These taxonomies include the benefits the economy obtains from educational research, the cultivation and discovery of (potential) talent, the increased "capability of people to adjust to changes in job opportunities," the preparation of teachers (a self-sustaining activity), and the provision of manpower for sustained economic growth (Schultz 1963: 39-42). In addition, schooling provides for better citizenship, the ability to appreciate and recognize a wider range of cultural and other services, and the chance to give the next generation better education and therefore a better future. Finally, Schultz (1975) argued that education might help people deal with disequilibria.

Basic Types of Educational Benefits

For analytical purposes, educational benefits can be conveniently partitioned into "consumption" and "investment" categories, and also into "private" and "social" categories. With regard to the first classification, a product (or service) is placed in the consumption category if it yields satisfaction (or utility) in a single period only. On the other hand, a good is placed in the investment category if it is expected to yield satisfaction in future periods only. There are, of course, goods for which it is difficult to draw a sharp distinction between the consumption and investment aspects—that is, goods that yield satisfaction now and are also expected to yield satisfaction in the future. Education is a product that is best characterized by the "in between" classification.

Studies of educational benefits typically exclude the consumption effects while focusing on the investment effects of education. There have been important omissions, however, even within the narrow focus of the investment component. In terms of consumption, education yields satisfaction to the student at the time the learning occurs. The magnitude of this satisfaction is likely to increase as the student progresses through various levels of formal education, which has important implications for higher education. In terms of investment, education also yields a future stream of "consumption"— that is, it provides even greater utility over time in the form of an increased ability and capacity to enjoy and appreciate certain things in life (such as art and literature), to make more effective use of leisure time, or to function more efficiently in various nonmarket activities.

"Private" benefits are those benefits that accrue to the individual being educated. Social benefits include private benefits as well as those benefits that accrue to other members of society. There are basically two types of benefits that belong in the social but not the private domain. These include (1) tax payments associated with the educational benefit (that is, income taxes paid out of one's lifetime income stream) and (2) "external" benefits, which are those benefits that are due to the educational investment but that the individual cannot capture. In practice, the difference between social and private benefits amounts to tax payments that, although a part of an individual's earnings, represent a portion of society's returns to education in that the individual is unable to retain them and therefore they are not included in private benefits. External benefits are extremely difficult to calculate, and hence they are almost always ignored.

Other Educational Benefits

There are several other educational benefits that most empirical studies do not consider. One such benefit is the "option value" open to students (Weisbrod 1962). This option refers to the fact that the completion of one level of schooling gives the student the opportunity to undertake the next step in education. A second class of benefits include nonfinancial options (Weisbrod 1962). A college professor, for example, enjoys certain nonfinancial advantages because of his or her position, including a substantial degree of freedom and flexibility or the satisfactions associated with teaching and research. Other options of this sort include the "hedging option" (that is, the flexibility of educated individuals in adapting to new job opportunities, which provides a "hedge" against unemployment) and the "nonmarket option" (that is, the fact that with education an individual can perform a variety of activities that could not have been done without it).

In addition, there may be possible educational benefits that will be felt only a generation later (Ribich 1968; Spiegelman 1968; Swift and Weisbrod 1965). The alleged intergenerational effects of education stem mainly from studies showing that persons are more likely to complete a given level of education if their parents are (or were) more highly educated. The intergenerational effect is the increment in a person's education that can be ascribed to the incremental education of the parent.

For the most part, research on human capital formation has been concerned with the identification and conceptualization of these educational benefits, both to the individual and to society. The very nature of these benefits suggests that their measurement will be a very difficult task and that placing a monetary value on their worth will be an even more difficult job. Although an extensive taxonomy of educational benefits has been developed over the years, benefit-cost studies have focused almost exclusively on the direct monetary returns from investments in education. These studies have applied benefit-cost techniques to measure the effects of education on lifetime income, using different methods involving the shape of age-earning profiles, earning differentials, and the discounted present value of lifetime income differentials.

Increased Lifetime Earnings

Different theories have been developed over the years to examine and explain the relationship between education and income. Although there is overwhelming evidence in support of the conventional human capital theory, other theories of income distribution (such as the "screening" and "dual labor market" hypotheses) are receiving increased attention today (Blaug 1976, 1985). The basic premise of the human capital approach is that variations in labor income are due, in part, to differences in labor quality in terms of the amount of human capital acquired by the workers. In short, investment in human capital leads to higher productivity of workers, which in turn causes higher earnings. This is consistent with "orthodox" economic theory, better known as the marginal productivity theory, which argues that wages are determined according to the workers' marginal contribution to the revenues of the firm, implying that more productive workers will be paid more, other things being equal.

Following the initial efforts of Houthakker (1959), Miller (1960), Becker (1960, 1964), and Hansen (1963), numerous studies have investigated the economic returns to investment in schooling. These studies have documented extraordinarily high private internal rates of return to public elementary schooling, ranging up to 155 percent (Hines, Tweeten, and Redfern 1970), and the much lower, but still substantial, private returns to public secondary schooling, ranging from approximately 13 (Mincer 1974) to 50 percent (Carnoy and Marenbach 1975). The social returns are lower, with estimates ranging from approximately 10 to 18 percent for both public elementary and secondary education.

Because economists have been much more interested in the returns to college education than in primary and secondary education levels, there are numerous empirical studies on the topic. Before these studies are discussed, some data on lifetime earnings by education are provided and then, using cost data shown in Table 9-1, some estimates of the net present value of social investment in higher education are presented.

NPV of College Education

As explained previously, the net present value of college education is measured by the difference between the sum of discounted lifetime benefits and discounted costs attributed to a given educational investment. The conventional approach to estimate the benefits side has been to compute the *difference* between the discounted lifetime income attributable to a college graduate and the discounted lifetime income attributable to a similar person who completed only

Table 9-3. Estimated Lifetime Earnings in 1979 for Men and Women, by Years of School Completed, Age, and Selected Assumptions for Discount and Productivity Rates (*in thousands of 1981 dollars*).

Years of School Completed/Sex/Age (when earnings stream commences)	Assumptions about the Discount Rate (R) and Productivity Rate (X)			
	$R = 0; X = 0$	$R = 5\%; X = 0$	$R = 5\%; X = 2\%$	$R = 5\%; X = 3\%$
	1	*2*	*3*	*4*
High school graduates 12 years: age = 18				
Males	861	289	419	512
Females	381	136	192	232
College graduates 16 years: age = 18				
Males	1,190	349	534	671
Females	523	180	258	314
College postgraduates 16 years: age = 22				
Males	1,187	419	599	725
Females	505	202	275	325
Some graduate education 17+ years: age = 22				
Males	1,288	438	636	776
Females	693	260	363	435

Source: U.S. Bureau of the Census (1983).

four years of high school. Some idea of the monetary benefits of higher education can be obtained from published Census Bureau data, despite the fact that the simple cross-tabulations provided do not take into consideration the likelihood that average high school graduates may differ from their college graduate counterparts in many important characteristics.

The data in Table 9-3 present estimates of lifetime earnings by level of education completed based on a number of different scenarios. Lifetime earnings vary according to the chosen rate of discount, the assumption of increased income over the life cycle due to improvement in productivity (that is, an attempt to convert the cross-sectional data into time-series data), the number of years of school completed, the age at which a given college education begins (not shown here), and gender.

The data indicate the presence of higher lifetime earnings when (1) a lower discount rate is chosen, (2) a person completes more years of schooling, and (3) the productivity rate is higher. Also, males have much higher lifetime earnings than females, though the ratio of male/female lifetime earnings appears to decline the higher the number of years of schooling completed. Finally, lifetime earnings, in general, are lower the later the age when earnings commence. Note that lifetime earnings for college graduates are almost identical regardless of whether we begin at age 18 or 22. This occurs because college students earn little or nothing while in school, and if earnings are calculated beginning at age 18, subsequent earnings are also discounted to that age, reducing the present value (at age 18) of earnings obtained after age 22.

To obtain the benefits attributable to education, lifetime earnings differentials are calculated. The first two rows in column 1 of Table 9-4 provide a comparison between discounted lifetime earnings of college and high school graduates, discounted at 5 percent, assuming a 0 rate of productivity increase. Higher discount rates would decrease the differentials, and higher rates of productivity increase would increase them. The last two rows of column 1 provide a comparison between individuals with some graduate work and college graduates.

The results indicate substantial benefits to college education, ranging from $19,000 (for males with some graduate education relative to college graduates) to $60,000 (for male college graduates relative to high school graduates). Note that these benefits are already net of forgone earnings because the earnings of high school graduates when students are enrolled in college—representing forgone earnings of college students—have been subtracted from the lifetime earnings of college graduates. The same is also true for the comparison between individuals with some graduate education and college graduates.

When the present value of costs (column 2) are subtracted from the present value of benefits (column 1), the net present values of college investment are obtained (column 3). The figures in column 2 were obtained from the cost data described above, assuming that the per-student cost figure for 1980 applies to all college students exam-

Table 9–4. Present Value of Benefits and Costs and Net Present Value of Benefits Due to College Education, 1979 Data (*in thousands of 1981 dollars*).[a]

	Present Value of Benefits[b]	Present Value of Costs[c]	Net Present Value (1) – (2)	Benefit/Cost Ratio (1) – (2)
	1	2	3	4
College graduates vs. high-school graduates				
Males	60	37	23	1.62
Females	44	37	7	1.19
Some postgraduate education vs. four-year college				
Males	19	19	0	1.00
Females	58	19	39	3.05

a. Except for column (4), which is a unit-less ratio.

b. Estimated lifetime income differentials, discounted at 5 percent, assuming 0 rate of productivity increase. Discounting of first two rows is to age 18 and of final two rows to age 22.

c. It is assumed that the costs of education per student for 1980 will apply for all years for which costs are incurred.

Source: Column (1) from column (2), Table 9–3; column (2) from column (5), Table 9–2, adjusted for 1981 prices.

ined here, and that the typical college graduate and postgraduate enroll in school on a full-time basis for four and two years, respectively. The cost figures also were discounted at 5 percent and rounded to the nearest thousand.

Results shown in Table 9–4 indicate that investment in four years of college education is, on the average, worthwhile. For males, the present value of benefits exceeds the present value of costs by $23,000, and for females the difference is only $7,000. As illustrated in column 4, a dollar of investment in four years of college yields, on the average, $1.62 and $1.19 in benefits for males and females, respectively.

The story is different, however, for postgraduate training. For females the returns are quite large, whereas for males the returns just equal the costs, implying no net benefit of graduate education.

Contributing to this result are forgone earnings, which are very high for college graduates, especially males. The data appear to indicate that one avenue for females to overcome at least some of the male/female earnings differential is to obtain some postgraduate training.

It was mentioned earlier that earnings differentials might overstate the returns to education because differences in other, nonschooling attributes between those with and those without college education might account for at least some of the apparent differences. Although the use of an earnings function might generate alternative streams of lifetime earnings, there is considerable disagreement in the literature whether use of an earnings function to reduce the nonschooling bias is appropriate. Griliches (1977), for example, found that the bias is very small, at most 10 percent. In what follows, a brief summary of internal rates of return (IROR) studies, many of which were computed on the basis of an earnings function, is provided.

IROR to College Education

Overall, the returns to four years of college education are somewhat less than the returns to secondary education. A summary of research results with regard to the returns to four years of college education is presented in Table 9-5. Historically, estimates of the private rates of return to four years of college education range, for the most part, from 10 to 15 percent. Estimates for the social rates of return are somewhat less, yielding approximately 11 to 13 percent. In recent years, the disparity between private and social rates has been diminishing. In addition, there was an apparent reduction in the internal rate of return to college education between 1940 and the early 1970s. Raymond and Sesnowitz (1975) argue that the 1970 rate is higher than what Becker (1964), Carnoy and Marenbach (1975), and others obtained for earlier years, but R.B. Freeman (1976, 1977, 1980) argues that the economic returns to college education began to decline in the early 1970s. Freeman's findings indicate a relatively sharp decline in the returns to college education during the five-year period from 1968 to 1973, when the private IROR dropped from 11 percent in 1968 to 7.5 percent in 1973.

Several researchers (McMahon and Wagner 1982; Rumberger 1980, 1984; Smith and Welch 1978; Witmer 1976, 1980) have challenged

Table 9-5. Private and Social IRORs to Investment in Four Years of College Education in the United States.

Author(s)	Sample Year	IROR (percentage)	
		Private	Social
Hansen (1963)	1950	11.4%	10.9%
Becker (1964)	1940	14.5	
	1950	13.0	
	1956	12.4	
	1958	14.8	
Hanoch (1967)[a]	1960	9.6	
Mincer (1974)	1960	10.0	
Carnoy and Marenback (1975)	1940	21.4	10.7
	1950	13.2	10.6
	1960	17.6	11.3
	1970	15.4	10.9
Raymond and Sesnowitz (1975)[b]	1970	17.9	14.3
Freeman (1977)[c]	1968	11.0-12.5	12.0-13.0
	1973	7.5-10.0	8.5-10.5
Witmer (1980)	1972		14.0
McMahon and Wagner (1982)[d]	1976	17.0	13.0

a. Northern whites only.

b. Male whites only; rates for other race-sex groups vary substantially.

c. IRORs differ according to method used to estimate growth in income over time.

d. *Expected* private rate of return for white males; realized social rate of return for all males.

the diminishing rates of return reported by Freeman, and a lively debate ensued during the late 1970s and early 1980s with regard to "overinvestment" in higher education. Much of the debate focused on whether the observed decline in the economic value of college education is a temporary or a permanent phenomenon. Freeman, for example, speculated on the effects of cohort size (the vintage effect) and on the effects of business cycles on earnings. Smith and Welch (1978) and Welch (1979) examined the effects of economic recessions and large cohort sizes on the earnings of recent entrants into the labor market. They explored the inability of the labor market to absorb relatively large numbers of college graduates in an efficient manner and suggested that the low rates of return to college education might have been due to temporary adjustments in the supply of and demand for college graduates.

Yet another perspective is offered by Cline (1982), who pointed out that the characteristics and skills of workers with different levels of schooling have changed dramatically over the years as increasing numbers of individuals have obtained more and more education. Cline argued that the reduction in the disparity in the earnings differential between college and high school graduates was largely a result of the changing composition of these two work groups.

In a recent comprehensive study, McMahon and Wagner (1982) examined the historical record of monetary rates of return to higher education. They argued that rate of return studies, to mitigate the effects of transitory recessions and large cohort sizes, should reflect a view of the entire life cycle. Based on their findings, they suggested that the economic value of college education has not declined over the years and concluded that the long-run private rates of return have remained relatively stable at approximately 13 to 14 percent, at least through 1977. The expected rates of return for 1976, reported in Table 9–5, which were estimated by students based on their own costs and anticipated earnings, averaged 17 percent. They also reported an estimated social rate of return of 13 percent for 1976. These rates of return to college education compared favorably with the average rates of return to financial assets, which were approximately 10 to 12 percent for this same period. Moreover, the rates of return to education appeared to be more stable than rates of return on financial assets.

McMahon and Wagner (1982) also considered differences in monetary returns in relation to costs by degree level, by major field (and its related occupations), and by type of institution. With regard to the returns to four years of college education, there was considerable variation across major fields and types of institution. Students who intended to become engineers (see Table 9–8), for example, expected a private rate of return (25.5 percent) twice as large as those who intended to become schoolteachers (12.3 percent). In addition, expected private rates of return for students planning to earn only a bachelor's degree (see Table 9–7) were low at private liberal arts colleges (8.7 percent) when compared to the rates of return at public and private four-year comprehensive colleges (21.0 and 18.5 percent, respectively). For the most part, these differences in expected private rates of return at the bachelor's degree level across major fields and types of institution were also reflected in the corresponding social rates of return.

Finally, since fringe benefits as a percentage of total compensation have increased in recent years, use of earnings data (rather than total compensation) could result in a downward bias in the estimated returns to education. In fact, Kiker and Rhine (1985) found that the omission of fringe benefits from the earnings function biased downward the returns to college by over 20 percent.

Returns to Graduate Education

The economic returns to graduate programs are generally much lower than for bachelor degree programs, as indicated by the research results reported in Table 9-6. Although the returns to graduate education are characterized by considerable variation, the private payoff, for the most part, ranges from 2 to 10 percent. Hanoch (1967) obtained an IROR of 7.0 percent for the category 17+ (at least some graduate education), for northern whites for the year 1960. Similar figures were also obtained by Mincer (1974). On the other hand, Bailey and Schotta (1972) report very low, even negative, returns to graduate education for academicians for 1966. Their results are disputed by Tomaske (1974), who claims that when summer and outside earnings are taken into account, the private IROR climbs to around 10 percent.

In addition to the research by Bailey and Schotta (1972), other studies (such as Rogers 1969; Maxwell 1970) have reported low, and sometimes negative, IRORs to graduate education. These findings suggest that there may be insufficient returns in the form of increased lifetime earnings to justify either private or public investment in graduate education. There are some exceptions, such as the IROR for a three-year Ph.D. program calculated by Ashenfelter and Mooney (1968)—10.5 percent; the higher IRORs for Ph.D. economists employed in business estimated by Siegfried (1971)—as high as 23.6 percent; and the average IRORs calculated by Weiss (1971)—over 12 percent.

Additional information with regard to the economic value of graduate education is provided by McMahon and Wagner (1982). They documented the considerable variation that characterizes the returns

Table 9-6. Private IRORs to Graduate Education in the United States.

Author(s)	Sample Year	IROR (percentage) 17+	M.A.	Ph.D.
Hanoch (1967)[a]	1960	7.0%		
Ashenfelter and Mooney (1968)	1958–60		4.8%	3.5–10.5[b]%
Siegfried (1971)[c]	1964			5.3–23.6
Weiss (1971)[d]	1966		12.2	12.3
Bailey and Schotta (1972)	1966	-1.0		
Tomaske (1974)[e]	1966	10.0		
Mincer (1974)	1960	7.3		
McMahon and Wagner (1982)[f]	1976		-0.7– 9.6[g] -0.8–12.7[h]	-1.8–19.3[g] -0.1–16.4[h]

a. Northern whites only.

b. IRORs vary depending on number of years in school.

c. Rates are for Ph.D. economists; rates differ by type of employment and by type of financial aid while individuals were in graduate school.

d. These are "average IRORs"; "marginal" IRORs are somewhat lower. Also, considerable variation of IRORs by field is observed.

e. This is a recalculation of Bailey and Schotta (1972), allowing for summer and outside earnings.

f. *Expected* rates of return for white males.

g. Rates varying depending on type of institution attended. See Table 9-7.

h. Rates varying depending on intended occupation. See Table 9-8.

to various graduate programs and found that expected private rates of return to graduate education varied from -0.7 to +9.6 percent for the M.A. degree, and from -1.8 to +19.3 for the Ph.D. degree, depending on type of institution attended. The rates also varied from -0.8 to +12.7 percent for the M.A. degree, and from -0.1 to +16.4 percent for the Ph.D. degree, depending on the intended occupation.

Although the costs of graduate education were highest for students at public and private research universities, the private rates of return for students who planned to pursue masters and doctoral degrees were highest there as well (see Table 9-7). The social rates of return were also highest at these types of institutions for students pursuing advanced degrees. With regard to major fields of graduate study, the expected private rates of return were highest in medicine,

Table 9-7. Mean Private (*P*) and Social (*S*) Expected Rates of Return for White Males by Degree Level and Type of Institution.

	Type of Institution									
	Research Universities				Comprehensive Four-Year Colleges				Liberal Arts Colleges	
	Public		Private		Public		Private		Private	
Degree Objective	*P*	*S*	*P*	*S*	*P*	*S*	*P*	*S*	*P*	*S*
Bachelors	19.0	15.5	a	a	21.0	17.7	18.5	15.9	8.7	7.1
Masters	9.6	8.0	a	a	6.2	4.8	-0.7	-1.4	7.7	6.9
Doctor/Professional	19.3	17.9	11.6	10.5	9.0	9.3	-1.8	-5.0	10.3	10.1

a. Fewer than six respondents in cell.
Source: Adapted from McMahon and Wagner (1982: table 5, 167–68).

Table 9-8. Mean Private (P) and Social (S) Expected Rates of Return for White Males by Intended Occupation and Degree Objective.

| | Degree Objective | | | | | |
| | Bachelor's | | Masters | | Doctor/ Professional | |
Occupation	P	S	P	S	P	S
Doctor/dentist					14.0	12.2
Lawyer					16.4	15.5
Engineer	25.5	18.9	12.0	10.0	8.6	7.4
Accountant	22.8	17.8	12.7	10.7		
Natural scientist			8.9	7.4	4.5	3.2
Social scientist					-0.1	-4.8
Schoolteacher	12.3	10.3	-0.8	-0.8	1.8	2.0
College professor					5.4	5.2

Source: Adapted from McMahon and Wagner (1982: tables 6 and 7, pp. 170 and 172–73, respectively).

law, engineering, and business, ranging from 12 to 16.4 percent (see Table 9-8). The expected private rates were lowest for advanced training in teaching, natural science, and social science, ranging from −0.8 to +8.9 percent. Again, the differences in these private rates of return were also reflected in the differences in social rates of return for the various occupational fields.

The considerable variation in the rates of return across occupational fields reflects oversupplies in some professions and shortages in others, suggesting that allocative efficiency could probably be increased in higher education. At the same time, the disparities and the ranges for these differences in the rates of return across occupational fields documented by McMahon and Wagner are consistent with findings in earlier studies that reported similar differences in rates of return across professions (for example, Eckaus, El Safty and Norman 1974). These differences in rates of return among major fields appear to persist over time, perhaps because of restrictive enrollment quotas and related underlying internal budgeting decisions that limit expansion in those fields where returns are high relative to costs. On the other hand, the low, and sometimes negative, returns to certain major fields raise questions about the efficiency of providing public subsidies to these areas. Without public subsidies (such as tuition rebates, assistantships, and fellowships), the private IROR to certain major fields would be extremely low and often negative. To promote greater efficiency in the creation of human capital, investments could be gradually (and judiciously) shifted toward those fields, levels, and institutions where social payoffs are the largest.

It is possible, of course, that interoccupational variations in private IRORs represent differences in nonmonetary returns as well as returns to nonschooling attributes, such as superior ability (to the extent that higher rates of return are found in areas where superior ability is required to obtain a degree—not just admission). Furthermore, low social rates of return may not signal the need to curtail programs if external benefits are large. The problem with all of these arguments is that it is quite difficult to estimate nonmonetary and external returns and to discern the required levels of ability to complete different degree programs (that is, there is a need to differentiate between a screening device, such as GRE or MCAT scores, which is merely used to *limit* enrollments, from a device that is also used to eliminate effectively enrollment by those who are not likely to succeed).

The overall level of returns to investment in higher education indicates that, in general, such an investment is profitable both for the individual and for society. At the same time, it must be recognized that college education is not universally profitable, with rates of return varying considerably by major fields and types of institution and also by such variables as "innate ability" and other nonschool factors. Even if the lower returns reported by Freeman should continue to persist over time, or even in the case of the well-documented low returns to certain graduate programs, several scholars have argued that these low IRORs might still be of sufficient magnitude to justify investment in higher education because of the existence of extensive private nonmonetary benefits and social external benefits.

Returns by Race, Sex, National Origin, and Religion

It has been claimed that the returns to education differ significantly among various groups in society, and considerable evidence has been accumulated to support such a contention. In addition, several studies that have investigated differentials in returns to education across particular groups have also focused on differences in returns across regions of the country. Most of these studies suggest higher overall returns to education in the urban north. Hanoch's (1967) results, for example, show almost uniformly higher IRORs for northern whites than for southern whites, whereas the north-south comparison for blacks is mixed. Adams and Nestel (1976) obtain results indicating that wages in the urban north exceed those for the urban south for both whites and blacks. In contrast, Lassiter (1966) obtains higher returns for southern whites and lower returns for southern blacks.

Black-White Differences. It has been commonly alleged that the IROR to education for blacks was considerably below that for whites. Hanoch (1967), for example, provided IRORs by race (white versus nonwhite). The IRORs were generally lower for blacks (who comprise the majority of the nonwhite group) than for whites—in many cases much lower. More recently, Adams and Nestel (1976) reported that the returns to college education for young blacks approached the returns for young whites. For older males, however, whites had about three times the returns to college education as compared to blacks. Adams and Nestel attributed much of the discrepancy in black-white returns to the quality of education received as well as to the geographic area in which individuals happen to live.

In recent years, the economic returns to blacks have increased in relative terms, as efforts toward integration, affirmative action, and other programs on behalf of minorities have become more effective (Welch 1973, 1980; Link, Ratledge, and Lewis 1976, 1980; Jud and Walker 1982). Hoffman (1984) examined black-white differences in returns to higher education for the 1970s and found that the earnings differential between the college-educated and the high school-educated decreased for young white males but at the same time increased for blacks. Hoffman's findings suggest that the black-white earnings gap has narrowed to the point that predicted earnings (based on 1977 data) would be equal for black-white college graduates. This study and others (Darity 1982; Kiker and Heath 1985) suggest that education is a much more important determinant of earnings for blacks than for whites. Other writers, notably Thurow (1975), Jencks et al. (1972), and H.M. Levin (1977a, 1977b), continue to argue that education has not improved the plight of the poor, especially blacks.

Male-Female Differences.   Some evidence on differential returns by sex is available. Hines et al. (1970), for example, provided IRORs by sex-race groupings. For whites, returns to education were almost uniformly higher for males. For nonwhites, however, returns were higher for males in the lower educational levels and higher for females in the higher educational levels. In addition, Christian and Stroup (1981) documented that the returns to higher education were much greater for black females, particularly for younger black females with some college, than for comparable white females in southern urban areas in 1970. Educational credentials proved to be a very important asset for black females who made sizable gains in both earnings and occupational status.

Although studies have shown differences in returns to education by sex, it does not necessarily follow that such differences were due to discrimination. Such differences may be due to various attributes of the male-female groups under examination, such as labor market experience, commitment to full-time participation in the labor force, continuity in employment, or types of skills and professions for which individuals are qualified. Daymont and Andrisani (1984) argued that a substantial portion of the gender differential in hourly earnings among recent college graduates can be attributed to differences between men and women in preference for occupations and in preparation (college major) for these occupations. Similarly, Ferber and McMahon (1979) suggested that increased education and a shift to "male" occupations may result in higher rates of return to women.

National Origin.   Of interest, too, are possible differences in returns to higher education by national origin of large groups of U.S. citizens. Niemi (1974) calculated IRORs for three levels of education (high school, college, and postgraduate) for California and Texas individuals by race (white, black, and Mexican). Niemi's results (for 1960) showed some differences in IRORs by race, but the differences were relatively minor and in some cases showed higher IRORs for nonwhites (especially for postgraduate education). A recalculation of the IRORs by Raymond and Sesnowitz (1976), using a different methodology, produced different results but preserved the pattern of relatively small differences in returns to education by whites, blacks, and Mexican Americans.

In a more recent study, Raymond and Sesnowitz (1983) investigated the returns to college education for Mexican Americans and

Anglos. When all major fields of study were combined, they reported that the rates of return were higher for Anglos than for Mexican Americans. One exception was noted, however, with Mexican Americans who majored in education receiving higher returns than Anglos who majored in education. Penley, Gould, and LaVina (1984) examined the relative salary position of Mexican Americans who graduated from college with a business major. When they controlled for certain key variables, (such as regional income variation, socioeconomic background, and degree of academic success), they found that adjusted income for Mexican Americans and their non-Hispanic counterparts was comparable. Mexican American males received higher incomes than non-Hispanic males, and both groups of males received higher incomes than females. Non-Hispanic females received higher incomes than Mexican American females.

Religion.   Recently, a few researchers have begun to investigate the effects of religious and denominational background on earnings. In a Canadian study, Tomes (1983) concluded that Jews made greater investments and received higher rates of return to schooling than did Protestants and Catholics. With regard specifically to higher education, however, the returns to a college degree were highest for Protestants, then for Catholics, with no significant rate of return to Jews for the degree. In effect, the rate of return for the degree to Jews was the same as for an additional year of college. Meng and Sentance (1984), who also explored the relationship between religion and earnings in Canada, supported the general findings of the Tomes's study.

In another recent study, Chiswick (1983) examined the earnings differential between non-Jewish and second-generation Jewish native born white males in the United States. Chiswick reported that American-born Jewish males had higher earnings, a higher rate of return from schooling, and a steeper experience-earnings profile than their non-Jewish counterparts. These patterns of differences across Jewish and non-Jewish males persisted after controlling for occupational distribution and self-employment status. Chiswick estimated that more than one-third of the effect of schooling on earnings for Jews may be attributed to their higher occupational status.

SUMMARY

Although in recent years significant advances in research on human capital formation have occurred that permit more accurate estimates of the "true" or "full" returns to investments in higher education, several caveats are still very much in order. A basic shortcoming of benefit-cost calculations of investments in higher education has been the inability to include external and nonmonetary benefits of schooling. These topics received considerable attention during the last decade (McMahon 1982; Michael 1982), and progress has been made in conceptualizing and even measuring some of these elusive educational benefits. But the inclusion of these types of benefits in the benefit-cost calculus promises to remain highly problematic.

Resolution of the current debate about "overinvestment" in higher education will be extremely difficult until additional knowledge about the effects of these important benefits is obtained. Initial attempts to quantify and value the nonmonetary private benefits associated with education suggest that estimates of the returns to schooling may be substantially understated. Haveman and Wolfe (1984) identified and discussed the various nonmarket effects of schooling (such as effects on family, health, learning, consumption behavior, migration, leisure, asset management) and attempted to place an approximate value on them. They speculated that benefit-cost studies that have focused exclusively on increased earnings may have captured only about 50 percent of the total value of an additional year of schooling. At the same time, other economists (Bowen 1978) have argued that substantial external benefits are associated with education, even though it may be impossible to empirically verify them.

There will always be disagreement over the magnitude of external and nonmonetary benefits. But just as research designs, methodological approaches, and measurement techniques have improved over the last two decades to enable more accurate estimation of the effects of schooling on earnings, research investigating the effects of schooling on the nonmonetary and external benefits of education might also improve substantially in the future.

Similarly, while much knowledge about the relationship between education and income has been gained, the precise contribution of schooling to earnings is unknown. The numerous studies reviewed in this chapter all concentrated on the quantity of schooling (years completed), rather than on the quality of schooling (expenditure levels), though both dimensions are clearly important. In addition, while analyses have become much more sophisticated over the years, there is considerable room for improvement in the quality of the data base. Finally, the calculated net present values and internal rates of return only provide aggregated averages that, for a variety of reasons, may vary significantly among individual people.

Despite the difficult conceptual and methodological problems that must be confronted, benefit-cost techniques have proved useful in estimating the returns to investments in higher education. The benefit-cost approach, admittedly, involves inherent shortcomings, and the types of analyses conducted are not as straightforward as many might suggest, but neither are they as complex as others might contend. Although benefit-cost analysis in education is far from perfect, the information one gleans from the analysis is still extremely valuable. The main advantage of using benefit-cost analysis is that the decisionmaking process of investment in education involves the best available estimates of costs and returns, so that the analyst and the decisionmaker are forced to take the facts into account rather than rest content with hunches, educated guesses, or rules of thumb. It should be emphasized, however, that benefit-cost analysis does not obviate the need to make decisions. Use of such techniques does not make such decisions easier; it should, however, make them better.

REFERENCES

Adams, Arvil V., and Gilbert Nestel. 1976. "Interregional Migration, Education, and Poverty in the Urban Ghetto: Another Look at Black-White Earnings Differentials." *Review of Economics and Statistics* 58 (May): 156–66.

Ashenfelter, Orley, and Joseph D. Mooney. 1968. "Graduate Education, Ability and Earnings." *Review of Economics and Statistics* 50 (February): 78–86.

Bailey, Duncan, and Charles Schotta. 1972. "Private and Social Rates of Return to Education of Academicians." *American Economic Review* 62 (March): 19–31.

Becker, Gary S. 1960. "Underinvestment in College Education?" *American Economic Review (Papers and Proceedings)* 50 (May): 345–54.

_____. 1964. *Human Capital—A Theoretical and Empirical Analysis with Special Reference to Education.* New York: National Bureau of Economic Research.

Blaug, Mark. 1976. "The Empirical Status of Human Capital Theory: A Slightly Jaundiced Survey." *Journal of Economic Literature* 14 (September): 827–55.
_____. 1985. "Where Are We Now in the Economics of Education?" *Economics of Education Review* 4(1): 17–28.
Bowen, Howard R. 1978. *Investment in Learning: The Individual and Social Value of American Higher Education.* San Francisco: Jossey-Bass.
Carnoy, Martin, and Dieter Marenback. 1975. "The Return to Schooling in the United States, 1939–69." *Journal of Human Resources* 10 (Summer): 312–31.
Chiswick, Barry R. 1983. "The Earnings and Human Capital of American Jews." *Journal of Human Resources* 18 (Summer): 313–36.
Christian, Jr., Virgil L., and Robert H. Stroup. 1981. "The Effect of Education on Relative Earnings of Black and White Women." *Economics of Education Review* 1 (Winter): 113–22.
Cline, Harold M. 1982. "The Measurement of Change in the Rate of Return to Education: 1967–75." *Economics of Education Review* 2 (Summer): 275–93.
Cohn, Elchanan. 1972a. "On the Net Present Value Rule for Educational Investments." *Journal of Political Economy* 80 (March-April): 418–20.
_____. 1972b. "Investment Criteria and the Ranking of Educational Investments." *Public Finance* 27(3): 355–60.
_____. 1979. *The Economics of Education*, rev. ed. Cambridge, Mass.: Ballinger.
Darity, William A., Jr. 1982. "The Human Capital Approach to Black-White Earnings Inequality: Some Unsettled Questions." *Journal of Human Resources* 14 (Winter): 72-93.
Daymont, Thomas N., and Paul J. Andrisani. 1984. "Job Preferences, College Major, and the Gender Gap in Earnings." *Journal of Human Resources* 19 (Summer): 408–28.
Eckaus, Richard S., A. El Safty, and V. Norman. 1974. "An Appraisal of the Calculation of Rates of Return to Higher Education." In *Higher Education and the Labor Market*, edited by M.S. Gordon, pp. 333–71. New York: McGraw-Hill.
Economic Report of the President. 1985. Washington, D.C.: U.S. Government Printing Office.
Ferber, Marianne A., and Walter W. McMahon. 1979. "Women's Expected Earnings and Their Investment in Higher Education." *Journal of Human Resources* 14 (Summer): 405–20.
Frankel, Martin M., and Debra E. Gerald. 1982. *Projections of Education Statistics to 1990-91*, Vol. I. Washington, D.C.: National Center for Educational Statistics, Department of Education.
Freeman, Richard B. 1976. *The Over-Educated American.* New York: Academic Press.

_____ . 1977. "The Decline in the Economic Rewards to College Education." *Review of Economics and Statistics* 59 (February): 18–29.

_____ . 1980. "The Facts about the Declining Economic Value of College." *Journal of Human Resources* 15 (Winter): 124–42.

Griliches, Zvi. 1977. "Estimating the Returns to Schooling: Some Econometric Problems." *Econometrica* 45 (January): 1–22.

Hanoch, Giora. 1967. "An Economic Analysis of Earnings and Schooling." *Journal of Human Resources* 2 (Summer): 310–29.

Hansen, W. Lee. 1963. "Total and Private Rates of Return to Investment in Schooling." *Journal of Political Economy* 71 (April): 128–40.

Haveman, Robert H., and Barbara L. Wolfe. 1984. "Schooling and Economic Well-Being: The Role of Nonmarket Effects." *Journal of Human Resources* 19 (Summer): 377–407.

Hines, Fred, Luther Tweeten, and Martin Redfern. 1970. "Social and Private Rates of Return to Investment in Schooling, by Race-Sex Groups and Regions." *Journal of Human Resources* 5 (Summer): 318–40.

Hoffman, Saul D. 1984. "Black-White Differences in Returns to Higher Education: Evidence from the 1970s." *Economics of Education Review* 3(1): 13–21.

Houthakker, H.S. 1959. "Education and Income." *Review of Economics and Statistics* 41 (February): 24–28.

Jencks, Christopher; Marshall Smith; Henry Acland; Mary Jo Bane; David Cohen; Herbert Gintis; Barbara Heyns; and Stephan Michelson. 1972. *Inequality: A Reassessment of the Effects of Family and Schooling in America.* New York: Basic Books.

Johnson, George E., and Frank P. Stafford. 1973. "Social Returns to Quantity and Quality of Schooling." *Journal of Human Resources* 8 (Spring): 139–55.

Jud, G. Donald, and James L. Walker. 1982. "Racial Differences in the Returns to Schooling and Experience among Prime-Age Males: 1967-1975." *Journal of Human Resources* 17 (Fall): 623–32.

Kiker, B.F., and Julia A. Heath. 1985. "The Effect of Socioeconomic Background on Earnings: A Comparison by Race." *Economics of Education Review* 4(1): 45–55.

Kiker, B.F., and Sherrie L.W. Rhine. 1985. "Fringe Benefits and the Earnings Function: A Test of the Consistency Hypothesis." Working Paper No. B–85–08. Columbia, S.C.: Division of Research, College of Business Administration, University of South Carolina.

Lassiter, Jr., Roy L. 1966. *The Association of Income and Educational Achievement.* Gainesville: University of Florida Press.

Levin, Henry M. 1977a. "A Decade of Policy Developments in Improving Education and Training for Low-Income Population." In *A Decade of Federal Antipoverty Programs*, edited by Robert H. Haveman, pp. 123–88. New York: Academic Press.

_____. 1977b, "A Radical Critique of Educational Policy." *Journal of Education Finance* 3 (Summer): 9–31.

Link, C., and Edward C. Ratledge. 1975. "Social Returns to Quantity and Quality of Education: A Further Statement." *Journal of Human Resources* 10 (Winter): 78–89.

Link, C., Edward Ratledge, and Kenneth Lewis. 1976. "Black-White Differences in Returns to Schooling: Some New Evidence." *American Economic Review* 66 (March): 221–23.

_____. 1980. "The Quality of Education and Cohort Variation in Black-White Earnings Differentials: Reply." *American Economic Review* 70 (March): 196–203.

Maxwell, Lynn. 1970. "Some Evidence on Negative Returns to Graduate Education." *Western Economic Journal* 8 (June): 186–89.

McMahon, Walter W. 1982. "Externalities in Education." Faculty Working Paper No. 877. University of Illinois at Urbana-Champaign.

McMahon, Walter W., and Alan P. Wagner. 1982. "The Monetary Returns to Education as Partial Social Efficiency Criteria." In *Financing Education: Overcoming Inefficiency and Inequity*, edited by W.W. McMahon and T.G. Geske, pp. 150–87. Urbana: University of Illinois Press.

Meng, Ronald, and Jim Sentance. 1984. "Religion and the Determination of Earnings: Further Results." *Canadian Journal of Economics* 17 (August): 481–88.

Michael, Robert T. 1982. "Measuring Non-Monetary Benefits of Education: A Survey." In *Financing Education: Overcoming Inefficiency and Inequity*, edited by W.W. McMahon and T.G. Geske, pp. 119–49. Urbana: University of Illinois Press.

Miller, Herman P. 1960. "Annual and Lifetime Income in Relation to Education: 1939-1959." *American Economic Review* 50 (December): 962–86.

Mincer, Jacob. 1958. "Investment in Human Capital and Personal Income Distribution." *Journal of Political Economy* 66 (August): 281–302.

_____. 1962. "On-the-Job Training: Costs, Returns, and Some Implications." *Journal of Political Economy* 70 (October Supplement): 50–79.

_____. 1974. *Schooling, Experience and Earnings.* New York: Columbia University Press.

Mishan, E. J. 1983. *Cost-Benefit Analysis*, 3d ed. London: George Allen & Unwin.

Morgan, James N., and Martin A. David. 1963. "Education and Income," *Quarterly Journal of Economics* 77 (August): 424–37.

Niemi, Jr., Albert W. 1974. "Racial and Ethnic Differences in Returns to Educational Investment in California and Texas." *Economic Inquiry* 12 (September): 398–402.

Penley, Larry E., Sam Gould, and Lynda Y. de la Vina. 1984. "The Comparative Salary Position of Mexican American College Graduates in Business." *Social Science Quarterly* 65 (June): 444–54.

Prest, A.R., and R. Turvey. 1965. "Cost-Benefit Analysis: A Survey." *Economic Journal* 75 (December): 683–735.

Ray, Anandarup. 1984. *Cost-Benefit Analysis.* Baltimore: Johns Hopkins University Press.

Raymond, Richard D., and Michael L. Sesnowitz. 1975. "The Returns to Investments in higher Education: Some New Evidence." *Journal of Human Resources* 10 (Spring): 139–54.

_____ . 1976. "Comment on Racial and Ethnic Differences in Returns on Educational Investments in California and Texas." *Economic Inquiry* 14 (December): 604–09.

_____ . 1983. "The Rate of Return to Mexican Americans and Anglos on an Investment in a College Education." *Economic Inquiry* 21 (June): 400–11.

Ribich, Thomas I. 1968. *Education and Poverty.* Washington, D.C.: The Brookings Institute.

Ribich, Thomas I., and James L. Murphy. 1975. "The Economic Returns to Increased Educational Spending." *Journal of Human Resources* 10 (Winter): 56–77.

Rogers, Daniel C. 1969. "Private Rates of Return to Education in the U.S.: A Case Study." *Yale Economic Essays* 9 (Spring): 89–134.

Rumberger, Russell W. 1980. "The Economic Decline of College Graduates: Fact or Fallacy?" *Journal of Human Resources* 15 (Winter): 99–112.

_____ . 1984. "The Changing Economic Benefits of College Graduates." *Economics of Education Review* 3 (1): 3–11.

Sassone, Peter G., and William A. Schaffer. 1978. *Cost-Benefit Analysis: A Handbook.* New York: Academic Press.

Schultz, Theodore W. 1961. "Investment in Human Capital." *American Economic Review* 51 (March): 1–17.

_____ . 1963. *The Economic Value of Education.* New York: Columbia University Press.

_____ . 1975. "The Value of the Ability to Deal with Disequilibria." *Journal of Economic Literature* 13 (September): 827–46.

Siegfried, John J. 1971. "Rate of Return to the Ph.D. in Economics." *Industrial and Labor Relations Review* 24 (April): 420–31.

Smith, James P., and Finis R. Welch. 1978. *The Overeducated American? A Review Article.* Santa Monica: Rand Corporation.

Solmon, Lewis C. 1973. "The Definition and Impact of College Quality." In *Does College Matter?*, edited by Lewis C. Solmon and P.J. Taubman, pp. 77–102. New York: Academic Press.

Spiegleman, R.G. 1968. "A Benefit/Cost Model to Evaluate Educational Programs," *Socio-Economic Planning Sciences* 1: 443–60.

Swift, W.J., and Burton A. Weisbrod. 1965. "On the Monetary Value of Education's Intergeneration Effects." *Journal of Political Economy* 73 (December): 643–49.

Taubman, Paul J. 1976. "Earnings, Education, Genetics, and Environment," *Journal of Human Resources* 11 (Fall): 447–61.

Thurow, Lester L. 1975. *Generating Inequality: Mechanisms of Distribution in the U.S. Economy.* New York: Basic Books.

Tomaske, John A. 1974. "Private and Social Rates of Return to Education of Academicians: Note." *American Economic Review* 64 (March): 220–24.

Tomes, Nigel. 1983. "Religion and the Rate of Return on Human Capital: Evidence from Canada." *Canadian Journal of Economics* 16 (February): 122–38.

U.S. Bureau of the Census. Various editions. *Census of Governments.* Washington, D.C.: U.S. Government Printing Office.

_____. 1983. "Lifetime Earnings Estimates of Men and Women in the United States: 1979." *Current Population Reports*, series P–60, no. 139. Washington, D.C.: U.S. Government Printing Office.

Weisbrod, Burton A. 1962. "Education and Investment in Human Capital." *Journal of Political Economy* 70 (October Supplement): 106–23.

Weiss, Yoram. 1971. "Investment in Graduate Education." *American Economic Review* 61 (December): 833–52.

Welch, Finis. 1973. "Black-White Differences in Returns to Schooling." *American Economic Review* 67 (December): 893–907.

_____. 1979. "Effects of Cohort Size on Earnings: The Baby Boom Babies' Financial Bust." *Journal of Political Economy* 87 (October): S65–S98.

_____. 1980. "The Quality of Education and Cohort Variations in Black-White Earnings Differentials: Reply." *American Economic Review* 70 (March): 192–95.

Witmer, David R. 1976. "Is the Value of College Really Declining?" *Change* 8 (December): 46–47, 60–61.

_____. 1980. "Has the Golden Age of American Higher Education Come to an Abrupt End?" *Journal of Human Resources* 15 (Winter): 113–20.

10 CAPITAL FUNDING IN HIGHER EDUCATION

Douglas R. Sherman and Ralph Nichols

A major concern of those holding leadership positions in higher education is the condition of the physical plant and equipment of the nation's colleges and universities. College presidents, in testimony before congressional committees and state legislatures, are carrying the message that academic buildings and equipment are deteriorating and becoming obsolete at a rate that vastly exceeds colleges' fiscal capacity to respond. The intensity of these presentations leads to the conclusion that a crisis now exists. Certainly the financial dimensions of the problem, as estimated by various experts and commentators, suggest a crisis. An investment of as much as $50 billion has been estimated as necessary to resolve the accumulated problem.

Despite the recent intensity of concern, the developing problem became apparent years ago. Indeed, in 1980 *Time* magazine provided an overview of the problem ("Dilapidation in Academe" 1980: 62). A significant amount of facilities neglect had occurred by the time that the national media learned of the problem; since then things have worsened.

By 1986 the problem was well recognized: U.S. campuses are aging. Nearly 25 percent of college and university space was constructed before 1950, while a second quarter was built during the fifteen years between 1950 and 1965 (Kaiser 1984a). That is, one-half of the square footage that higher education currently uses is more than twenty years old and one-quarter exceeds thirty-five years.

217

Another cause of inadequate capital maintenance and renewal is the lack of adequate funding. An integral component of the postwar building boom in higher education was the federal government's active participation in financing much of that construction. Since the mid-1970s that source of low-interest loans and direct grants has virtually disappeared. Almost coincidental with the withdrawal of federal government support was a period of severe economic conditions from 1973 to 1984, when deep recessions and high inflation squeezed the resource base of higher education.

Another factor, the energy crisis, emerged during this same period. It not only contributed to the economic malaise by adding budgetary strain in the form of higher utility costs, but it also provided a new component to the facilities agenda: energy conservation projects. The same was true for a variety of code-compliance projects.

In sum, the rapid aging of university buildings and equipment produced an enormous need for incremental capital investment at precisely the time that the financial capacity of higher education was under maximal strain to support current operations. As a budget balancing strategy, it was easier to forgo necessary capital expenditures than to reduce academic programs and support services. The result was that the capital stock of colleges and universities throughout the country was consumed in a very real sense.

Campus administrators now are facing the reality of facility failure. This is manifested in several different forms. One is outright systems breakdowns—leaking roofs, broken pipes, overloaded electrical circuits, and the like. Another form, subtler but equally debilitating to the academic enterprise, is the inability of the facilities to accommodate the functions they house. Technological innovation has greatly altered educational and research processes. Theoretical physicists of two decades ago needed access to chalkboards and legal pads to conduct their research; now they use the computer to conduct experiments that simulate particle behavior. These changes have a direct impact on facilities, which must accommodate the changes. In virtually every discipline, building and equipment needs have been affected by new technology, and all too often the changes require additional investment.

Another force that creates large-scale facility misfit is the changing interests of students as reflected in their academic program choices. In Illinois, baccalaureate degrees in education awarded by public colleges and universities declined from 22 percent of the 1974 total to 10 percent of the 1984 amount. During the same period, degrees in engineering and computer science grew from 5.9 percent to 10.3 percent (Illinois Board of Higher Education 1985). The facility implications of this magnitude of change are enormous.

These difficulties are precisely what college presidents have in mind when they refer to the crisis in university facilities. The toll of long-term underinvestment now threatens the core activities of the enterprise. Some are suggesting that instructional and research program quality are being compromised by the inability to support the work of students and faculty in facilities and with equipment appropriate to their expertise. In fact, the National Science Foundation is supporting a study to "determine the long-term impact of outmoded buildings on the quantity and quality of research in the nation's universities" (University of Michigan 1985).

The confluence of these complex interactions—student program preference, technological change, and the larger environmental forces—have created a difficult set of challenges for college and university administrators. They are not the whole story, however. In the remainder of this chapter, capital needs are examined from several perspectives: the dimensions of need, associated capital funding matters, and several key management questions. After a brief discussion of how this problem is unique to higher education, the chapter concludes with an agenda of items for additional review and discussion.

DIMENSIONS OF NEED

In his thoughtful comments, Chancellor Charles Young of UCLA (1984) reported that the University of California required $4 billion in capital funds over the next decade to meet the needs associated with building deterioration, program change, enrollment shift, historic space shortages, and code compliance. Young divided the total into four categories of need: $1.6 billion for new construction and renovation of general academic/administrative facilities and hospitals; $900 million to keep existing buildings functioning safely (including seismic corrections); $500 million for a variety of self-supporting facilities, including housing; and $1 billion in increased funding for maintenance. Chancellor Young also extrapolated the California situation to the fifty states, concluding that as much as

$60 billion might be required to meet the accumulated national need (Young 1984).

Other estimates of the size of the national problem have been made. *The Chronicle of Higher Education* (Wilson 1985: 17) reported that "An estimated $50 billion worth of repairs and renovation may be needed on college campuses according to the sketchy data that are available." *The Chronicle* also noted that "the cost of needed renovation and repair has doubled since 1974." Kaiser (1979) estimated that $35 billion was needed simply to offset the existing backlog of deferred maintenance. And *Time* magazine ("Dilapidation in Academe" 1980: 62), quoting the National Association of College and University Business Officers, said that a $30 billion investment was required "to catch up with accumulated neglect of campus buildings."

The public estimates for individual institutions appear to confirm the enormity of the problem. President Frank H. T. Rhodes of Cornell (1984) indicated that on his campus were accumulated facility needs totaling $100 million with no funding in sight. The University of Washington estimated that $60 million was needed for renovation and repair, while Michigan State University President John DiBaggio identified a $74 million gap (Wilson 1985). From a different perspective, Hans Jenny (1981) suggested that $3.5 billion per year might not be adequate to meet the ongoing needs for capital renewal and replacement.

Data

One cannot help but be impressed by the financial magnitude of the problem in university facilities as described above. Yet a good deal more must be done to communicate the dimensions of the crisis in a form that makes it possible to formulate commensurate responses by policymakers, donors, and friends. There is no common methodology for estimating capital needs in higher education. Each of the quoted figures was derived using a local construct of what is or is not included, which stymies attempts to make "clean" estimates of the need for operating funds to maintain existing facilities appropriately, as opposed to capital construction funds for new buildings. Chancellor Young's estimate included both operating and capital funding for academic and self-supporting enterprises.

There is a dearth of systematic information on the annual expenditure of funds for physical facilities at colleges and universities, a major gap in the information base necessary to enhance the quality of decisions in this arena. Existing information on the current capital investment in higher education is not sufficient to demonstrate to the community what is "at risk."

Developing an estimate of the facilities need based on a uniformly applied set of guidelines from each of the nation's campuses would be an enormous task; but it would greatly assist policymakers by providing the true dimensions of the challenge. Appropriately defined and collected, such information would help funding units understand the components of the need and focus on the most critical elements at each institution. This latter point is particularly important in helping match critical capital needs to the various funding constituencies that institutions might approach for support.

These comments are not intended to suggest that the problem has been overstated or that institutions are "crying wolf." Quite the contrary, it is likely that the need is larger than the current estimates.

Recent experience in Michigan is instructive in this regard. As part of their agenda, the Governor's Commission on the Future of Higher Education asked each campus to submit a list of necessary deferred maintenance projects. Those lists were then turned over to a group assembled by the Michigan Society of Professional Engineers, to "investigate, review, and comment upon the costs and validity of them." The projects submitted by five of the fifteen campuses were examined in detail, following reclassification to separate the deferred maintenance from other kinds of projects like code requirements, energy conservation, and capital improvements. According to the review committee report (Michigan Society of Professional Engineers 1984: 294):

> The projects generally are necessary and of high priority. . . . In general, we feel that the estimates shown on the list have been made on a reasonable basis, however, our investigation indicates that some may be low. It should also be recognized that if funding is delayed, the more these costs will be escalated.

Several key points come through in this report, the most important being that the need is real and large and requires solutions of commensurate size.

Estimate Credibility—Three Project-Related Aspects

Having established a basis for asserting the need for a substantial infusion of new funds, it is essential nevertheless that individual campuses present credible facility-related requests derived from credible planning processes.

The "bottom line" for all capital funding is the individual project. Thus, if individual projects are well conceived and developed, resulting estimates of overall need based on totaling the costs of these individual projects should also be on target. Hence, larger estimates usually are tested in practice by a more detailed review of projects. Three project guidelines are useful:

1. *Has the planning process measured the overall capital need appropriately?* The concern is that individual projects are truly needed and priorities appropriately set. It is unfortunate that examples of poor planning can be readily identified. In one instance, an institution with 4,000 classroom student stations and an enrollment of 3,850 FTE requested a new building with 1,200 classroom student stations. All of the proposed classrooms were general purpose in nature, and no existing facilities were to be withdrawn from the space inventory! The school requested state funding for the project and had already expended its own funds for initial architectural work. This sort of proposal can lower the credibility of the planning process that generated it, but it will also taint any subsequent estimates of overall capital need.

2. *Is the project plan geared to overall campus efficiency?* Legislators and other reviewers must believe that the planning (which must reflect the "personality" of the institution) is also geared to efficiency. Differences in the physical plant sizes of institutions that cannot be explained by programmatic or enrollment differences can create credibility problems unless they can be justified. Consider the situation in one state. Institution A has 4,200 FTE and a total nonhousing area of 240,000 net square feet. Institution B, with an enrollment of 5,500, has a nonhousing net square footage of 750,000. The two are regarded as comparable institutions offering similar academic programs and degrees. A responsible state legislator could not be faulted for expecting B to justify its significant space advantage. Higher education officials

must be prepared to demonstrate that facility requests based on current parameters also incorporate maximum efficiency and effectiveness.

3. *Can the projects be accomplished within the timeframe proposed by the plan?* As a practical matter, most campus environments can accommodate only a certain amount of construction activity in a given period of time. Parking, traffic, pedestrian systems, and, most important, the academic programs are disrupted by construction. When disruption is not considered, institutions overestimate the amount of work that can be accomplished and propose overly ambitious programs.

Similarly, it is not unusual now for a college or university to discover that all of its science buildings require renovation and renewal. While it may be feasible to renew all of these structures, what happens to the academic program during construction? Often some modest *new* construction is initially required to unlock the log jam. However, if the planning has not proceeded to this level of operational detail, the estimates of time needed and total cost may not reflect the practical requirements.

THE FUNDING QUESTION

What Is Facility Funding?

While specific practices of facility funding vary from one organization to another, the public sector, particularly colleges and universities, has long followed the practice of dividing expenditures into two categories: operating allocations and capital funding. As they relate to facilities, *operating allocations* include the activities associated with custodial services, repair and maintenance, utilities and heating plant operations, and the like. In addition, the personnel involved in capital planning, project management, space assignment, and information data base development and maintenance are also supported from operating revenues. One particular area of inadequate facilities spending and building maintenance—deferred maintenance—is included in the operating category. Now a cliché, deferred maintenance is used to characterize the backlog of regular maintenance that could not be accomplished during the year when it was scheduled, thus being deferred to the future. The accumulation of neglected maintenance often produces projects too large to be considered part of on-going operations. At that point, the projects must be moved to the capital category as renovation, renewal, or new construction projects. This should not be regarded as a cost-free bookkeeping transfer, however. It has been estimated that inadequate maintenance reduces the expected life of a building by as much as 20 percent (Roege 1982).

Lack of funding also can limit such facility management activities as developing and maintaining facility data bases and long-range planning. The importance of an accurate data base cannot be under-estimated: Organizations that do not know what they have simply cannot manage it. Underinvestment in information and other management failures, such as poor project definition, inaccurate forecasting, and inadequate attention to long-range priorities, result in the misguided expenditure of available capital funds.

Capital allocations are usually developed in a project-by-project framework. Capital needs are discussed here in terms of the "facility drivers," or the categories that generate them.

The first category, emergency projects, is common to all organizations. While individual emergencies cannot be predicted, accurate historical records (the importance of a data base) make it possible to estimate the amount of dollars that an organization should plan to spend in a normal year. Such estimates are directly related to the organization's success in making sufficient investments in building maintenance over time. These expenditures are capital costs, but they only sustain the status quo of facilities.

The second driver category, "fix-it" projects, refers to capital projects generated by other completed capital projects: The facilities must be fixed to make them fully functional. Inappropriate room sizes, inadequate cooling, insufficient power, and incorrectly installed equipment are examples of projects in this category. While lack of funding (in the original building project) may be blamed, the difficulties often can be attributed to inadequate project definition and poor project management. Again, these represent capital costs that do not advance an organization's mission but nonetheless involve substantial expenditures.

The third category, special-purpose projects, includes such work as code compliance and energy conservation projects. While such projects may be valuable to the organization, if undertaken as single projects, they seldom help an organization meet its objectives.

The fourth and final category encompasses renovation, building renewal (which traditionally includes meeting the needs of the intended occupant), and new construction. This category alone promises to meet the future needs of the institution. Even in this category, though money can be wasted. Two points deserve mention.

First, every organization wants to accommodate its various units in facilities appropriately related to one another. Since various units grow at different rates, some relocation is always necessary on a college campus or in a private sector organization. However, this continuing relocation can sometimes get out of hand. The resulting "churn rate" in some private sector organizations exceeds 50 percent; this means that one out of every two employees is moved each year. Such rates in higher education can lead to unnecessary expenditures of capital funds.

Second, it is easy for colleges and universities to expand their facilities when existing space is sufficient. To be sure, "perfect matches" are seldom possible, and it is better to have slightly more space than to face the problem of space shortages. Nevertheless, the record is clear: Academic units expand to occupy whatever space is available. Thus, management needs to monitor facility requirements closely, for excess space (or excess facility sophistication) merely consumes resources that could be better allocated.

It is possible within any organizational framework to expend scarce capital funds in ways that do not bridge the gap between where an organization is now and where it is going. These are the types of capital expenses that should be avoided (and that depend on solid facilities management).

Equipment Needs. Note that equipment has not been included in the above categorization. This is a conscious omission intended to raise a flag of caution, rather than engage in a debate with the accounting profession on the classification of assets. The important consideration is the linkage between financing equipment purchases and expected useful life. Microcomputers are capital equipment items, but their useful life expectancy is significantly shorter than the ten- or twenty-year bonds often issued to finance capital acquisitions. Hence, it would be an imprudent business decision to include short-term equipment purchases on a long-term bond issue. The importance of good information in this area cannot be overstated.

Table 10-1. Outline of Alternative Sources of Finance.

Type of Financing	Typical Source of Funds
A. Equity financing: payment up front	
University, school or departmental reserves	Accumulated from: • Funded depreciation charges, if any • Part operating surpluses • General gifts
Restricted gifts or grants from private services (lead or "name" gift, other gifts)	Obtained from: • Individuals • Foundations • Corporations
Line items in sponsored research or instruction agreements (grants or contracts)	With: • Corporations • Foundations • State and local government • Federal agencies
Joint ventures for research or instruction	With: • Corporations • Foundations • State and local government
State appropriations (public institutions only)[a]	State government
Federal facilities grants	Federal government
B. Debt financing: payment over time	
Tax exempt bonds and notes[b]	The following applies to all types of debt financing: Interest payments:
Taxable bonds and notes[c]	• Indirect cost recovery (external interest is allowable on Federal grants and contracts) • Line items in sponsored agreements • General income, gifts, etc. • Restricted gifts

Table 10-1. continued

B. Debt financing: payment over time
  (*continued*)

Government loans (subsidized or unsubsidized) [d]	Principal repayment:
	• Indirect cost recovery (depreciation charges)
	• Line items in sponsored agreements
	• General income, gifts, etc.
	• Restricted gifts
Government guaranteed bonds and notes (tax exempt or taxable) [b]	

a. Some states provide some capital funds to private institutions.

b. Access of private institutions to tax exempt financing would be eliminated under the Treasury II tax reform proposal. Public institutions would be unaffected. The result would be to further increase the gap between the tuition and fees and the indirect cost rates of private and public institutions.

c. Used mainly by private institutions when access to tax exempt financing cannot be obtained.

d. The federal government currently has no general programs applicable to research facilities.

Source: Massy (1985).

Sources of Funding

Table 10-1 lists all fund sources available for capital purposes. Since this table applies to both public sector and private sector institutions, it is particularly valuable. Virtually all possible funding sources are identified—including all of Kaiser's (1984a) sources as well as those mentioned by Young (1984) and Millett (1984). Hence, this table is a valuable tool for understanding the practical range of available funding sources.

A review of various proposals for creative financing now being proposed and promoted reveals nothing really new. The best example of a "new" fund source is the financing of energy conservation projects through savings in energy costs. Nothing else seems to be in that category. Rather, most so-called creative approaches are simply new combinations of older sources, or a rewriting of existing rules. Millett (1984) exemplifies this latter position in his discussion of the steps being taken in many states to "get around" prohibitions on borrowing. Most of these approaches enable the institutions to buy time or deal with present symptoms rather than resolve the problem.

The Nature of Capital Funding

Capital funding has distinctive patterns. While there is a tendency to focus on the amount of dollars provided, other factors—such as the regularity of funding, the basis of funding, and the control framework—are equally interesting and important. Each of these items is described here. For a complete review of present practices, an excellent analysis of funding for public higher education was made by the University of Idaho (1985) and is recommended to the interested reader.

Capital funding typically is irregular for both private and public institutions. Most states issue bonds for capital purposes at irregular intervals. Pay-as-you-go capital appropriations are most often regarded as budget balancers and are completed only after other more urgent budgetary matters (typically, the whole operating budget) have been attended to. Major capital funding for private schools is just as irregular, since major gifts and grants typically develop according to their own life cycle rather than institutional needs.

This irregularity, however, is not uniform. West Virginia, for example, provides funding for public higher education capital needs through student fee revenues. Thus, while the total amount of funding may not be adequate, its flow is predictable.

Some states have moved to formula funding for building renewal. Using this method provides a regular and disciplined approach that generally has been lacking. Yet no states have fully funded their formulas. Thus, the formulas have served more as a method to allocate funds than as determinants of the funds required.

The basis for the funding also varies widely. In some states, the approval process focuses on the projects themselves and funding levels are based on project authorizations. Those states using a formula approach may provide funds in a lump sum without reference to projects or stated needs. Some approaches are quite "informal" in terms of facilities needs: The use of FTE students as a starting point for capital funding would be a good example. The control framework for public institutions is equally varied. On the one hand, some states attempt to keep tight control on the use of capital funds allocated. Detailed justifications at each step of the project are required simply to release the funds. A very different approach is used by one state that provides capital funding in a lump sum and then imposes only loose controls making management of those funds (for land purchase, new construction, renovation, or equipment procurement) the sole responsibility of the institution.

The best approach may be a course between these two extremes, ensuring some ongoing external review of the management practices of the institutions. Note the careful choice of the word *review* rather than *control*. The latter typically leads to inefficiencies, such as the spending down of unused funds rather than letting them lapse. Contrast this with the situation where an institution has the ability to "bank" the funds for some other high priority capital need but knows that that decision will be subject to audit by the funding authority.

Future Fund Availability

If one compares the capital needs of higher education—both immediate and long term—to the present funding picture, there seems little reason for optimism. Chancellor Young (1984) maintained that if the funding levels of the past five years continue, only 20 percent of the critically necessary capital improvements will be accomplished. But thus far governmental bodies have been generally unresponsive. George Keyworth, science adviser to the president (1984), maintains that the federal government should not and is not likely to develop a dominant role in the support of buildings. In the course of one federal hearing, a discussion by several representatives about these needs implied that higher education's appetite is far larger than the resources that can reasonably be committed to facilities and equipment (Rhodes 1984). William Roege and Gerald Faverman (1985), in an insightful analysis of the infrastructure problems in the state of Michigan, concluded that Michigan is not in a position to appropriate the required capital funding. Similar pronouncements in

Missouri (Missouri State Coordinating Board for Higher Education 1983) and elsewhere suggest that the necessary funding may not be forthcoming from state governments.

At the same time, higher education is urged to do more to press for "larger contributions for faculty and less for plant" because "donors . . . tend to favor plant disproportionately" (Joint Economic Committee 1969). Thus, even current capital funding sources may be "raided." The realistic picture therefore seems grim. Some different approaches are required, and the initiative for appropriate change, particularly for comprehensive management of capital assets, is becoming mandatory for the higher education community.

MANAGEMENT QUESTIONS

An earlier discussion focused on the external environmental forces (mostly financial) that led to the higher education facilities crisis. The problem is not evenly distributed among institutions of higher education, and significant differences exist among generally comparable institutions *within* a state. While one can make adjustments for differences in initial plant quality and in funding patterns, these do not fully explain the gap between institutions, suggesting that institutional management is an important factor in the facilities equation.

The Role of Facilities Within an Organization

It is important to establish a context in which to examine capital facilities and their contribution to organizational performance, and this begins with the mission of the organization. Accepting that "making a profit" is a primary motive for business organizations, the central mission of, for example, a "Big Three" auto company relates to the design, manufacture, distribution, and sale of automotive vehicles. Universities engage in a mission centered on knowledge — its discovery, transmission, and application. In contrast to profits, higher education exists to provide needed services for society.

Facilities, like human capital and information, are the necessary supporting elements used by organizations to fulfill their missions. Of course, financial resources are needed to acquire all three. The requirements for each of the elements differ according to the mission; if the quantity or quality of the supporting elements is deficient, the organization's success will be constrained.

The converse, however, is not necessarily true. That is, the availability of excess resources does not guarantee the fulfillment of mission. Rather, having too many facilities or unnecessarily sophisticated equipment simply results in higher costs. Hence, facility needs, like all the other necessary resources of the higher education enterprise, must be determined in relation to organizational mission.

Six Management Issues

The first management issue might be called the short-run/long-run budget dilemma. After all, financial problems arise in all organizations from time to time. In such emergencies, reductions in building maintenance expenditures and curtailment of capital project activity are logical reactions, for it is in these areas that dramatic and immediate savings can most easily be effected.

A practice that may be appropriate for the short term, however, can become disastrous over the long term. Continuing too long with short-term "solutions" (usually in the hope that the cause of the financial crisis will be resolved) can result in the institution being hopelessly entangled in a substantial long-term problem.

A second issue is the prevailing institutional attitude about physical facilities. In higher education, facilities are almost exclusively regarded as *tools* to carry out the institution's mission.

There is ongoing pressure to have facilities that can be made available on a moment's notice to meet the needs of the various academic programs and the institution as a whole. Hence, counterproductive behavior is observed: Old, exhausted, fully depreciated buildings are not demolished but are left standing while the organization develops a use for such space. On a smaller scale, academic departments are loath to relinquish currently underused (excess) space, the prevailing argument being "we might be able to use it some day, somehow."

Contrast this attitude with some private (corporate) sector settings where there may be an overriding tendency to view space *only* as a cost. There is constant pressure on operating units to reduce space.

This emphasis is not without problems and has contributed to ineffective operations and poor bottom-line performance in the organizations where it occurs.

There is clearly a need for a middle ground between these two extremes. For higher education, that suggests the need for establishing cost parameters for facilities on the basis of their use and assignment and integrating that information into the resource allocation process.

The *rate* of deterioration of facilities is a third issue. "Alumni and administrators rarely see or quite believe the slow, steady decay that goes on" ("Dilapidation in Academe" 1980: 62). Thus, it is easy psychologically to delay capital cost in favor of funding other areas, where the need is more apparent ("squeaky wheels").

Among all the competing priorities on a college campus, building problems, especially deterioration of existing facilities, are unique in that they have no clear or natural constituency. Students react to scholarship changes or tuition increases; faculty react to course assignments and pay; alumni may stop contributing when athletic teams do not perform up to expectations. But buildings just "go on" until something stops working. Even where building issues have effective spokespersons, these individuals suffer from the disadvantage of having no constituency support.

There is, in some cases, a tendency of management to underestimate the importance of "facility fit" in higher education. This often is observed when the facilities professionals are allowed to function without adequate understanding of the academic program. No mechanism is developed to help the planners understand the critical relationships between academic program and capital facilities. The buildings, as houses for the programs, must be constructed to fit these programs. To accomplish this, the professional in charge of facilities must have almost as much academic as facility orientation.

Where such professional talent is present at an institution, a different approach to planning and problem solving is evident. Instead of merely reacting to departmental requests, projects are developed that effectively meet program needs while minimizing costs; money is expended in ways that yield better results.

Finally, there are many rules and practices in place that work against effective management of capital facilities and funds. In many states, institutions find that if money is left over from projects at the end of the year, it must be returned to the state. Aside from a spending spree at year's end, this kind of rule simply announces that there is no reward for good management. In other states, appropriations of maintenance funds are based on the number of square feet of physical plant an institution has in its inventory. In this case, if no other factors are considered, institutions have every incentive to increase square footage. These kinds of policies and practices are counterproductive.

Some state public institutions stand out as having superbly managed facilities. One such institution had relatively few facility problems: Older buildings had been effectively renewed, and structures were sound and effective. Yet a thorough review of capital funding over a twenty-year span revealed that this campus had received substantially *less* funding than comparable state institutions. It became clear, after further investigation, that the president of this campus had established effective plant operations as a priority. The benefits that faculty and students reap from this kind of management are obvious. Depending on the prevailing values, benefits can also be viewed as ephemeral compared to the excitement generated by the announcement of a new building. If presidential performance is measured by the number of new buildings constructed, rather than by the overall quality of the facilities and their ability to support the academic enterprise, then effective management will be thwarted.

Is This Problem Unique to Higher Education?

Articles over the past ten years have pointed out similar problems throughout the private and public sectors. Indeed, lack of appropriate facilities has forced many corporations and entire industries to expend millions to renew existing plants and to create new complexes for competitive production. There are things about higher education that set it apart from other organizational types, however, and these have facility implications. Three aspects are described below.

The Nature of Change. Private sector organizations do not necessarily manage their facilities more effectively than higher education institutions do. In fact, there is some evidence of better management in higher education than in the private sector. This may be explained, in part, by different expectations about the future.

Comparing higher education to other sectors, the differences in the nature of change *of the organization* are striking. Some corporations, for example, begin as manufacturing enterprises and evolve into sales organizations. Others add and delete major product lines with astonishing speed. This shift in basic operations generates renovation and new construction needs totally unrelated to building deterioration and normal program obsolescence. Change in some businesses is so regular and drastic that facility problems are much different from those in higher education.

In higher education, organizational change is extremely slow by comparison. Although methods in chemical research and teaching have changed drastically in the past thirty years, the department of chemistry still exists to perform those functions. Thus, change in higher education tends to be incremental in nature. Computer usage in the sciences is a case in point. Scientists at some universities were using computers thirty years ago; today, computers are ubiquitous.

It is important to understand the facilities implications for an environment dominated by slow incremental change. There is a bias toward responding to growing demand by overloading existing buildings, an appropriate temporary action, unless it is taken in lieu of an analysis of the underlying trends that are developing.

Locational Immobility. It is rare for a college or university to voluntarily relocate. Contrast this with other organizations that periodically abandon one location in favor of another as they seek reduced costs, market advantage, or improved service to customers. The facility implication from this difference should be clear. Higher education can continue to use older facilities on the familiar campus.

Emotional Attachment to Buildings. The environment and process of higher education produces an emotional attachment to campuses and buildings, especially old buildings. This feeling is a part of college life and it can be useful during fund-raising campaigns. It also emphasizes the importance of renovating and renewing campus facilities.

Higher education is unique because of these factors. Hence, the "wear out" of campuses creates problems and elicits emotional reactions within and outside the higher education community without parallel.

WHAT NEXT? SOME CONCLUDING COMMENTS

From the foregoing discussion, it appears that a major facility problem faces higher education today. Solutions seem remote at best. To significantly affect the facility situation, higher education must undertake serious additional work. What, then, should be done? The following suggestions are presented.

What is the framework within which the problem exists?   Initially, a much better data base of "facts" is required. For example:

What is the current replacement value of the various kinds of buildings now in place on our campuses? equipment?

What percentage of this total plant was built and is supported by the various financial constituencies (federal government, state government, foundation sources, other institutional funds)?

What is the annual depreciation "cost" associated with the above values?

What is the history of capital fund expenditures for the past twenty years?

How much of the funds available for the past twenty years have been directed toward the renewal or replacement of the physical plant?

The point of such a data base is not only to dramatically point out what is "at risk" but to identify the practical limits of higher education.

Identify specific needs.   It appears that the problem is not uniformly distributed. In some situations, equipment may be the paramount concern; in other situations, the basic problem may be with dysfunctional buildings; in others, the amount of space available is inadequate. Thus a detailed analysis (even if done on a sampled basis) is in order.

Such an investigation should lead to the discovery of significant patterns of strength and weakness. Further, the presence of discernible patterns would permit the ensuing financial responsibility to be assigned to a specific constituency in a reasonable format.

An equivalent of "depreciation" should be funded annually as a part of the operating budget.   Several current, good formulas can be useful in this case. Failing this, some regular depreciation method could be used to determine the appropriate amount to fund. In any event, such an approach is similar to private sector practices that recognize depreciation as a regular cost of doing business.

Such funds should be earmarked for renovation and renewal purposes with restrictions against appropriating these monies for other purposes. Since these funds are a "regular cost of doing business," they are appropriately categorized in the operating budget.

"Smaller" can also spell relief.   There are many costs associated with higher education's predisposition to add space to the inventory. The costs of operating space are the most obvious, but the capital renewal and replacement costs must be considered also. Hence, there is the potential for significant savings from a program of downsizing the physical plant in some campus settings. Since the savings from such a program are real, this strategy should serve as a source of modest support for meeting the capital needs described earlier.

Incentives must be provided for good management.   It is unlikely that any major source of additional funding will become generally available unless funding agencies can be assured that higher education is prepared to avoid those actions that led to the current situation. A key step toward this objective is to ensure that good management is rewarded. *Only* if there is incentive to manage the facility situation effectively is there any practical assurance that this situation will not recur. Further, such management rewards must be a part of a current solution.

National leadership is necessary.   While many national organizations in higher education are concerned about this problem, a designated group must "adopt" the problem and assume the necessary work and expense involved in collecting data, conducting studies, making analyses, drawing conclusions, and approaching the various financial constituencies. The size of the problem and implications of not resolving it demand the full commitment of some group. Without this, the future seems bleak.

The theme running through these suggestions is the belief that the overriding need for higher education at this critical juncture is the establishment of credibility. If the present facility situation in higher education is both real and critical, it is essential that this argument be convincing. As a start for serious discussion, this agenda represents a step in the right direction.

REFERENCES

"Dilapidation in Academe." 1980. *Time* (March 17): 62.

Illinois Board of Higher Education. 1985. "A Background Report for the Study of Undergraduate Education in Illinois Colleges and Universities." Springfield, Ill. Mimeo.

Jenny, Hans. 1981. *Hang Gliding, or, Looking for an Updraft.* Boulder: John Minter Associates.

Joint Economic Committee. 1969. *The Economics and Financing of Higher Education in the United States.* Washington, D.C.: U.S. Government Printing Office.

Kaiser, Harvey H. 1979. *Mortgaging the Future: The Cost of Deferring Maintenance.* Washington, D.C.: Association of Physical Plant Administrators.

_____. 1984a. *Crumbling Academe: Solving the Capital Renewal and Replacement Dilemma.* Washington, D.C.: Association of Governing Boards of Universities and Colleges.

_____. 1984b. "How Can We Afford This: Funding and Financing Means." Syracuse, N.Y.: Syracuse University. Mimeo.

Keyworth, George. 1984. "Statement." In *Improving the Research Infrastructure at U.S. Universities and Colleges,* Committee on Science and Technology, U.S. House of Representatives. Washington, D.C.: U.S. Government Printing Office.

Massy, William F. 1985. "Alternative Sources of Finance." Paper presented at the Conference on Academic Research Facilities, Washington, D.C., July 22–23.

Michigan Society of Professional Engineers. 1984. "Task Force Report to the Commission on the Future of Higher Education of the State of Michigan." From the Complete Issues Papers of the Governor's Commission on the Future of Higher Education in Michigan, James K. Robinson, Chairman. December 13, p. 294.

Millett, John D. 1984. *Conflict in Higher Education: State Government Coordination versus Institutional Independence.* San Francisco: Jossey-Bass.

Missouri State Coordinating Board for Higher Education. 1983. "Missouri General Revenue and Higher Education Appropriation Trends and Projections." Jefferson City, Mo. Mimeo.

Roege, William. 1982. Public Statement. Michigan Bureau of Facilities, Division of Technical Services.

Roege William, and Gerald A. Faverman. 1985. "Michigan's Deteriorated Infrastructure." Lansing, Minn.: Public Sector Consultants.

Rhodes, Frank H.T. 1984. "Statement before the Committee on Science and Technology, U.S. House of Representatives, on behalf of the Association of American Universities, National Association of State Universities and Land Grant Colleges, American Council on Education, Association of Graduate Schools, and Council of Graduate Schools." 98th Cong., 2nd Sess.

University of Idaho. 1985. "Financing Academic Capital Improvements in the Fifty States." Moscow. Mimeo.

University of Michigan. 1985. *University Record* (Ann Arbor) (November 11).

Wilson, Robin. 1985. "Colleges Seek Federal Aid to Repair Crumbling Buildings." *Chronicle of Higher Education* 31(2) (September 11): 17.

Young, Charles. 1984. "Statement." In *Improving the Research Infrastructure at U.S. Universities and Colleges*, Committee on Science and Technology, U.S. House of Representatives, pp. 49–55. Washington, D.C.: U.S. Government Printing Office.

11 WHO'S GOING TO PAY TO MAINTAIN RESEARCH EXCELLENCE AT U.S. UNIVERSITIES?

Howard Gobstein

Scientific advances are being made in university research laboratories with increasing momentum. Techniques impossible a decade ago are commonplace as more powerful instrumentation is developed and disseminated. Access to supercomputers will soon transform entire fields because what used to take weeks now can be done in hours.

This momentum of research progress is threatened, however. Rising research costs combined with a slowing growth in research funding are slowing the pace of scientific advance. Billions of dollars are claimed to be needed to treat the inadequacy of present research equipment. The need for equipment may be eclipsed by the amount of money required to rebuild the research facilities of "crumbling academe" (Kaiser 1984). Indirect costs continue to increase their share of the research dollar. Finally, there is the specter of federal funding freezes or even cuts brought on by efforts to stem federal budget deficits.

Research momentum has not been the sole victim of the increase in research costs and of the allocation of research funds. The thirty-five-year partnership between the federal government and the nation's research universities is being put to the test. For example, universities that try to claim higher indirect costs for research-related activities find themselves trying to answer questions such as, If scholarship (or research) is integral to the self-defined mission of research universities, why do universities demand that someone else pay these costs? From another perspective, as the federal government

239

hesitates to provide funds for rebuilding and re-equipping university research facilities, it finds itself answering queries on how universities are to contribute basic knowledge and educated graduates to support the nation's security, health, and international competitiveness. Additional concerns arise from the attempts by a few universities to garner federal funding by direct congressional appropriations, a procedure that threatens to topple what has been an extraordinarily productive system of awarding research funds based predominantly on merit.

The solicitation of direct congressional appropriations also focuses the spotlight on the divisions within the academic community as institutions striving to join the top-ranked universities' struggle to obtain scarce funds. There is a new stridency in arguments against allocations of funds that result in "the rich institutions' getting richer" (Silber 1985). Smith and Karlesky (1977: 82) reported in 1977 that lower-ranked departments were having less success winning a sufficient amount of research dollars to maintain their research efforts. The unanswered question then was whether the U.S. research effort would contract to a more select group of top-tiered university research departments—and whether this would be "good" for the national research enterprise. Dr. William McElroy, former chancellor of the University of California at San Diego and former director of the National Science Foundation (NSF), raised similar questions (University of Georgia 1984: 5):

> From about fifty major research universities producing about 80% of the Ph.D.'s after World War II, we went to well over 125 Ph.D. granting institutions. There is no way, with the present mechanism of funding by the federal government, we can maintain excellence in all these research universities. . . . [W]ith funding today we will do well to support fifty of the major research universities in this country.

These are the major funding issues confronting academic science in the mid-1980s: the level and rate of increase of funding, research equipment and facility needs, and indirect costs.

PATTERNS OF FUNDING

The interdependency between universities and the federal government is demonstrated simply with a few statistics. In fiscal year 1984

Figure 11-1. Expenditures for Academic R&D by Sponsor (*in current dollars*).

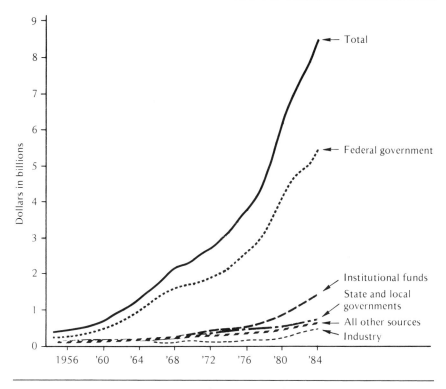

Sources: National Science Foundation (1985: table b-1).

the nation depended on universities to perform about half of basic research, to conduct a little over 10 percent of the nation's applied research, and to educate future scientists and engineers. The universities' dominant contribution to basic research compares to the 20 percent share performed by industry and the 15 percent share performed by the federal government. The universities, on the other hand, have depended on the federal government to provide the bulk of their research funds, or about 64 percent of the funds for academic research and development (R&D) in fiscal 1984.

Growth in university R&D funding has been dramatic over the past thirty years, as shown in Figure 11-1. In fiscal year 1954 universities and colleges spent $290 million on R&D. This sum quadrupled to $1.3 billion in fiscal 1964, more than doubled to $3 billion in fiscal 1974, and has almost tripled again to $8.5 billion in fiscal 1984.

The share of support provided by various sponsors has not varied much over this period. The federal government provided between 55 percent to 65 percent of the funds for R&D to 1961, which steadily rose to a peak of 74 percent in 1966, then slowly but steadily declined to slightly under 64 percent in fiscal 1984. Internal university funds were used for about 14 percent of R&D in 1953, slipped to 8 percent in the early 1960s, then have subsequently increased to about 16 percent in fiscal 1984. At the start of this period, direct state and local government funding supported between 14 and 15 percent of R&D but had fallen to less than 8 percent by fiscal 1984. Industry funding ranged between 6 and 8 percent in the early 1960s, then dropped to 2 to 3 percent as federal funding continued to grow rapidly in the mid-1960s. Industry funding picked up steadily over the past decade and exceeded 5 percent in fiscal 1984. Funding from other sources, principally foundations and nonprofit health agencies, averaged 9 to 10 percent in the 1950s and has been between 6 and 8 percent since 1960 (NSF 1985).

These aggregate data must be used with care, for major differences between the private and public universities in their dependence on funds from the federal government are masked. Private institutions received 77.3 percent of their research funding from the federal government in fiscal year 1977, and 75.7 percent in fiscal 1984. Comparable data for public institutions were 61.3 percent in 1977 and 56.8 percent in fiscal 1984 (NSF 1985). The percentage of R&D supported by industry was about the same for both sets of institutions: For private institutions it was 3.9 percent in 1977 and 6.2 percent in 1984, and for public institutions it was 3.1 percent in 1977 and 5.0 percent in 1984 (NSF 1985).

Growth patterns do not appear to be as robust after considering the effect of inflation. When viewed in constant 1972 dollars, funding growth looks quite different, as shown by Figure 11–2. Funding increased rapidly until 1968. Inflation contributed mightily to a decade long plateau of steady funding from 1968 through 1978. Funding growth has been sporadic since fiscal 1978.

Distinct stages of growth in funding for the past twenty-five years are depicted on Figure 11–3. The boom years of the early and mid-1960s were paced by average annual federal funding growth of over 20 percent in constant 1972 dollars, through 1964, then 11 percent

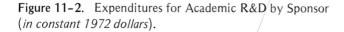

Figure 11-2. Expenditures for Academic R&D by Sponsor
(*in constant 1972 dollars*).

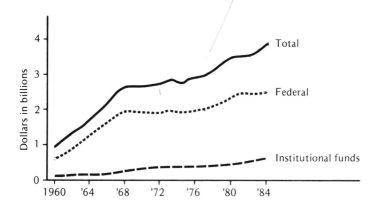

Sources: National Science Foundation (1985: table b-1); National Science Board (1983: 305). 1984 constant dollar figures were calculated from a fiscal year deflator based on quarterly data in the *Economic Report of the President 1985*.

through 1968. From 1969 through 1976 average annual funding rose little, if at all, in constant dollars. Total growth resumed to an average rate of increase of over 4 percent from 1977 to 1980, then dropped to about 3 percent from 1981 to 1984, depressed by federal growth, which averaged slightly above 1 percent in constant 1972 dollars.

Academic research spending has been concentrated in major research universities. Over the past decade concentration has remained remarkably constant, as shown by Table 11-1. In fiscal 1984, 184 institutions performed more than $5 million of R&D. Over 100 institutions spent more than $10 million in the life sciences (agriculture, biology, and medicine). About fifty institutions spent over $5 million in engineering and the physical sciences respectively (NSF 1985). The major findings of this brief review of funding patterns include the following:

Overall academic R&D funding is growing slowly;

Federal funding for academic R&D is growing very slowly, if at all, in constant dollars;

The federal government still supports over 60 percent of academic R&D;

Figure 11-3. Average Annual Changes in Expenditures for Academic R&D by Four-Year Period (*in constant 1972 dollars*).

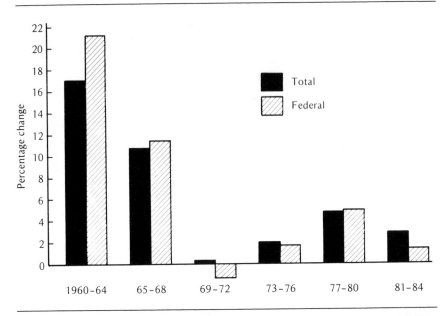

Sources: National Science Foundation (1985: table b-1); National Science Board (1983: 305). 1984 constant dollar figures were calculated from a fiscal year deflator based on quarterly data in the *Economic Report of the President 1985.*

Table 11-1. Relative Concentration of R&D Expenditures at Leading Doctorate-Granting Institutions by Rank, 1975, 1978, 1981, 1984 (*in percentages*).

Source and Ranking	1975	1978	1981	1984
All sources				
First 10	22.0%	20.2%	22.6%	22.1%
First 20	36.9	34.5	36.4	36.2
First 100	84.7	83.9	84.4	84.5
Federal support only				
First 10	24.1	23.1	26.2	26.6
First 20	40.6	37.9	40.4	41.4
First 100	84.7	84.1	85.1	86.7

Source: National Science Board (1983: 302); 1984 figures computed from NSF (1985: tables B-6, B-28, and B-37).

There are major differences in dependency on federal funds between
  public and private institutions;

The relative concentration of funding remains about the same as a
  decade ago, but a large number of institutions other than the
  major universities are undertaking substantial amounts of research.

MAINTAINING THE RESEARCH INFRASTRUCTURE

A major public policy question is whether the nation and its universities can afford the present scale of university research. The cost of
equipment has soared as the technology for doing research in many
fields has changed in as little as five years. A chronic underinvestment in renovation and deferred maintenance may have bailed universities out of short-term fiscal exigencies but may have severely
damaged long-term capacity to conduct modern research. Stanford
University President Donald Kennedy (1985: 480) sees R&D as

> crossing a significant watershed . . . an important transition from people to
> property, and from operating to capital budgets—at which point we must
> start worrying more about one time equipment costs and facilities renewal
> than we do about salaries.

The following discussion focuses on three principal issues relating
to university research infrastructure—research equipment, research
facilities, and indirect costs. These pressing issues may sorely constrain the capacity of universities to perform research.

Research Equipment

University scientists are concerned about the tremendous backlog of
needs for research equipment. As Donald Langenberg, then deputy
director of the NSF, stated in 1982 (NAS 1982b: 10):

> There is an emerging consensus . . . that there is a critical and growing need to
> replace obsolete and worn-out research apparatus and laboratory facilities
> in the nation's research universities. . . . A rough but reasonable, estimate of
> the lower level of the deficit is $1.0 billion. Upper boundaries of the problem
> have been placed in the $4.0–$6.0 billion range.

The rapid advances in technology combined with the fiscal pressures on universities, the federal government, and state governments have made it difficult for researchers to keep pace.

In the past several years several federal agencies have increased their spending on research equipment. Dr. George Keyworth, formerly President Reagan's science advisor, expected the government to spend more than $800 million on university research equipment over the 1984 and 1985 fiscal years (Congressional Research Service 1984).

The unanswered question is whether these new funds will alleviate the research equipment problem. To answer this, equipment need must be defined. Evidence of need exists in the following key past reports.

One of the first efforts to draw attention to the current need for research equipment was the 1965 National Academy of Sciences (NAS) report: *Chemistry: Opportunities and Needs.* The NAS concluded that the deficiency in instrumentation for chemistry at the 125 departments granting a Ph.D. in chemistry was between $20 million and $35 million. The upper figure was extrapolated from the difference between the average stock at the existing departments and an assessment of what was required of a good department of moderate size. The lower figure was based on requests for "urgently needed equipment" in response to a 1963 letter of inquiry sent by the NSF to 121 chemistry departments.

In 1971 the NSF called on the NAS to conduct a far broader and more ambitious survey of university instrumentation needs. The resulting report was entitled *An Assessment of the Needs for Equipment, Instrumentation, and Facilities for University Research in Science and Engineering.* The objectives of the study were to collect data on the types of major equipment needed to conduct an effective program of research at a sample of major university departments (across ten disciplines) and to evaluate these equipment needs in relation to the total department budget, sources of support, size and capability of the research staff, and critical significance to the research for which it would be employed.

Departments were requested to list their equipment needs, defined according to two criteria: that the equipment could be used for research during the 1971–72 academic year and that no additional staff would be required to operate any new equipment. Following the survey, NAS selected teams of scientists and engineers from outside the surveyed departments to determine the validity of equipment needs by conducting site visits. Through the peer review by these site visits, cuts were made to the department chairs' lists of their equipment needs of from 5 to 40 percent!

The study concluded that equipment needs indicated by the various departments were, for the most part, valid and that "a pressing need for equipment in the $100,000–$300,000 price range" existed in university science and engineering centers to support existing research. The total national need was estimated at that time to be over $200 million.

In this study, the critical point is not the total needs derived but the methods used to derive them. The first chemistry report used an average amount for the equipment that each department should have and then implicitly assumed that the total number of *all* departments, whatever their current research efforts, ought to be used in calculating the total national need. Additionally as a lower boundary, the report relied on a simple self-assessment by chemistry department chairs. The second report contained methods that unfortunately have not been duplicated since in equipment assessments. The criteria for need were conservative, and the self-assessed needs of department chairs were then reduced through site visits of their peers.

Not until 1980 — almost fifteen years after the chemistry report — did an equipment study attract significant attention. Commissioned by NSF, the Association of American Universities (AAU) study contained the broadest range of information on university equipment yet published. Incorporated were a wide assortment of data, subjective assessments by the almost 400 researchers and research managers interviewed in five fields of science, and the conclusions of the team of scientists undertaking the study. The report (AAU 1980) showed that

1. The fraction of NIH and NSF research project support allocated to permanent equipment declined after 1966 — NIH support went from 11.7 percent in 1966 to 5.7 percent in 1974; NSF support went from 11.2 percent in 1966 to 7.1 percent in 1976;

2. The constant level of overall research support of the late 1960s and 1970s, and decline in relative equipment support, occurred as the costs for instrumentation increased, sometimes over 20 percent per year;

3. The median age of instrumentation purchased from 1960 to 1978 at a sample of the best ten universities (across five disciplines) was twice that of the instrumentation in a sample of *two* of the best industrial laboratories.

This latter point has been cited in countless testimony and found its way into *Business Week* four years later. By that time the point had become a bit more definitive: "Today, equipment in academia is twice as old as that found in industrial and government labs" ("The Dangerously Decrepit Condition of University Labs" 1984: 90b).

A 1982 study by the Geological Sciences Board of the National Research Council (the operating arm of the NAS) indicated a need for over $100 million per year for installation, maintenance, and replacement of basic geochemical instruments and for development of frontier instruments. This study called for development of simpler, cheaper equipment and for retrofitting existing equipment to fill a large portion of the present need (NAS 1982a: 66):

> Undoubtedly, some laboratories can use profitably all the "bells and whistles," but others could manage quite well with simpler instruments that cost less to buy and operate. Particularly important is development of instruments out of modular components which can be exchanged if service cannot be accomplished easily by the user; service calls by technicians are too expensive (commonly $1,000) and freight service would be much cheaper.

NSF was charged in its 1980 authorization act to "develop indices, correlates or other suitable measures or indicators of the status of scientific instrumentation in the United States and of the current and projected need for scientific and technological instrumentation" (Westat 1984: 1). The baseline survey results for the first of two phases were published as *Academic Research Equipment in the Physical and Computer Sciences and Engineering* and covered the academic year 1982–83 at a stratified sample of forty-three universities. Phase II will cover the agricultural, biological, and environmental sciences of these same forty-three universities, and a separate sample of twenty-four medical schools. Phase II data are based on the 1983–84 academic year.

Of the extensive information published in the first report on such factors as the age, use, costs, and sharing of research equipment, several disturbing figures have been extensively cited: Only 16 percent of the instrument systems in the 1982 stock in these three fields was classified as state-of-the-art; one-quarter of the existing inventory of instruments physically present was inoperative all year either because the instruments were technologically or mechanically obsolete; and 90 percent of the department heads surveyed stated that, as a result of lack of needed equipment, research personnel could not conduct critical experiments.

The situation may not be as severe as it first appears. As the document states elsewhere (Westat 1984: 22):

> By itself, the existence of substantial amounts of non state-of-the-art research equipment is not a problem. Even the best-equipped research facilities would be expected to have such equipment—for use in routine analyses, as backups for more advanced instruments, etc. Non state-of-the-art equipment is a problem only in situations where the users of such equipment do *not* have access to more advanced equipment when needed.

For almost 60 percent of the non–state-of-the-art equipment in use at large universities, more advanced instruments are available to users when needed (59 percent for large private universities and 57 percent at large public universities). Researchers at smaller universities have access to more advanced equipment—46 percent of the time for those in private universities and 42 percent for researchers in public universities (Westat 1984: 83). The public policy question is whether it should be national science policy that every university scientist have access to state-of-the-art equipment.

Similarly, the figure of 25 percent of equipment being obsolete and inoperable but still physically present and on the property inventories can be interpreted variously. This continued listing on inventories may be due to tardiness in cleansing inventory roles, the acquisition of more current equipment, the retention of obsolete equipment as a source for parts or for use as a counter top. Including this equipment in the inventory also increases the total stock and affects the other statistics.

Finally, 90 percent of department heads reported that investigators were inhibited from conducting critical research in their areas because of a lack of needed equipment. Undoubtedly there is unused potential due to inadequate research equipment—but there is also untapped potential that goes unfunded altogether. Has funding for research ever kept up to the total demand? If a constant need for equipment is a fact of research life—if a good researcher will always wish to be advancing, periodically needing upgraded (probably more expensive) equipment—then how much of relatively limited budgets should be spent on equipment?

Since 1981 funding for academic research equipment has increased from $414 million to $435 million in 1983 and to $518 million in 1984. The federal government contributed $265 million in 1981, $273 million in 1983, and $335 million in 1984—or 64 percent of the total in 1981, 63 percent in 1983, and 65 percent in 1984. Federal funds for research equipment increased by 23 percent from 1983 to 1984 (NSF 1985).

These key reports demonstrate that although there is a consensus that a major problem exists, the analytical base is not sufficient to identify a course of action. Several questions remain unanswered. If total academic research funding levels off or continues to grow slowly, how much of this funding should be taken from program support and allocated to equipment purchases and maintenance? Should efforts be made to maintain or upgrade the more up-to-date equipment at more research intensive universities, since they perform a larger portion of the nation's research? Are larger equipment programs needed in federal agencies, or will researchers and universities be able to internally allocate sufficient funds? When will the need for research equipment have been met—when state-of-the-art research equipment moves up to 30 percent of equipment present or when only 75 percent of department heads report that researchers are hindered by the lack of available equipment?

Research Facilities

Concerns over research facilities appear to be widespread. The NSF reported university and college capital expenditures for science and engineering of over $1.2 billion in 1984, following similar expenditures of close to a billion dollars in each of the preceding three years (NSF 1985). (These figures include spending for facilities and major equipment for research, development, *and* instruction.)

Most evidence suggests that present facilities problems represent the culmination of years of accumulated neglect of physical plant needs. When a choice needed to be made during prior years of financial difficulty, the capital need was delayed "temporarily" to minimize more painful decisions on personnel or program cuts. Indeed, financial indicators for universities still do not adequately portray the state of the capital portion of the institutions (Jenny, Hughes, and Wynn 1982).

Investments in facilities were made somewhat more difficult as federal support for university R&D plant dropped dramatically. Federal expenditures peaked at about $160 million in 1966 and dropped rapidly to between $40 and $60 million (in current dollars) from 1969 on (NSB 1984). This is also demonstrated by the federal share of all capital expenditures for scientific activities at universities and colleges being about 12 percent since 1982 (NSF 1985).

Chronic delays in tending to physical plant needs and the decline of the federal role in funding have come concurrently with at least several other factors that have made facility needs apparent. First, there is the periodic maintenance to keep up with normal deterioration of physical plant—painting, replacing roofs, and floors, and so forth. Second, tremendous changes have been made in the technologies used to do research, and there is an attendant need to alter existing facilities or construct new facilities to house the new equipment. Third, changes have taken place in the nature of fields of science (such as more interdisciplinary work) and enrollment shifts (such as renewed emphasis on computer science and engineering). Finally, facilities must be updated to meet changing regulatory (such as animal care facilities) or health and safety codes (Congressional Research Service 1984).

A disturbing development is illustrated by the dozen universities that have sought facility funding by direct congressional appropriation without any form of merit review by scientists. These institutions have argued that these drastic actions have been necessary because no alternatives existed to them. Major science and university associations have deplored this direct political approach, fearing that its relative success to date could create a snowballing of requests. Increased reliance on this approach could threaten to eliminate or do severe damage to the present credibility and success of competitive award mechanisms for science based on merit. AAU President Robert Rosenzweig (1985:13) warns how a political award process for facilities would carry over to awards for projects:

> I would argue that it is the likelihood—that the habit of treating scientific *facilities* as economic goods will lead to treating scientific projects as economic goods. . . . It is inconceivable to me that facilities bargained for in the Congress on the basis of their connection to the condition of local economies

will be allowed to lie fallow because the scientists in them are unable to compete successfully for project funds from . . . federal agencies.

Neither the research nor the efforts of these institutions provide firm figures of the funding needs for facilities for academic R&D. Existing estimates are based on admittedly crude extrapolations of limited surveys, assuming an even need across fields and institutions. These estimates cluster around $1 to $1.5 billion annual investments for up to ten years to meet present needs (Government-University-Industry Roundtable 1985). In view of the inadequacies of existing data, in late 1985 Congress gave NSF the mandate to perform a full-scale facility study and maintain a data base of the conditions and needs for academic research facilities. The first report was due September 1986.

The present estimates of research facility needs are large and perhaps imply a potentially debilitating effect on R&D efforts. The interest in the issue is large, with some leaders calling research facility needs the most serious long-range problem facing research universities. However, there is no consensus on the relative priority of research facilities in budgetary terms. In hearings on the University Research Facilities Revitalization Act of 1985 (H.R. 2823), no agreement was reached on one of the key provisions of the proposed act—mandating that federal science agencies set aside a portion of their R&D funds to support university R&D facilities programs. Adamant opposition was expressed to the proposal that this set-aside be taken out of existing R&D program support. The favored approach was to provide new funds. This add-on of federal funding seems unlikely in any appreciable amounts, given efforts to stem federal budget deficits.

This resistance to redirecting federal research program funds to support facility construction appears consistent with a survey of a small number of current NSF principal investigators and administrators in five fields of science and engineering on their perception of the state of the research facilities in which they were conducting their research. The results of this survey, presented at the June 1984 National Science Board meeting, showed that 70 percent of the facilities had been renovated in the past ten years, with only 7 percent of the funds provided by the federal government; and 50 percent of the facilities were slated for renovation in the next three years, with only 6 percent of the funds expected to be provided by the federal government (NSB 1984). The NSF facilities study will provide further information to see if the survey results simply reflected state government funding of state university facilities and if private universities that do not have access to public funds are being left out of this seeming renovation and building boom. Indeed, Vice President Dan Zaffarano (1985) of Iowa State University stated at the hearings on the facilities bill that it should not be a federal responsibility to provide money for facilities for existing fields of science—that this base support should be covered by state funding. He argued the need was in the new fields of science and that federal funding should be forthcoming only to assist in constructing facilities that would be used in new areas of research that could demonstrate an economic payoff in the long term.

Without additional direct federal funding for facilities however, increases in expenditures for research facilities from other sources eventually do detract from R&D program funds by increasing indirect costs. These other alternatives range from new state and industry giving, increases in the rate of indirect cost recovery for building use and depreciation, creation of independent authorities to finance research buildings, or use of other forms of debt financing. These latter two approaches likely would increase indirect cost recovery, probably with the added expense of interest tacked on. Many of these approaches would force the redirecting of a portion of R&D program funds into capital renewal and add to the concern over rising indirect costs.

Indirect Costs

Indirect costs have become one of the most controversial and frustrating issues associated with federal funding of university research. Meant to support overhead such as administration, operations and maintenance, and use of facilities and equipment, indirect costs have gained much attention over the last two decades. Repeated government and institutional disagreements over faculty time and effort reporting and negotiated settlements of disagreements on assignments of costs and cost sharing have made this a constant source of friction between the federal government and universities.

The debate began to shift approximately five years ago on what apparently has been the central (albeit mostly tacit) issue all along: How should the full costs of federally sponsored academic research be paid? How should costs be defined? To paraphrase an official from the White House's Office of Science and Technology Policy (OSTP), it is no longer a question of how to calculate the allocations on particular costs but of which costs should the government pay at all (private conversation 1985). That the debate had become acute and more focused on this basic issue was inevitable, given that indirect cost growth has consistently claimed an increasing share of federal funding for university research.

Universities beset by fiscal pressures apparently are claiming more of the costs allowed them under OMB Circular A-21. Meanwhile attempting to stretch its research dollars, the National Institutes of Health (NIH) unsuccessfully proposed in its authorizing legislation for fiscal years 1983 and 1984 that it pay only 90 percent of the amount of indirect costs due universities based on their negotiated rates. Congressional committees did not agree to this proposed unilateral cut by NIH. Partly as a result, OSTP is considering indirect costs governmentwide as part of the broader study conducted by the White House Science Council on the federal role in the health of research universities. Future conflict is sure to occur, as demonstrated by the unsuccessful attempt of the Senate Appropriations Committee (reportedly with administration support) to freeze indirect cost rates for NIH recipients for fiscal year 1986. Fortunately for the universities, the freeze did not survive the conference committee (U.S. House 1985).

Comprehensive trend data on federal indirect cost reimbursements to universities have not been maintained centrally. Existing data for NIH and NSF *grants* (excluding contracts and cooperative agreements) show that since 1965, when caps on indirect costs were lifted, indirect costs as a percentage of total research costs climbed rapidly during the early 1970s (at the same time that federal research funding was level). The indirect cost share for NSF was 16.3 percent of total research costs in 1966, 26.3 percent in 1977, 25.3 percent in 1980, and 25.9 percent in 1982, the last year for which data were available. Indirect costs as a portion of NIH research costs rose steadily from 15.3 percent in 1966 to 30.5 percent in 1983. NIH's Federal Assistance Accounting Branch projects that the indirect share will increase to 31.7 percent in 1985 (Thomas and Lederman 1984).

Indirect cost rates are calculated by seven cost pools based on OMB Circular A-21: operations and maintenance, general administration, departmental administration, sponsored project administration, use allowance or depreciation for research equipment and facilities, libraries, and student services. The aspect of indirect costs that will likely receive the predominant future attention is the amount attributed to infrastructure, or facility and equipment construction, renewal, operations, and maintenance. Donald Kennedy (1985) claims that these are the quickest rising components of indirect cost rates, citing Stanford's figures as an example. Between 1974 and 1983 the annualized growth rate of the administrative costs (general, departmental, sponsored projects, and student services) was 0.30 percent per year, while during this same period, the sum of building-related costs (operations and maintenance, equipment, depreciation, and use charges) was 8.41 percent. (Kennedy notes that these figures were taken directly from the indirect cost *pools* before cross-allocations were figured in. For example the indirect cost *rates* would show different growth rates due to the charging of operations and maintenance on the buildings in which administrative activities were performed.)

Kennedy's assertion is corroborated by HHS estimates based on the major research universities that negotiate their rates with HHS. In 1982, on the average, use allowance and depreciation and operations and maintenance accounted for 36 percent of the total indirect cost rates for these universities. The four administrative cost pools (general, departmental, sponsored projects, and student services) accounted for 57 percent of the total indirect cost rates. In 1984 the equipment- and facility-related rates went up to 38 percent of the total costs, while the administrative portions of the rate slipped to 55 percent of the total. Using base data, the average infrastructure indirect cost components grew by 10 percent over this period, while the administrative components grew by 2 percent (Kirschenmann 1985). (These figures already include the cross-allocations, so that the trends would be expected to be more toward infrastructure if based on actual cost pools.) GAO figures based on a sample of 82 NIH grantees showed indirect costs related to these administrative pools increasing 28 percent from 1980 to 1982, the indirect costs related to infrastructure increasing 33 percent over the same period of time (U.S. GAO 1984). These increases in the infrastructure components may be only a start. Interest on construction has been allowed only since 1982, and an increasing amount of construction for research appears to be using debt financing.

The focus on the infrastructure portion of indirect cost recovery will surely continue, especially if present proposals are accepted to use indirect cost recoveries to put more funds into infrastructure.

These proposals would speed up recovery for investment in buildings and equipment by boosting the annual use charges built into indirect costs. Thus, the R&D enterprise would be forced to set aside money for infrastructure by capturing these increased indirect costs from program funds. Decisionmaking for facilities would be integrated with the research efforts at individual campuses—thus bringing trade-offs between research programs and facilities to the operating level where consequences must be felt, rather than at the more abstract agency level, where they would be if there were to be federal facilities programs.

However, forcing tradeoffs at the institution level may put off facility decisions as in the past, since it pits faculty against administration. Tension may also increase among departments, as researchers from one department help pay for the new equipment and facilities in more capital-intensive departments. Several issues are related to the calculation of indirect costs. Should separate indirect cost rates for different disciplines reflect their differences in capital intensity? Should the social sciences be taxed for expensive capital equipment of the physical, engineering, and life sciences? Are university administrations strong enough in leadership and resolve to hike indirect cost rates for infrastructure in spite of dominant faculty identification with their field and department, rather than their home institution (Alpert 1985)?

Finally, funding infrastructure predominantly through indirect cost recovery is inequitable under the current system for setting rates. There are differences in the indirect cost rates for universities among the ten HHS regions and between HHS and DOD schools. The differences seem to be based on negotiation toughness and allowable indirect costs. (HHS has responsibility for negotiating the indirect cost rates with institutions that perform about 90 percent of the federally funded research; DOD has the remaining institutions, which tend to be very large research universities.) Determining where university research facilities are to be built and upgraded on the basis of the skills of their indirect cost negotiators is not good national policy. Additionally, funding the R&D infrastructure in this manner places the burden on the universities to raise or borrow the funds up front for facility construction. This may be easier for public universities with state governments to appropriate funding, as opposed to private institutions that depend on donations. The implications for quality R&D activities and competition for funds are illustrated in a

1982 faculty quality ratings of departments that found that six of the seven highest-rated institutions were private, as were nine of the top fifteen (Geiger 1986).

TO MAINTAIN THE CAPITAL BASE

To scientists, the need to upgrade research equipment is obvious. To university administrators, the need to replenish aging facilities is obvious. To researchers, federal officials, members of Congress, and the public, rising indirect cost rates obviously withdraw funds from research support. To many, the need to maintain the infrastructure of the major research universities is obvious. To others the need to spread the research potential and build up the capabilities of developing institutions is just as obvious.

Funding for academic science is growing only slightly—hardly enough to accommodate all of these needs. The need to decide among the many choices is obvious.

REFERENCES

Alpert, D. 1985. "Performance and Paralysis: The Organizational Context of the American Research University." *Journal of Higher Education* 56(3) (May/June): 241–81.

Association of American Universities. 1980. *The Scientific Instrumentation Needs of Research Universities.* Washington, D.C.: National Science Foundation.

Congressional Research Service. 1984. *Summary and Analysis of Hearing on Improving the Research Infrastructure at U.S. Universities and Colleges.* Report for the House Committee on Science and Technology, 98th Cong., 2d Sess.

"The Dangerously Decrepit Condition of University Labs." 1984. *Business Week* (September 3): 90b–90c.

Geiger, R. 1986. "Hierarchy and Diversity in American Research Universities." In *The University Research System: The Public Policies of the Home of Scientists*, pp. 77–100, edited by A. Elzinga and B. Wittrock. Stockholm: Almqvist and Wiksell.

Government-University-Industry Research Roundtable. 1985. "Academic Research Facilities Financing Strategies." Washington, D.C.: National Academy of Sciences. Mimeo.

Jenny, H., G.C. Hughes and G.R. Wynn. 1982. "Taking Capital Requirements into Account." In *New Directions for Higher Education: Successful Responses to Financial Difficulty* (no. 38), edited by C. Frances, pp. 39–44. San Francisco: Jossey-Bass.

Kaiser, H.H. 1984. *Crumbling Academe: Solving the Capital Renewal and Replacement Dilemma.* Washington, D.C.: Association of Governing Boards of Universities and Colleges.

Kennedy, D. 1985. "Government Policies and the Cost of Doing Research." *Science* 127 (February 1): 480–84.

Kirschenmann, H.G. 1985. "Statement before the Task Force on Science Policy." House Committee on Science and Technology, 99th Cong., 1st Sess. (May 21).

National Academy of Sciences. National Research Council. 1965. *Chemistry: Opportunity and Needs.* Washington, D.C.: National Academy Press.

_____. 1971. *An Assessment of the Needs for Equipment, Instrumentation, and Facilities for University Research in Science and Engineering.* Washington, D.C.: National Academy Press.

_____. 1982a. *Report of the Ad Hoc Committee on the Status of Geochemical/Mineralogical Instrumentation.* Washington, D.C. Mimeo.

_____. 1982b. *Revitalizing Laboratory Instrumentation.* Report of the Ad Hoc Working Group on Scientific Instrumentation. March 12–13. Washington, D.C.: National Academy Press.

National Science Board (NSB). 1983. *Science Indicators 1982: An Analysis of the State of U.S. Science, Engineering, and Technology.* Washington, D.C.: U.S. Government Printing Office.

_____. 1984. *Discussion Issues 1984: Academic Science and Engineering: Physical Infrastructure.* Vols. I & II. NSB 84–160. Washington, D.C.

National Science Foundation (NSF). 1985. Preliminary Release of FY 84 data on Academic Science Expenditures. Washington, D.C.: Division of Science Resources Studies. Mimeo.

Rosenzweig, R.M. 1985. "Testimony on Science in the Political Process." Before the House Task Force on Science Policy, Committee on Science and Technology. 99th Cong., 1st Sess. (June 26).

Silber, J.R. 1985. "Testimony." Before the House Task Force on Science Policy, Committee on Science and Technology. 99th Cong., 1st Sess. (June 26).

Smith, B.L.R., and J.J. Karlesky. 1977. *The State of Academic Science: The Universities in the Nation's Research Effort.* New Rochelle: Change Magazine Press.

Thomas, E.C., and L.L. Lederman. 1984. "Indirect Costs of Federally Funded Academic Research." Washington, D.C.: National Science Foundation. Mimeo.

U.S. General Accounting Office. 1984. *Assuring Reasonableness of Rising Indirect Costs on NIH Research Grants—A Difficult Problem.* GAO/HRD-84-3. Washington, D.C.: U.S. Government Printing Office.

U.S. House of Representatives. 1985. House Report 99–402. Conference report on HR3424. November 21.

University of Georgia. 1984. "A New Age for University Research." Report of the National Conference on the Future of University Research, edited by A.L. Lawson. University of Georgia, Athens, Georgia. October 1–3.

Westat, Inc. 1984. *Academic Research Equipment in the Physical and Computer Sciences and Engineering.* Washington, D.C.: National Science Foundation.

Zaffarano, D.F. 1985. "Testimony on the University Research Facilities Revitalization Act of 1985." House Subcommittee on Science, Research and Technology, Committee on Science and Technology. 99th Cong., 1st Sess. (October 24).

12 HIGHER EDUCATION REFORM
Recommendations for Research and Practice

Frances Kemmerer

Institutions of higher education, caught as their secondary counterparts in the web of their own successes, are in the process of reexamining the nature and the quality of the services they offer. The reexamination comes at a time when colleges and universities are serving students who differ markedly from earlier cohorts in numbers, composition, educational preparation, and academic and vocational interests. The growth of large heavily subsidized state systems clearly helped to accommodate the baby boom cohort. But in addition to cohort-driven increases in enrollments, enrollment rates—particularly from traditionally underserved populations—increased. In 1950 less than two out of every five high school graduates enrolled in college (NCES 1981). Now three out of every five graduates enroll (NIE 1984). To a large extent, this increase in numbers reflects the democratization of higher education. Federal civil rights and financial aid initiatives, as well as the previously mentioned growth in state systems in the late 1960s and early 1970s, opened the gates of the academy to women, ethnic minorities, and older students. At the present time over 60 percent of all undergraduates are women, 17 percent are ethnic minorities, and 40 percent are over age 25 (NIE 1984).

In response to the demands for access and the mood of the time, institutions diversified their programs to accommodate the new cohorts of students who often differed from their predecessors in

261

both academic preparation for college and interests. The national reports *Integrity in the College Curriculum* (AAC 1985), *Involvement in Learning* (NIE 1984), and *To Reclaim a Legacy* (Bennett 1984), which are the subject of this chapter, address the questions of what has been lost in diversification, whether diversification was or is the appropriate response to differences in student characteristics, and what is and should be the value added to an individual's stock of knowledge and skills by attendance at college. A summary of these reports is followed in this chapter by an examination of the relationships between the issues raised and the recommendations. The chapter concludes with a statement of the implications of the reports for research and practice.

THE REPORTS

Not surprisingly, the literature on the reform of higher education has followed the same historical pattern as that on compulsory schooling (Kemmerer 1984). Both sets of literature reflect changing societal pressures and periodic efforts to redress the balance of values that ultimately shape what is taught and how it is taught. Perched at the apex of the educational system, institutions of higher education are alternatively accorded the credit or the blame for the character and skills their graduates bring to the marketplace or, more globally, the value added to the culture. To a large extent, however, both the goals and curricula of colleges are determined by the quality and effectiveness of precollegiate institutions.

One of the central problems in higher education, therefore, and one only partially controlled by institutional selectivity, is how to deal with this relationship. The extent to which the academic preparation and interests of students, as opposed to the standards dictated by the academy itself (and presumably reflective of national needs and aspirations), should determine the college curriculum remains an open and debated question.

In addressing this question, all three reports agree that the recent past has been marked by an imbalance in favor of a demand-driven curriculum. In support of their position, the reports point to the smorgasbord of equally valued electives offered by most institutions; the widespread phenomena of grade inflation; the decline both in the number of required liberal arts courses and the number of majors in the humanities; the decline in scores on eleven of the fifteen subject areas tested by the Graduate Record Examinations; and the facts that fewer than 25 percent of higher education institutions require study of European history or American history and literature and fewer than 50 percent require foreign language study. *Involvement in Learning* (NIE 1984) suggests that high dropout rates and the large numbers of high school graduate students who do not choose to attend college should also be considered "warning" signs of inadequate quality.

All three reports consider that clear articulation of goals and the translation of these into validated curricula are the first step toward realizing quality improvements in higher education. *Involvement in Learning* (NIE 1984), the broadest of the reports, focuses on the contextual variables demonstrated to influence student achievement. Both *Integrity in the College Curriculum* (AAC 1985) and *To Reclaim a Legacy* (Bennett 1984) speak directly to curricular reform. The first of these reports specifies a set of competencies that should be acquired in college, while the second focuses on the substance and implementation of the humanities portion of the curriculum.

The reports differ in audience and substance from the nine or so major reports on precollegiate education published in the past few years. They are directed, for the most part, to administrators, faculty, and students rather than state legislators. The choice of audience stems not so much from an acknowledgment of the differences in governance structures between levels (which, in fact, seem to be disappearing) but from a recognition that true reform is effected in lecture halls and seminar rooms.

While the reform movement at the secondary level has addressed issues related to exposure to and coverage of material, the reports on the reform of higher education advocate change in both what is taught and the way in which disciplines are approached. They claim that content has been emphasized to "the neglect of the style of inquiry on which the content is based" (AAC 1985: 2). "Faculty should make greater use of active modes of teaching and require students to take more responsibility for their learning" (NIE 1984: 27). "Excessive concentration in one area . . . often abetted by narrow departmentalism, can promote provincialism and pedantry. . . . Conversely, . . . going too far toward breadth could make the curriculum a mere 'bus trip of the West' characterized by 'shallow generalization and stereotypes'" (Bennett 1984: 7, 8).

On the issue of program evaluation and student assessment, the higher education reports come much closer to their precollegiate counterparts. Advocacy of standardized testing is, however, tempered by recognition of legitimate differences in institutional goals and objectives and the difficulty in measuring many of the outcomes of postsecondary education. The fear that such assessment will eventually dictate the curriculum underlies the marked preference for internal versus external evaluation.

The weaknesses of the reports lie in five directions and owe much to the narrow charge given to the different study groups. While criticism of publications for not addressing issues outside their stated scope is a questionable practice, the impact of reports such as these on public opinion and national and state policy decisions justifies at least some recognition of what has been left out. Specifically the reports tend to ignore:

1. The substantial differences in the missions of four-year, two-year, and community colleges. In so doing, they disregard the differences in aspirations of students and the variety of reasons for which individuals enroll in postsecondary institutions.

2. The financial implications of their policy recommendations. For instance, the societal, institutional, and student costs of increasing the amount of time students spend in postsecondary schooling are certain to be prohibitive.

3. Emerging equity issues such as the decline in both the absolute and relative numbers of black enrollments and the relative numbers of Hispanic entrants (Wagner 1985) despite the growing proportional representation of these groups in the population.

4. The link between what is learned in college and how it is used on the job. The assumption seems to be that quality increases of whatever nature will bring about improvements in the job performance of graduates.

5. The excellence that already characterizes many institutions. On the precollegiate level, emphasis on schools with poor programs and results has led to "legislated learning" for all schools. It has also encouraged legislators and governors to spread scarce new resources across all schools rather than targeting resources on those most in need of both technical and material assistance.

THE ISSUES AND RECOMMENDATIONS

While the issues underlying the recommendations are not easily categorized, it is useful to divide them into three groups: those related to
institutional standards, instructional methods, or assessment. For the
purpose of this chapter, *institutional standards* is defined to include
the set of decisions related to the selection, promotion, or graduation
of faculty and students. Decisions regarding the allocation of faculty
time, student time, and material resources for particular purposes are
considered under the category of *instructional methods.* The category of *assessment* encompasses institutional and faculty decisions
related to the evaluation of programs, student progress and achievement, and effective teaching. The specific recommendations for each
of these categories are outlined in Table 12-1.

Institutional Standards

The subset of recommendations regarding institutional standards
addresses issues related to curriculum, remediation, and the emphasis
placed on faculty teaching. The intent of these recommendations is
to increase the value of the postsecondary degree.

Minimum Required Curriculum.   While the reports generally recognize the legitimacy of the differences among institutional goals and
objectives, the recommendations shown in Table 12-1 indicate that
all either explicitly or implicitly endorse the notion of a minimum
required curriculum. Defined alternatively as two years of liberal
education, a basic set of competencies, or a grounding in Western
philosophy and literature, the authors of the reports view changes in
requirements for awarding a college (in particular a bachelor's)
degree as fundamental to any reform effort. Together with the
changes in curricular objectives and emphasis on the development of
higher-order skills, the reports agree that greater emphasis should be
placed on "good" teaching in the selection, promotion, and tenure
of faculty.

The recommendations for liberal education and the humanities
are considered both as a means of ordering curricular objectives and
also as a value statement. The suggestion, however, that the content

Table 12-1. Recommendations for Reform in Higher Education.

Involvement in Learning	Integrity in the College Curriculum	To Reclaim a Legacy
Institutional Standards		
1. List the skills and capacities graduates are expected to have. 2. Require two full years of liberal education, regardless of major. 3. Emphasize the development of analytic skills. 4. Require noncredited remediation where students do not test at the twelfth-grade norm. 5. Increase the weight given to teaching in hiring and retention of faculty.	1. Develop a minimum curriculum that emphasizes inquiry; logic; critical analysis; historical consciousness; understanding numerical data, scientific issues, and the scientific approach; appreciation of art; international and multicultural experiences; and study in depth. 2. Increase the weight given to teaching in the hiring and retention of faculty.	1. Require careful reading of several masterworks of English, American, and European literature; proficiency in a foreign language; and an understanding of philosophical issues. 2. Maintain balance between curricular breadth and depth. 3. Increase the weight given to teaching in the hiring and retention of faculty.
Instructional Processes		
1. Reallocate resources to freshmen and sophomores: (a) reduce part-time faculty; (b) reduce use of T.A.s. 2. Use active modes of teaching. 3. Increase faculty/student contact in the use of new technologies. 4. Create learning communities. 5. Support cocurricular activities.	1. Exploit the use of new technologies and expose students to diverse technologies. 2. Integrate the academic and cocurricular programs.	1. Reduce the use of part-time faculty and T.A.s.

Assessment

1. Implement a systematic program to measure student gains in the knowledge, capacities, and skills listed as curricular objectives.
2. Require participation in the development, administration, and scoring of the new tests so that faculty members acquire skill in the use of assessment as a teaching tool.
3. Improve the means used to assess faculty teaching.
4. Provide for regular student evaluations of programs and learning environments.

1. Require faculty to design and monitor assessments of students, programs, and teaching.
2. Encourage interinstitutional cooperation in assessment activities.

should be primarily related to Western civilization (Bennett 1985) seems strangely at odds with both the population profile and the fact that pluralistic forces have and continue to shape U.S. history and culture. The debate about whether to emphasize Western civilization or give free rein to pluralism is an old one. Admittedly, the pluralistic position was not strengthened by the addition of many weak "ethnic" courses in the past decade. This does not mean, however, that a multicultural approach should be abandoned but rather that such programs should be evaluated on the basis of objectives and substance.

Much the same can be said about the AAC's preference for higher skill development over curricular coverage and course weightings. The separation of the substance of the curriculum from skills development is virtually impossible. In fact, by definition, a successful course or program is characterized by a good fit between content and learner tasks (see, for example, Stodolsky 1983).

Remediation.   Only one of the reports considers, however, the implications of a minimum required curriculum for the selection and retention of students. Based on the principle that not only should there be open access to college but that all should attend, the NIE report lays the responsibility for remediation clearly on the shoulders of postsecondary institutions. "In no case should standards of performance in remedial courses in English be normed at less than twelfth grade levels" (NIE 1984: 48). Since none of the state systems with requirements for competency testing before high school graduation sets such a high standard, it is likely that large numbers of freshman college students would be eligible for remediation. Remediation requirements combined with the requirement to take two full years of liberal arts, regardless of major, may add over a year to college studies. The financial implications of these recommendations for states, institutions, and students, in terms of direct costs and opportunity costs, are staggering.

In addition to the financial costs, the research indicates that implementation of these recommendations might also result in substantial social costs due to lower enrollment rates and increased attrition within some segments of the potential college-going pool. Socioeconomic status, as measured by parental education and income, has been shown to be consistently and positively related to an individual's decisions about whether to attend college and which college to attend (Manski and Wise 1983; Terkla and Jackson 1984; Chapman 1981). The direct effect is, of course, on the student's financial ability to support both the tuition costs and opportunity costs (forgone earnings) related to continuing in school. The indirect effect operates through both home contributions to and expectations for learning and the quality of compulsory schooling the student receives (Kemmerer 1980). The quality of prior schooling is, in turn, related to academic achievement (Chapman 1981).

While it is difficult to partial out the financial component of students' decisions to persist, students' perceptions of their academic progress appear to be significantly related to remaining in college (Blane, DeBuhr, and Martin 1983; Pascarella forthcoming; and Pascarella, Smart, and Ethington forthcoming). This finding suggests that extra time spent in noncredited remediation would reduce both the incentives for enrollment and persistence in higher education.

Tinto reflects on the stability of the dropout rate (roughly 45 percent) over the past hundred years despite the enormous amounts spent on "enhancing the likelihood that students will enter and persist in college" and concludes "that there is some value to being discriminating in educational judgments without being discriminatory in the manner in which we make them" (Tinto 1982: 694–95). If institutional judgments about the value of certain students remaining in a given program are to be respected, then so, too, must be students' decisions about whether to enroll in higher education and whether to persist to graduation. The social benefits derived from higher education are not so great that they dictate a need for doubling the societal investment (or whatever may be required) to encourage all to attend. The antithesis of the point of view that all should attend college is that the society is now "overeducated" (Tsang and Levin 1985; but see also Wagner 1984). It can be argued that both extremes do violence to fairness and efficiency (McMahon and Wagner 1982). The concern expressed in the recommendations for effectively lengthening the college period thus might be better addressed by more efficient use of the time available for instruction.

Weight Given to Teaching. Although all three reports recommend that greater attention be given to evidence of "good" teaching as opposed to good research in the hiring, promotion, and tenure of faculty, good teaching remains largely undefined. A preference, however, is shown for reducing the use of both part-time faculty and teaching assistants (Professor Wayne Booth cited in Bennett 1984: 15):

> We have chosen—no one required it of us—to say to the world . . . that we do not care to teach nonmajors . . . so long as the troublesome hordes move on. . . . [W] e hire a vast army of underpaid flunkies to teach the so-called service courses, so that we can gladly teach, in our advanced courses, those precious souls who survive the gauntlet.

While there is no uniform definition of part-time, it is estimated that "nearly one in every three faculty is employed" on a part-time basis (Gappa 1984: 1). Over half of all part-timers are found in community colleges (Gappa 1984: 23). As both Booth's remarks and Gappa's research indicate, the primary reasons for hiring part-time rather than full-time faculty are cost and flexibility. Part-time faculty are paid by the course and are rarely eligible for nonsalary benefits. At the same time, part-timers act as a contingent labor force that can be drawn on quickly to mount new programs or substitute for faculty on leave (Gappa 1984: 70, 76).

Although the relative effectiveness of part-time faculty instruction is widely debated, the available research results are contradictory. When effectiveness is measured as experience, use of media, availability to students, and grading practices, full-time faculty are superior to their part-time colleagues. Other measures of effectiveness, such as changes in student attitudes, student performance in subsequent courses, and student attrition rates, apparently do not support this difference (Gappa 1984: 82, 83). Research findings aside, however, it is certainly true that institutions could do much more than is typically done to promote the accessibility and efficiency of part-timers by providing office space and adequate support services.

The use of graduate teaching assistants is a qualitatively different issue from the employment of part-time faculty, since no matter how well such assistants perform, they generally do not have credentials comparable to full- or part-time faculty. In distinction from part-time faculty, teaching assistants are not viewed as a substitute for full-time faculty but rather as a resource that can be used to increase the effectiveness of scarce faculty resources. The role of the graduate assistant, therefore, is best considered in relation to instructional processes.

Instructional Processes

The reports take serious issue with current practices regarding the allocation of resources among students and the way in which faculty time, student time, and materials are combined in the teaching and learning situation.

Effective Distribution of Experienced Faculty. All three reports explicitly or implicitly endorse a more effective distribution of the time of experienced full-time faculty members among freshmen, sophomores, juniors, and seniors. Unfortunately, little research has been done on the relationship between exposure to different instructional methods and persistence in college. Indirect evidence provided by the correlation between faculty contact and persistence (Pascarella 1980, 1984, forthcoming) suggests, however, that the large faculty lecture/small teaching assistant seminar format, which typifies many entry-level courses in large universities, may have a negative effect on persistence.

One of the primary reasons for the use of the large lecture/small teaching assistant seminar format is cost. One hour of faculty time combined with several hours of teaching assistants' time is far less expensive than alternatives that employ only full-time faculty inputs. If it is conceded that the issue is the *quality of instruction* (and not the use of graduate students per se), then a number of other possibilities can be considered. These possibilities require a shift in the responsibility for the content and the delivery of instruction from the teaching assistant to materials designed by faculty.

Programmed Instruction. A number of new approaches to combining resources for instruction show promise of more effectively distributing faculty time and increasing student involvement in learning. The audio-tutorial system (A–T) uses some form of media to deliver faculty designed material. Probably the most widely known example of this approach is the audio-tutorial system developed by Professor S.N. Postlethwait in the early 1960s at Purdue University. Interactive media, self-pacing, and support by a live instructor are characteristic of the A–T model (Heinich et al. 1982).

A variety of forms of programmed teaching and learning have been implemented successfully throughout the world at the elementary level (see Pasigna 1985). The approach used most commonly in higher education in the United States is personalized systems of instruction (PSI). PSI is based on faculty-designed programs consisting of modularized, competency-based instructional materials. Mastery is determined by criterion-referenced tests that students take when they feel ready. Graduate assistants and student proctors provide opportunities for small group discussion and feedback. In Ellson's (1976) analogy, the faculty member serves as the composer, and the teaching assistant as the performer.

A 1976 review of the literature attests to success of the PSI approach to instruction in psychology, engineering, and biochemistry. In thirty-eight of the thirty-nine studies examined, PSI students significantly outperformed control group students. Nine out of nine studies indicated that PSI students retained more information, and four out of five studies confirmed student preference for PSI rather than lectures (Kulik, Kulik, and Smith 1976).

PSI, as well as other types of programmed learning, has been criticized on the grounds that the modules emphasize rote learning as opposed to higher-level skills (Caldwell 1985). Where this is, in fact, the case, two explanations are possible. First, the students entering new fields may need to master additional "learning-to-learn" skills, which require practice. Practice using simple algorithms is almost by definition a lower-level cognitive activity. This is not to say, however, that it is not a necessary activity. Such practice may be the only way to provide the discipline and the foundation for later application of higher-order skills.

The second explanation is that the particular program may have been poorly designed. The objectives may underestimate student capabilities, or there may be dissonance between stated objectives and learner tasks. Either situation indicates poor formative evaluation. Since PSI objectives are stated and translated into tasks, deficits can be fairly easily remedied. It is much more difficult, however, to correct the level of content and lack of fit problems in traditional formats because objectives and learner tasks are rarely specified in sufficient detail (Caldwell 1985).

Another criticism of existing programmed learning systems (and PSI, in particular) is the possibility they afford for cheating (Caldwell 1985). In an era, however, when term papers are easily purchased, it would seem that cheating is a much more general problem. It is not clear that greater external control (and less student responsibility) is the appropriate remedy. Creating a closer knit faculty and student community in which cheating becomes a violation of trust might well act as a stronger disincentive for such behavior.

In addition to these approaches, many colleges and universities are experimenting with the use of such instructional media as computers, interactive videotapes, and satellite telecommunication—all of which promise the possibility of reducing the cost of allocating excellent faculty to larger numbers of classes and seminar halls. Jackson (forthcoming) discusses ways in which technological devices stimulate learning while effectively using scarce faculty time.

The concern raised by the reports that students not be abandoned to technology is well taken. The literature on distance education indicates that both learner-learner contact and faculty-learner contact are required for program success (Thiagarajan 1978).

Congruency and Feedback.   Regardless of whether traditional methodologies or new technologies are used to define the learning situation, the congruency or fit of selected properties such as teacher or student pacing, student interaction, materials feedback, and options determine its effectiveness (Grannis 1978; Gump 1967; Stodolsky 1983). An example of lack of congruence would be a situation in which the instructor has assigned work for students to do on their own but has made no provision for those who work more slowly or quickly and has made no feedback available.

In research at the elementary classroom level, Stodolsky (1983) found that students allocated more time to learning basic skills if they could proceed at their own pace and get assistance as needed. Where students were asked to work on their own but had no access to feedback, involvement was low. Stodolsky also found that the highest involvement rates were associated with formats almost never used in teaching basic skills—namely, cooperative peer group work. While many of the formats typical of the elementary classroom are less commonly found in the college classroom (such as seatwork and recitation), analogues such as library work do exist. This suggests that much could be learned from additional research relating the individual's actual learning environment in the college or university to his or her progress in mastering skills and content.

Cocurricular Programs.   Recognizing the lost opportunities for experiential learning caused by the separation of the curriculum into academic and cocurricular segments, the authors of the reports further recommend that efforts to integrate the two would enrich the classroom and promote greater student interest and involvement. The authors of *Integrity in the College Curriculum* suggest ways in which resources beyond the campus can be tapped to enrich the baccalaureate experience. The authors of *Involvement in Learning* emphasize the strong holding power of the cocurricular programs and recommend the expansion of existing programs to accommodate part-time and commuter students. Frank Newman (1986), president of the Education Commission of the States, expresses a similar view in recommending that college students should work while they are enrolled. Research from the related areas of nonformal education (such as Bock and Papagiannis 1983), experiential learning (Marks and Davis 1975; Thiagarajan 1980), and simulations and games (Bredemeier and Greenblat 1981) support the motivational and instructional potential of this approach and also provide suitable prescriptions for fully exploiting its potential.

Assessment

The reports recommend that institutions place a great deal more emphasis on the evaluation of programs, student progress, and faculty teaching than is currently the case. These recommendations imply that assessment activities receive little weight in colleges, a point of view to which many faculty and students would take exception.

Program Evaluation. Deans and faculty in state universities commonly complain of the length of time it takes to obtain the necessary approval for program and even course changes. Typically, the changes are reviewed both at the departmental and university level. In some states, such as New York, the recommended changes must also be endorsed by the state department of education. The strength of this system lies in the requirement for broad peer review of the congruency between academic standards and new or altered programs. Its weakness in practice results from the fact that it encourages proving the worth of a program rather than improving the worth of a system.

An alternative approach would be to initially require only departmental approval for an experimental course or program. Then, if and when formative and summative assessments justify inclusion of the experimental course into the formal curriculum, the recommendations might be forwarded with the evaluation data to appropriate universitywide and external agency committees. This type of flexibility is necessary if faculty are to become involved in, and accept responsibility for, the learning environment. In addition, both universitywide and external agency committees would surely make better decisions if presented with data rather than idealized descriptions of the potential effectiveness of new programs or courses.

The NIE Report (1984) also suggests that students play a more active role in evaluating programs and the learning environment. However, the research on student course evaluations does not indicate that a great deal of reliance should be placed on this form of assessment (Centra 1980). One alternative to this type of evaluation is to obtain student preferences among instructional formats, the types and kinds of feedback found most useful, and the forms of assignments most conducive to learning. Given that more and more students commute to college, structures should be created to encourage ongoing faculty and student exchange on these issues. A secondary benefit of these discussions is that they would do much to promote the realization of the recommended "learning communities."

Faculty Evaluation. Student ratings of teacher effectiveness have been shown to be strongly correlated with student achievement and with factors beyond the control of the faculty member, such as class size (Centra 1980). The first correlation indicates that students confuse their own success with the quality of the teacher, while the second indicates that characteristics of the instructional format are not distinguished from the teacher's role.

Despite the well-known unreliability of student ratings, these evaluations are used routinely in promotion and tenure decisions. As is the case with a great deal of easily quantifiable data, the dangers in overinterpreting differences in ratings among faculty and placing too much reliance on the measures may outweigh the benefits derived from student feedback.

Acceptance of the limitations of student evaluation of faculty teaching does not mean, however, that the effectiveness of such teaching cannot be evaluated. A number of alternative approaches have been used successfully to assess teaching, especially when the intent of such assessment is formative (that is, to help the teacher improve his or her practice) rather than summative (to make salary, tenure, or promotion decisions). These approaches include the following:

1. *Standardized observation systems.* A number of observation systems that identify and record critical classroom transactions are available (such as Simon and Boyer 1967, 1970), and these could form the basis for describing and evaluating teacher performance in various instruction settings.

2. *Computer-assisted teacher training systems.* The combination of standardized observation systems, expert observers, and microcomputers permit the delivery of "real-time" feedback to teachers on behavioral categories of their own choice (such as student involvement and time spent lecturing or questioning) (Semmel 1972). Such an approach allows faculty to measure their progress toward self-defined performance goals.

3. *Student achievement data.* The most valid measure of teacher performance is, perhaps, the amount students learn. Faculty evaluation procedures that are based on external assessment of student achievement as a secondary indicator of teacher impact are available but are seldom utilized.

4. *Simulated teaching performance tests.* To compare the performances of different teachers, it is possible to use performance tests that involve real students but simulated content (incorporating the range of cognitive demands from the ideal higher-education curriculum). Such standardized performance tests enable teachers to discover their strengths and weaknesses as a first step in improving their competencies.

Student Evaluation. The principal dilemma in the evaluation of student progress is posed by the fact that the evaluators (faculty and administrators) are often untrained in the skills necessary to design valid and reliable test instruments. Kelly (1985: 54, 55) indicates that this is but one of ten issues that should be considered prior to advocating an increase or change in testing practices. The other nine are:

2. The confusion of aptitude and achievement;
3. The untrustworthiness of grade-equivalent scores;
4. The untrustworthiness of gain scores;

5. The overgeneralization of test results and the question criteria validity;
6. The confusion of testing with evaluation;
7. The difference between using tests to detect effects and using tests to quantify the intended outcomes of instruction;
8. The arbitrary institution of minimal standards versus the identification of appropriate criteria;
9. Current confusions about what tests measure;
10. Inference, attribution, and the post hoc fallacy.

Given the seriousness of these issues and the fact that the problems they raise are not likely to be solved in the immediate future, Kelly recommends the use of multiple measures of both student progress and achievement. These include both faculty evaluation of student mastery of the subject matter and skills, as well as the use of external criterion-referenced tests. As student evaluation is incorporated into an overall scheme of program evaluation and faculty assessment, the credit or blame for achievement gains can be more equitably distributed among the factors associated with the production of skills and knowledge.

The fear of external testing expressed in the reports seems unjustifiable, since testing is already required for graduate work and curricula are already subjected to external agency review for accreditation purposes. The external agencies, in fact, appear to be quite sensitive to differences in mission among postsecondary institutions and the wide variation in the preparedness of the students they enroll.

IMPLICATIONS FOR RESEARCH AND PRACTICE

Although limited in their scope, the reports calling for improvement in higher education raise questions about mission, effectiveness, efficiency, and equity that go to the heart of the enterprise itself. Considered separately, each report argues forceably for a particular set of answers. Taken together, their differences in approach and solution indicate potential controversy regarding:

1. *Who is to be served?* Those academically prepared in the traditional sense or all? What types of remediation are different types of institutions best suited to provide?

2. *What is to be taught?* Who should decide the adequacy of the curriculum and its fit with the larger needs of the marketplace and the culture?

3. *How should it be taught?* Are there certain traditional methodologies or new technologies that result in greater individual and average gains in learning than do others?

4. *Who should evaluate programs, faculty, and students?* What is the role and responsibility of the institution? Of external agencies? What assessment techniques should be used to evaluate faculty teaching, student learning, institutional climate?

5. *Who should pay for reform?* What are the cost implications of the reform recommendations? How should the financial burden be distributed among the institutions, students and families, and external agencies?

Institutions and external agencies will wrestle with these questions, each in the light of its own mission. Some of their answers (curricular) will proceed from value judgments; others (structural and financial) will be determined in the political arena. Many questions, however, will remain unanswered unless a new generation of research on higher education is initiated. Cost and lack of access have served as major barriers to the microlevel research needed to identify the program specific correlates of college student involvement in learning and achievement. Yet unless all the questions are answered, and none ignored, the reform literature will simply take its place on the shelf— the last in a long line of paper lions.

REFERENCES

Association of American Colleges (AAC). 1985. *Integrity in the College Curriculum: A Report to the Academic Community.* Washington, D.C.: Association of American Colleges.

Bennett, William J. 1984. *To Reclaim a Legacy: A Report on the Humanities in Higher Education.* Washington, D.C.: National Endowment for the Humanities.

Blane, R.A., L.E. DeBuhr, and D.C. Martin. 1983. "Breaking the Attrition Cycle." *Journal of Higher Education* 54(1) (January/February): 80–90.

Bock, John C., and George S. Papagiannis. 1983. *Nonformal Education and National Development: A Critical Assessment of Policy, Research and Practice.* New York: Praeger.

Bredemeier, Mary E., and Cathy S. Greenblat. 1981. "The Educational Effectiveness of Simulation Games: A Synthesis of Findings." In *Principles and Practices of Gaming Simulation*, edited by Cathy S. Greenblat and Richard D. Duke, pp. 155-69. Beverly Hills: Sage.

Caldwell, Edward C. 1985. "Dangers of PSI." *Teaching of Psychology* 12(1) (February): 9-12.

Centra, John A. 1980. *Determining Faculty Effectiveness*. San Francisco: Jossey-Bass.

Chapman, David W. 1981. "A Model of Student Choice." *Journal of Higher Education* 52(5) (September/October): 490-505.

Chapman, David W., and Ernest T. Pascarella. 1983. "Predictors of Academic and Social Integration of College Students." *Research in Higher Education* 19 (3): 295-322.

Dowell, David A., and James A. Neal. 1982. "A Selective Review of the Validity of Student Ratings of Teachers." *Journal of Higher Education* 53(1) (January/February): 51-62.

Ellson, Douglas G. 1976. "Tutoring." In *The Psychology of Teaching Methods: The Seventy-fifth Yearbook of the National Society for the Study of Education*, edited by N.L. Gage, pp. 130-65. Chicago: NSSE.

Gappa, Judith M. 1984. *Part-time Faculty: Higher Education at a Crossroads*. ASHE-ERIC Higher Education Research Report No. 3. Washington, D.C.: Association for the Study of Higher Education.

Grannis, Joseph C. 1978. "Task Engagement and the Consistency of Pedagogical Controls: An Ecological Study of Differently Structured Classroom Settings." *Curriculum Inquiry* 8(1): 33-36.

Gump, Paul V. 1967. *Classroom Behavior Setting: Its Nature and Relation to Student Behavior*. Final Report to the U.S. Office of Education, Project Number 2453. Lawrence: University of Kansas Press.

Heinich, R., M. Molenda, and J.D. Russell. 1982. *Instructional Media*. New York: John Wiley.

Jackson, Gregory A. Forthcoming. "Learning Technology and Pedagogical Models in Higher Education." In *Educational Technology and the Adult Learner: Widening Access or Erecting Barriers*, edited by Alan P. Wagner and Ernest A. Lynton. State University of New York at Albany. Mimeo.

Kelly, Edward F. 1985. "The Role of Testing in American School Reform." In *National Educational Reform and New York State: A Report Card*, Rockefeller Institute Conference Proceedings, pp. 51-76. Albany, New York: The Nelson A. Rockefeller Institute of Government.

Kemmerer, Frances. 1980. "Towards Specification of a Student Time Supply Function." Ph.D. dissertation, University of Chicago.

_____. 1984. "The National Reports: Research and Recommendations." In *Challenge from Without: Analysis of the Recommendations Advanced by Five National Education Task Forces and Their Policy Implications for Precollege and Higher Education*, Rockefeller Institute Special Report Series, pp. 33–72. Albany, New York: The Nelson A. Rockefeller Institute of Government.

Kulik, James, Chen-Lin C. Kulik, and Beverly B. Smith. 1976. "Research on the Personalized System of Instruction." *Programmed Learning and Educational Technology* 13(1) (February): 3–30.

Manski, Charles F., and David A. Wise. 1983. *College Choice in America.* Cambridge, Mass.: Harvard University Press.

Marks, Stephen E., and William L. Davis. 1975. "The Experiential Learning Model and Its Application to Large Groups." In the *1975 Annual Handbook for Group Facilitators*, edited by John E. Jones and J. William Pfeiffer, pp. 161–66. San Diego: University Associates.

McMahon, Walter W., and Alan P. Wagner. 1982. "The Monetary Returns to Education as Partial Social Efficiency Criteria." In *Financing Education: Overcoming Inefficiency and Inequity,* edited by W.W. McMahon and T.G. Geske, pp. 150–80. Urbana: University of Illinois Press.

National Center of Education Statistics. 1981. *Digest of Education Statistics.* Washington, D.C.: U.S. Government Printing Office.

National Institute of Education. 1984. *Involvement on Learning: Realizing the Potential of American Higher Education.* Washington, D.C.: U.S. Government Printing Office.

Newman, Frank. 1986. *Higher Education and the American Resurgence.* New York: Carnegie Foundation for the Advancement of Teaching.

Pascarella, Ernest T. 1980. "Student-Faculty Informal Contact and College Outcomes." *Review of Educational Research* 50(4) (Winter): 545–96.

_____. 1984. "College Environmental Influences on Learning and Cognitive Development." In *Higher Education Handbook on Theory and Research,* edited by John Smart, pp. 1–61. New York: Agathon Press.

_____. Forthcoming. "Racial Differences in the Factors Associated with Bachelor's Degree Completion: A Nine-Year Followup." *Research in Higher Education.*

Pascarella, E. T., J. C. Smart, and C. A. Ethington. Forthcoming. "Tracing the Long-term Persistence/Withdrawal Behavior of Two-Year College Students: Test of a Causal Model." *Research in Higher Education.*

Pasigna, Aida. 1985. "Success Story: Liberia's Improved Efficiency of Learning Project." *Performance and Instruction* 24(9): 7–8.

Semmel, Melvin I. 1972. "Toward the Development of a Computer Assisted Teacher Training System." In *Classroom Behavior of Teachers,* edited by N. Flanders and G. Nutthall, pp. 127–38. Hamburg, Germany: UNESCO Institute for Education.

Simon, A., and E. G. Boyer, eds. 1967. *Mirrors for Behavior: An Anthology of Classroom Observation Instruments.* Vols. 1–6. Philadelphia: Research for Better Schools.

_____. eds. 1970. *Mirrors for Behavior: An Anthology of Classroom Observation Instruments.* Vols. 7–14. Philadelphia: Research for Better Schools.

Stodolsky, Susan S. 1983. *Classroom Activity Structures in the Fifth Grade.* Final Report. NIE Contract No. 400–77–0094. University of Chicago. Mimeo.

Terkla, Dawn G., and Gregory A. Jackson. 1984. "State of Art in Student Choice Research." Cambridge, Mass.: Harvard University. Unpublished.

Thiagarajan, Sivasailam. 1980. *Experimental Learning Packages.* Englewood Cliffs, N.J.: Educational Publishers.

_____. 1978. "The Loneliness of the Long-Distance Learner." In *Learning Via Telecommunications*, edited by Howard Hitchens, pp. 44–45. Washington, D.C.: Association for Educational Communications and Technology.

Tinto, Vincent. 1982. "Limits on Theory and Practice in Student Attrition." *Journal of Higher Education* 53(6): 687–99.

Tsang, Mun C., and Henry M. Levin. 1985. "The Economics of Overeducation." *Economics of Education Review* 4(2) (Winter): 93–104.

Wagner, Alan P. 1984. "An (Almost) Sure Bet: The Payoff to a College Degree." Paper presented at the College Board Annual Meeting, New York, October 29.

_____. 1985. "College Enrollments by Race 1970–1983: The Trends in the New CPS Data." State University of New York at Albany. Mimeo.

_____. Forthcoming. "Technological Innovations in Education for Adults: The Nature and Distribution of Costs." In *Educational Technology and the Adult Learner: Widening Access or Erecting Barriers*, edited by Alan P. Wagner and Ernest A. Lynton. State University of New York. Mimeo.

13 TRENDS AND EMERGING ISSUES IN FUNDING PRIORITIES FOR HIGHER EDUCATION

John D. Millett

The Twentieth Century: An Almanac (Ferrell 1985) concludes with a section titled "An Era of Anxiety, 1974– ." Certainly these past few years have been a period of uncertainty and confusion for institutions of higher education, public and private. Three factors predominantly contributed to the instability of the past decade: demographic and social trends, economic trends, and governmental trends. These complexities were compounded by other difficulties: small enrollment size at many institutions, geographical location, an increased emphasis on quality, and continuing pressure for better faculty salaries. Financial well-being has never been assured for colleges and universities; the future is not likely to be an exception.

The first half of the 1980s provided evidence of two kinds about institutions of higher education: First, their capacity to survive under adverse circumstances should not be underestimated; second, even in a threatening environment, change comes slowly. Drastic action does not fit the academic ethos. Incremental change, stimulated or enforced by external forces, prevails in most institutions. The colleges and universities of 1985–86 were not essentially different from those of a decade earlier. It would be rash to expect substantial change in the decade ahead.

283

DEMOGRAPHIC AND SOCIAL TRENDS

The changing numbers of the traditional college population ages 18 to 22 was clearly forecast in the 1970s, even as the "coming tidal wave of students" was forecast in the 1950s. The 18-year-old population in the United States numbered 2.6 million persons in 1960; by 1970 the number had grown to 3.8 million persons; by 1980 it had increased to 4.3 million persons. As of 1985 the number of 18-year-olds had declined to 3.7 million, and the projection was 3.3 million 18-year-olds by 1995.

Breneman (1982) warned that the 18-year-old population in 1986 would be 18 percent less than in 1979, 26 percent less in 1991, and 22 percent less in 1995. The projections by regions and states varied around these national averages. The 18-year-old population in the northeast was expected to be 40 percent less in 1994 than in 1979; in the north central region it was expected to be 32 percent less. On the other hand, the southeast and south central regions were expected to have only 13 percent fewer 18-year-olds in 1991 than in 1979, and the western region would have 16 percent fewer 18-year-olds. The projected changes state by state ranged from 43 percent fewer 18-year-olds by 1994 in Connecticut, Massachusetts, and New York to a 1 percent increase in Texas, a 12 percent increase in Utah, and a 21 percent increase in Wyoming. Breneman forecast 18-year-old population declines as follows: under 10 percent, five states; from 10 to 19 percent, nine states; from 20 to 29 percent, sixteen states; and over 30 percent, fifteen states and the District of Columbia.

As of the autumn of 1985, however, no overall enrollment loss had been experienced in the United States. Total enrollments had stabilized for three years at 12.3 or 12.4 million students, and the proportions of this enrollment remained about the same for undergraduate and graduate students, for students in four-year and two-year institutions, and for students in public and private institutions. But there were changes. The proportion of 18-year-old men enrolling appeared to have declined, while the proportion of 18-year-old women enrolling had increased. The number of students of the traditional college age had declined, while the number of older students had increased. The number of full-time students had declined, and the number of part-time students had increased. Although the data were not readily available, it appeared that the residential institutions were tending to maintain their enrollment or to lose enrollment slowly, while the enrollment in commuting institutions fluctuated. The moderately selective and more highly selective institutions were tending to maintain their enrollment, while the less selective and open-door institutions were tending to lose enrollment. As of 1985 there were fears that the number of foreign students might decline because of troubled economies in many other countries and the relatively high value of the dollar.

The enrollment experience nationwide and state by state concealed many different individual institutional experiences. Some institutions increased enrollment, some lost enrollment, and some remained stable. The number of minority students depended in large part on the availability of student financial assistance. The increased emphasis on quality in institutional performance had not yet had an enrollment impact as of 1985.

The changing circumstances of enrollment experience tended to make institutions more sensitive to their particular competencies in attracting and retaining students. Some institutions began to talk about "marketing" their special features. It was not always clear that such marketing served the ends of student needs rather than the ends of institutional survival.

SOCIAL TRENDS

A common criticism of neo-Marxist writers has been that U.S. higher education reflects characteristics of the dominant society (Clecak 1977). The accusation is that the dominant society is exploitive of persons and of human values; the alternative of a just and humane society is extolled. The usually cited evidences of exploitation are the persistence of unemployment and poverty, the unequal distribution of income and wealth, the higher standard of living in the United States than in other countries, and the high level of consumption by the United States of the world's finite resources. The critics seem uncertain about either the process or the result of social change but nonetheless insist that the mission of higher education must be to bring about a new social order.

The critics generally fail to analyze the fundamental characteristics of the dominant society: social pluralism, a mixed economy, and liberal democracy. The strengths and benefits of these characteristics are ignored, as well as the social changes that have taken place under this dominant society. Moreover, the critics would prescribe a role for higher education that colleges and universities lack the power to perform. It is difficult to conceive of any organization or process of higher education that is not a reflection of the society that sponsors and nurtures it.

The Carnegie Commission on Higher Education in one of its more persuasive reports, *The Purposes and Performance of Higher Education in the United States* (1973), set forth as its fifth and last enumerated purpose "evaluation of society for self-renewal—through individual thought and persuasion." The commission acknowledged that U.S. society did not fully understand or accept this purpose and also that "some elements on some campuses" exploited the opportunity for criticism unwisely and illegally. The doctrine of academic freedom was developed in the United States to protect the privilege of academic criticism, and in large measure that doctrine does appear to enjoy widespread acceptance. One basic characteristic of U.S. society is its commitment to constitutional rights and to limited government. This characteristic is reinforced by a diffusion of power in government and society. Higher education in the United States needs to offer no apology for its role in underlying the values of a free society, even though that society may fall short of perfection.

Society in the United States, as elsewhere, is divided into classes. For purposes of this discussion, the taxonomy of Banfield (1970) is preferable to that of the sociologists. Banfield proposed four major categories of class identification: upper class, middle class, working class, and poverty class. While class distinctions are based on social status, income, and type of work performed, any attempt at quantification of class structure has usually been neglected in the United States. Some governmental statistics present data on socioeconomic status in three categories—high, middle, and low—without precise definition or enumeration. And it must be acknowledged that class identification appears to be less evident in the United States than group affiliation.

Rushing in where sociologists fear to tread, the following estimates of change in the class structure of the United States are hypothesized:

Percentage Distribution of Families

	1930	1980
Upper class	2	4
Middle class	18	46
Working class	50	35
Poverty class	30	15

The importance of such data is simply the proposition that class structure in the United States does change over time. And the corollary proposition is that higher education has been an important factor in assisting any such change. At the same time it must be acknowledged that rather than a massive redistribution of income and jobs, governments in the United States, in concert with economic growth, have sought to advance social change through education, especially higher education.

If anything, the social expectations placed on higher education in the promotion of social change, and especially in the expectation of income distribution, have been excessive. Jencks (1972: 265) warned "that as long as egalitarians assume that public policy cannot contribute to economic equality directly but must proceed by ingenious manipulation of marginal institutions like the schools, progress will remain glacial." And elsewhere Jencks (1979: 311) concluded his study of the determinants of economic success with these words: "Thus, if we want to redistribute income, the most effective strategy is probably still to redistribute income."

A concern with higher education as an instrument of social mobility was dominant in the 1960s and 1970s. In the 1980s this concern is being replaced by a growing interest in the quality of educational performance. Beginning with the report of the National Commission on Excellence in Education, *A Nation at Risk* (1983), a sizable number of reports and studies about elementary/secondary and higher education have developed the theme that the drive for equality in educational opportunity had endangered or undermined attention to quality. The usual evidence for this deterioration was the record of declining scores of high school seniors on standardized tests of academic ability.

The consequences of this concern for educational quality have included changes in the expected high school course preparation for college study at public four-year institutions, some rethinking of the general education component of an undergraduate education, and some new state government appropriations in support of academic excellence. The discussion has tended to ignore several factors, however. As enrollments increased in secondary and higher education, considerable diversity in student interests and abilities was bound to occur. One response on the part of elementary/secondary education to this diversity was a tracking of students according to their interests and abilities. Among colleges and universities, public and private, considerable differences in admission standards and in expected student performance appeared. It is doubtful that the quality of student achievement at the most selective institutions declined seriously in the 1960s and 1970s.

Nonetheless in the 1980s the battle lines were drawn for the remainder of the century. How was higher education to reconcile the competing claims of quality and equality in instructional performance? Should colleges and universities become more selective in admission and provide instructional service to a lesser number of students? Should higher education spend more money to assist students of lesser ability in an effort to advance their educational achievement? How was higher education to compensate for an environment of poverty, of family and peer indifference to educational attainment, and of a struggling secondary school effort experienced by some students? As of 1985–86 there were many attempted answers to such questions but no assured solutions. Only an affluent nation could expect to cope with these issues, and few legislators or others desired to limit access to some kind of higher education opportunity.

It seemed likely that meritocracy in social and economic achievement would receive a new emphasis in the 1980s and 1990s. The role of higher education in social mobility would require new assessment. At the same time there appeared to be no likelihood that higher education would become less widely available in U.S. society. The fear was that U.S. society might be unwilling to bear the cost of diversity and of high standards in some institutions. The hope of the situation was that new attention might be directed to the "value added" to student intellectual and other performance by different kinds of higher education institutions.

ECONOMIC TRENDS

No aspect of U.S. life in the 1970s and early 1980s prompted more uncertainty and anxiety than the performance of the economy. These years produced various shocks: an oil embargo and an end to cheap fuel as a source of energy; increased capital investment in needed pollution controls, sometimes at the price of expanded production facilities; increased production of U.S.-labeled goods in foreign countries; a shift in some domestic production from the northeast and north central regions to the south and southwestern regions; increased foreign imports; large foreign trade deficits; a troubled farm economy; a perverse rise in the value of the U.S. dollar in foreign currency; a new attention to automated production in the United States; a decline in manufacturing employment; horrendous inflation; slow economic growth; mounting federal government budget deficits; and a continuing concern about unemployment and poverty.

As of 1985–86 only one of these economic maladies had been brought under control; inflation had substantially abated from the 1979–80 peak. Otherwise all of these concerns continued to perpetuate an environment of anxiety. Business executives, union leaders, public administrators, and governmental executives and legislators struggled to find policies and actions that would somehow resolve these various problems in ways that would benefit most Americans.

Institutions of higher education found it increasingly necessary to cope with this troublesome economic environment. On the one hand, they had to meet the higher costs of energy and to try to keep pace with the ravages of inflation. On the other hand, they had to face the threat of a declining federal government commitment to student financial support and the perplexing circumstances of fluctuating state government finances. Particularly in the years from 1979 to 1983 many state governments experienced economic slowdown, declining revenues, inflation, and increased attention to unemployment and poverty. A movement for tax reduction in several states such as California further exacerbated current circumstances. Appropriation support for higher education was reduced in efforts to balance state budgets. When the economic situation improved in 1983 and again in 1985 in many states, higher education institutions began to recover lost ground.

No economic challenge to higher education was greater, however, than the challenge of a changed economic expectation on the part of state government leaders and others. This change was nothing less than a fundamental alteration in the expected economic benefits to be derived from higher education. During the 1960s and 1970s the primary expectation of economic benefit from higher education was the preparation of educated talent for a changing labor market. A secondary benefit was derived from scientific research and technological development that advanced economic growth and employment. In the 1980s, from the point of view of state governments, these priorities were suddenly reversed. The primary economic concern became not the preparation of educated talent but the production of jobs.

As of 1950 the total employed civilian labor force in the United States came to 58.9 million persons. By 1980 this employed labor force numbered 99.3 persons, and by 1984 it numbered 105.7 million persons. Within these totals, however, the composition of the labor force had substantially changed, as shown in Table 13–1. Employment in agriculture, fisheries, and forestry decreased from 13 percent of the labor force to 3 percent in 1980. Employment in mining, construction, manufacturing, transportation, and utilities declined from 44 percent to 33 percent of the labor force. On the other hand, jobs in wholesale and retail trade, financial services, other services (such as health care), and government increased from 43 percent of the employed labor force in 1950 to 64 percent in 1980.

The contrast is even more evident when one examines the kinds of occupations filled by persons in the labor force. Farm work, crafts and trade jobs, operatives including truck drivers, common labor, and service jobs provided employment for 62 percent of the employed labor force in 1950. These same kinds of jobs provided work for 45 percent of the labor force in 1980. On the other hand, so-called white-collar jobs had advanced from 38 percent of all employment in 1950 to 55 percent of all employment in 1980.

As of 1985 the Bureau of Labor Statistics (1980: 17) projected that 68 percent of all professional and technical workers, 36 percent of all managers and administrators, and 22 percent of all sales workers would have completed four years or more of higher education. These proportions could be expected to increase in the remaining

Table 13-1. Civilian Employment in the United States (*in thousands*).

	1950	1960	1970	1980
By type of employer				
Agriculture	7,160	5,458	3,463	3,364
Mining	901	712	623	1,027
Construction	2,364	2,926	3,588	4,346
Manufacturing	15,241	16,796	19,367	20,285
Transportation, utilities	4,034	4,004	4,515	5,146
Wholesale, retail trade	9,386	11,391	15,040	20,310
Finance, insurance, real estate	1,888	2,629	3,645	5,160
Services	5,357	7,378	11,548	17,890
Government	6,026	8,353	12,554	16,241
By type of occupation				
Farm workers	7,408	5,176	3,126	2,704
Crafts, foremen	7,670	8,554	10,158	12,529
Operatives	12,146	11,950	13,909	13,814
Laborers	3,520	3,553	3,724	4,456
Service workers	6,535	8,920	9,712	12,958
Sales workers	3,822	4,224	4,854	6,172
Clerical workers	7,632	9,762	13,714	18,105
Professional, technical	4,490	7,469	11,140	15,613
Managers, proprietors	6,429	7,067	8,289	10,919

Source: By type of employer: *Economic Report of the President* (1985: 266, 275). By type of occupation: *Statistical Abstract of the United States* (1970: 225); *Statistical Abstract of the United States* (1981: 401).

years of the century and affect clerical employment as well (which was projected to be 7 percent college educated as of 1985).

In the 1980s the Bureau of Labor Statistics began to classify jobs in a somewhat different set of categories. As of 1983 (*Statistical Abstract 1985*: 402-03) the major categories and the number of employed persons in each category were reported as follows:

	Millions of Persons
Farming, fisheries, forestry	3.7
Precision production, crafts, mechanics	12.3
Operators, fabricators, laborers	16.1
Service occupations	13.9

	Millions of Persons
Technical, sales, administrative support	31.3
Technicians	3.1
Sales occupations	11.8
Administrative support, including clerical	16.4
Managerial and professional	23.6
Executive, administrative, managerial	10.8
Professionals	12.8

In this classification scheme, it will be observed that 54.9 million jobs out of a total of nearly 101 million were to be found in the last two major categories. These kinds of positions were those increasingly being held by graduates of two years or four years and more of higher education. It was this large increase in the categories of technical, sales, administrative support, professional, and managerial positions that helped to encourage the substantial enrollment increase in higher education from 2.6 million students in 1950 to the 12.3 million students of 1985.

In economic terms, the most important output of U.S. higher education from the 1950s to the 1980s was the preparation of educated talent for a changing labor force. In agriculture and the health sciences, the contributions were also especially notable in research and in technological transfer. Other contributions were made in space exploration, national defense, and nuclear energy. Yet the output of educated talent remained the paramount achievement.

Unfortunately, unemployment also rose in these years, from 3.3 million persons in 1950 to a high of 10.7 million persons in 1983. In 1984 unemployment fell back to around 8 million persons. Changing technology in farming, mining, and manufacturing required fewer workers in these industries. In service jobs the type of employment changed from domestic service to new positions in protective services, food service, health service (such as nursing aides and orderlies), building services, and personal services. Educational expectations affected these employment categories as well as the more highly technical and professional occupations.

Yet impressive as has been the record of higher education in meeting the economic needs of a changing labor force over the past thirty-five years, a new emphasis on the creation of jobs was emerging in the 1980s. The whole subject of manufacturing enterprise in the United States is far too complex to be considered here. A combination of high wages, reduced productivity gains, foreign competition (much of it encouraged by governmental political objectives), and other factors had changed the labor market for jobs in manufacturing industry. The economic problem then became one of persuading older industries to change their productive technology and of encouraging new industries to develop. One means of accomplishing these ends was to rely on higher education for assistance through scientific research, technical development, and technological transfer.

A shift in the economic expectation placed on higher education began to occur. The task of preparation of educated talent remained, but now higher education was asked to create jobs more than to educate people for jobs. And whereas education for jobs fell on all public and private institutions—doctoral-granting, comprehensive, general baccalaureate, specialized, and two-year—the task of creating jobs fell primarily on the doctoral-granting institutions and especially on their subsection, the major research universities. These universities, perhaps as many as 100 in number, held in their hands the economic fate of higher education in the remaining years of the twentieth century.

GOVERNMENTAL TRENDS: FEDERAL

During the 1970s the role of the federal government in relation to higher education was clarified. That role centered on science research and student financial assistance. While there were other programs peripheral to these two central thrusts, they remained fairly modest in scope. Some programs authorized by the Higher Education Act of 1965 and its various extensions were never funded, and others were funded on an almost intermittent basis. The difficulty for institutions of higher education was the uncertainty of federal government action from year to year in appropriating funds, especially funds for research and student aid.

For a time in the middle and late 1970s federal appropriations for research appeared to be leveling off and even to fall below the rate of inflation. In the 1980s research appropriations began to increase once again, and uncertainty was evident in the support of student financial assistance. This financial aid to students was critical to higher education institutions in encouraging wider access, especially for minority students. As charges to students increased because of

Table 13-2. Federal Appropriations for Student and Institutional Assistance (*in billions of dollars, by fiscal years*).

	1984 Actual	1985 Estimate	1986 President's Budget
Student assistance	$8.843	$9.350	$7.497
Pell grants	2.800	3.575	2.691
Guaranteed loans	2.254	3.078	2.714
Work-study	0.555	0.592	0.850
Supplemental grants	0.375	0.413	0.000
Direct loans	0.181	0.215	0.028
State grants	0.076	0.076	0.000
Graduate support	0.014	0.017	0.000
Veterans education	1.490	1.276	1.064
Health professions	0.098	0.108	0.050
Scientific research	6.241	6.978	6.952
NIH	2.248	2.575	2.427
NSF	1.323	1.501	1.569
Defense	0.840	0.861	0.971
Energy	0.960	1.071	1.032
NASA	0.713	0.801	0.834
Other	0.157	0.169	0.119
Health research and training	0.436	0.466	0.429
Arts and humanities	0.323	0.286	0.244
Institutional grants	0.875	1.048	0.787
Developing institutions	0.302	0.324	0.229
Libraries	0.007	0.007	0.000
Agricultural research and extension	0.472	0.633	0.516
Other	0.094	0.084	0.042

Source: *Budget of the United States Government, Fiscal Year 1986* (1985).

inflation and because of cost demands, student aid was indispensable if educational opportunity was not to be curtailed.

The recent course of federal appropriations and of budget requests indicates the reasons for institutional concern. This information is set forth in Table 13-2. The research appropriation to the National Institutes of Health has been arbitrarily reduced by one-half to account for in-house research. The Congress in fiscal years 1984 and 1985 provided more funds for student assistance than was recommended by the president, and once again the president proposed a reduction for the fiscal year 1986. The president's budget for higher education for 1986 came to a total of just under $16 billion, a 14 percent reduction from the appropriations made for the fiscal year ending September 30, 1985. There was a 20 percent reduction proposed for student assistance, a less than 1 percent reduction in research support, and an 18 percent reduction in the other three major categories of programs. It should be noted that for 1985 these miscellaneous programs amounted to just 10 percent of total federal support.

The history of federal government assistance to higher education during the past decade has been one of presidential reductions and of congressional increases. The emergence in 1985 of the federal budget deficit as a major political and economic problem posed the question of whether this past experience was likely to continue in the future. If the budget deficit was to be reduced and substantial increase in federal taxation was to be avoided, then curtailment of federal appropriations was the only choice of action. In any such action, the federal government support of higher education would become a major target for reduction.

GOVERNMENTAL TRENDS: STATE

As a major sponsor of institutions of higher education in the United States and as the principal provider of financial support for public institutions, state governments have had troublesome economic and other problems to contend with in the past decade. An economy of slow growth along with intense recessions, inflation, fluctuating state revenues, and substantial unemployment have combined to complicate state support of higher education. An intense competition among the states for new enterprises and for manufacturing location has brought higher education to the fore as a possible instrument for encouraging economic betterment.

In a threatening economic environment, state governments have been compelled to confront other issues. With each state having multiple institutions of higher education—from 135 in California, ninety-eight in Texas, and eighty-six in New York to six in Vermont, five in Delaware, and three in Rhode Island—the issue has arisen whether or not a particular state has more institutions than it needs or can "afford." Other questions have included issues about small enrollment size and about program duplication. How shall state governments respond to the new concern about educational excellence? What proportion of institutional support should be borne by public subsidy and what proportion by charges to students? Can charges to students be increased without an adverse effect on enrollment and educational opportunity (Hearn and Longanecker 1985)? Should state programs of student financial assistance be expanded when and if federal programs are contracted? Should state governments undertake to provide assistance to private institutions? And how shall a state government organize itself administratively to conduct state relationships with multiple institutions of higher education (Millett 1984)? It is impossible here to review the many approaches that have been attempted in the search for solutions to these problems in various states. It is sufficient here to observe only that the quest has been continual if spasmodic and that politically acceptable actions have been difficult to discover.

The political environment of state government will continue in the years ahead to be troublesome for both public and private institutions of higher education. There is competition for support as between higher education and other major state programs: mental health, public welfare, law enforcement and prison administration, financial assistance to elementary/secondary school districts, and support of local governments. Within higher education there is competition among programs (institutional support, student assistance, and aid to private institutions) and competition among public institutions including student instruction, research, public service, and especially the cost of teaching hospitals. There is no prospect as of 1985–86 that any of this competition will be simple to adjust. Rather, the competition can only become more intense in the next decade.

It must be emphasized that state governments have a different budget structure for higher education than do public institutions of higher education. State governments do not usually support financially the sum total of public colleges and universities. Institutions derive their major support for research activities from the federal government, business corporations, and private foundations. State governments do not usually support student residence facilities, a student health program, and student social and recreational programs. These activities are supported by charges and special fees. The state appropriations for higher education reflect state government interests rather than the sum total of institutional operation.

One trend in state government support for higher education in the past decade has been the increasing proportion of the appropriations for other than student instruction at public institutions. These increasing proportions have gone for student financial assistance, teaching hospitals, research, public service, aid to private institutions, and even debt service on academic facilities. It seems likely that this trend will not be reversed in the near future.

State government support for higher education reflects many factors: population size, enrollments, enrollment distribution between public and private institutions, the public and political expectations from higher education, the political interest in higher education support in comparison with other state services, and the decision about the desirable division in costs between state subsidy and charges to students (McCoy and Halstead 1984).

As indicated in Table 13–3, state appropriations for higher education vary substantially from state to state. When percentage increases over a two-year period are examined, the range is from minus 3 percent to a plus 53 percent. The increase for 1985–86 was made possible by a generally improved economic climate in most states and by enlarged state revenues, made possible in some instances by increased state taxation in 1983, 1984, or 1985. The increases also provided evidence of state government concern for economic competition state by state; state governments feared that a lessening of higher education support would have an adverse impact on the hope for state economic development. There were twenty states in 1985–86 above the national average for increased support. In terms of appropriations per capita of population the range was from a low of $52 to a high of $495. Appropriations per $1,000 of personal income varied from $4 to $27.

It has been estimated that some 90 to 92 percent of all state appropriations for higher education on the average go to public institutions of higher education, including research support, public service support, and teaching hospitals. The remaining 8 percent or less in a particular state goes mostly to student financial assistance, aid to private institutions, and the state administrative agency for higher education.

State governments could be expected to continue to be different one from another in the value attached to higher education, and in

Table 13-3. State Appropriations for Higher Education.

	1985–86 Appropriations in Millions	Two-year Increase in Percentage	Appropriations per Capita	Appropriations per $1,000 of Personal Income
Alabama	$625.6	53%	$158	$16
Arizona	235.8	8	495	27
Arkansas	299.2	52	128	13
California	4,209.0	31	166	11
Colorado	406.4	11	130	9
Connecticut	329.9	21	105	6
Delaware	91.4	18	151	11
Florida	1,129.8	18	104	8
Georgia	664.6	18	115	10
Hawaii	208.6	15	213	15
Idaho	121.8	21	122	12
Illinois	1,314.4	19	115	8
Indiana	607.3	19	111	9
Iowa	385.3	7	132	11
Kansas	349.5	14	145	11
Kentucky	433.1	8	117	11
Louisiana	572.7	14	129	12
Maine	100.9	31	88	8
Maryland	532.5	21	124	8
Massachusetts	711.1	31	123	8
Michigan	1,146.0	26	127	10
Minnesota	722.8	16	174	13
Mississippi	398.9	15	155	17
Missouri	453.9	25	91	7
Montana	108.2	5	132	12
Nebraska	215.0	10	135	11
Nevada	94.4	25	105	8
New Hampshire	50.3	22	52	4
New Jersey	847.7	27	113	7
New Mexico	234.6	17	167	16
New York	2,545.5	17	144	10
North Carolina	1,078.8	25	178	16
North Dakota	124.4	13	184	15
Ohio	1,085.3	23	101	8
Oklahoma	425.9	9	131	11
Oregon	312.2	14	117	10
Pennsylvania	1,063.6	16	89	7

Table 13-3.   continued

	1985-86 Appropriations in Millions	Two-year Increase in Percentage	Appropriations per Capita	Appropriations per $1,000 of Personal Income
Rhode Island	110.4	13	115	9
South Carolina	505.1	29	156	15
South Dakota	62.0	16	89	8
Tennessee	547.8	35	117	11
Texas	2,204.4	-3	139	11
Utah	249.4	26	152	16
Vermont	44.6	12	84	8
Virginia	767.1	24	140	10
Washington	588.9	5	137	11
West Virginia	233.1	17	119	12
Wisconsin	655.4	10	138	11
Wyoming	110.4	7	218	18
Total United States	30,747.2	19	132	10

Source: *The Chronicle of Higher Education* (October 30, 1985); data prepared by M.M. Chambers and Edward R. Hines.

the willingness to provide generous support. The future of state government support will depend largely on the economic circumstances of each state and in the public perception that higher education has in fact been helpful in economic development.

FINANCING INSTITUTIONS

It is at the institutional level that the whole story of financing higher education in the United States comes together. Bowen (1980) has observed that institutions of higher education spend for their multiple outputs—student instruction, research, public service (including hospitals), and student aid—whatever they are able to obtain from multiple sources of income. One unique characteristic of institutions of higher education is that they do produce more than one kind of educational service. A second unique characteristic is that they do draw on multiple sources of funding: charges to students, governmental subsidies (federal, state, and local), philanthropy (both endowment income and current giving), and sales and service.

Each year individual colleges and universities make their particular decisions in the light of their available income about the magnitude and scope of their programs, the priorities attached to each kind of program, and the values to be observed in their expenditure pattern. There must, of course, be a capital budget in addition to a current operating budget. If capital improvements are financed by borrowing, then debt service charges (mandatory transfers) will appear in the current operating budget. Attention here, however, is directed only to current operating income and expenditure.

It is estimated that in 1985–86 institutions of higher education in the United States will receive around $95 billion in income. Table 13–4 presents data about the number of institutions by type, their estimated enrollment, and their estimated income. In terms of full-time equivalent enrollment public institutions were expected to enroll 75 percent of the students (contrasted with 77 percent of all students in the autumn of 1985) and to receive 66 percent of all current funds income. The difference in income resulted in part from the large number of students enrolled in public two-year institutions. Over the past decade it has been evident, however, that private institutions spend more per full-time equivalent student than do public institutions; in 1980–81 private institutions spent $10,800 per student contrasted with $6,800 per full-time equivalent student in public institutions (NCES 1984b: 84). The difference resulted from varying enrollment patterns, from the sizable federal research support (including independent operations) at private institutions, and from the heavy residential characteristic of many private institutions.

The data about numbers of institutions, enrollment, and income tell us little if anything about the quality (however defined) of public and private institutions or about the quality of any type of institution. In general, it is known that qualitative factors vary from one public or private institution to another. Comparison of expenditures per student among institutions must be made with great care.

Table 13–5 represents an effort to estimate the varied sources of income for public and private institutions by major type. There are many obvious conntrasts: the lesser proportion, of income from tuition at public compared with private institutions, the heavy dependence of public institutions on state government support, the larger proportion of federal government support at private than at public institutions, the concentration of local government support on two-year public institutions, the importance of philanthropic support for

Table 13-4. Number of Institutions, Estimated Enrollment, and Estimated Current Funds Income by Type of Institution.

	Number of Institutions 1982–83	Estimated Enrollment 1985–86 (in millions)			Estimated Income 1985–86 (in billions of dollars)
		Full-time	Part-time	FTE	
Public					
Doctoral-granting	106	1.2	1.0	2.1	$27
Comprehensive, baccalaureate, specialized	443	1.6	1.3	2.0	25
Two-year	925	2.4	2.0	2.7	11
Total	1,474	5.2	4.3	6.8	63
Private					
Doctoral-granting	61	0.4	0.4	0.6	15
Comprehensive, baccalaureate, specialized	1,275	1.4	0.4	1.5	16
Two-year	281	0.2	0.0	0.2	1
Total	1,617	2.0	0.8	2.3	$32

Source: Number of institutions, National Center for Education Statistics (1984a: 108). Estimates calculated by author on projected data of the National Center for Education Statistics.

Table 13-5. Estimated Distribution of Current Funds Income by Major Types of Institutions, 1985–86 (*in percentages*).

	Public Institutions			Private Institutions		
	Doctoral Granting	Comprehensive, Baccalaureate, Specialized	Two-year	Doctoral Granting	Comprehensive, Baccalaureate, Specialized	Two-year
Sources of income						
Tuition and fees	13	12	14	28	44	60
Governments						
State	42	49	52	2	2	2
Federal	15	13	6	19	9	5
Local	—	1	16	1	1	—
Philanthropy	4	2	—	14	16	12
Sales and services						
Educational	3	2	3	3	1	2
Auxiliary	13	10	6	10	15	17
Hospitals	8	9	—	13	6	—
Independent operations	2	—	—	7	4	—
Other	—	2	3	3	2	2

Source: Author's calculations based on data of the National Center for Education Statistics (1984a). Blanks indicate less than 1 percent.

private institutions, the magnitude of income from the sales and service of teaching hospitals, and the considerable involvement of private institutions in independent operations (mostly for the federal government).

The sum total of institutional support obtained from the federal government according to this table is around $12 billion, contrasted with some $18 billion of appropriations by the federal government. Institutions of higher education have been confused about how to report federal grants to students. Since many of these grants are made to students on the basis of eligibility criteria fixed by federal agencies rather than by the institutions, the predominant tendency has been to treat any such income flowing through the institution as "agency fund" income rather than as current funds income. Some institutions report tuition income in subcategories: paid by students, paid by the federal government, paid by a state government, paid from endowment and gift income, paid by institutional income. As of 1985–86 there was still a good deal of confusion about how to report federal and state student financial assistance. It was important for institutions to know the sources of tuition income.

The income pattern in Table 13–5 presupposes an income pattern in 1985–86 comparable to the income pattern prevailing in 1981–82. If there should be any substantial departure from earlier experience, the estimates for sources of 1985–86 income will be faulty.

Table 13–6 sets forth an estimated distribution of current funds expenditures for 1985–86. The estimates of student financial aid outlays again presume that much of federal and state government student support will not appear in institutional current funds reporting. Certain contrasts are again evident. Public and private doctoral-granting institutions are the large performers of separately budgeted research. Public service expenditures are sizable at public doctoral-granting institutions because this category includes most of the 1862 land-grant institutions operating agricultural extension services. Private institutions spend a larger proportion of total outlays for student financial aid, partly because of the need to offset their higher tuition charges and partly because of the endowment and gift income available for this program. The size of support expenditures are affected by student development costs at open-door institutions and by the small size of some institutions.

The financial reports of institutions of higher education represent a composite of several component budgets, each of which is both a

Table 13-6. Estimated Distribution of Current Funds Expenditures by Major Types of Institutions, 1985–86 (*in percentages*).

	Public Institutions			Private Institutions		
	Doctoral Granting	Comprehensive, Baccalaureate, Specialized	Two-year	Doctoral Granting	Comprehensive, Baccalaureate, Specialized	Two-year
Educational and general						
Instruction	31	35	48	27	28	28
Research	15	5	—	15	4	—
Public service	6	3	2	2	2	—
Student aid	2	3	2	6	7	7
Support	23	30	40	21	32	47
Mandatory transfers	1	1	2	1	2	—
Auxiliary enterprises	13	12	6	9	14	17
Hospitals	8	10	—	12	6	—
Independent operations	—	—	—	6	4	—
Other transfers	1	1	—	1	1	1

Source: Author's calculations based on data of the National Center for Education Statistics (1984a). Blanks indicate less than 1 percent.

budget of income and a budget of expenditures. The princ
ponent parts of an institutional composite budget are sti
struction (including overhead), research, public service, stuc
hospitals, independent operations, and auxiliary enterprises
ever the income for one component is inadequate to meet une corresponding expenditures, then an internal transfer of income is necessary. Increased attention to component budgeting will be essential
in order to advance faculty and other understanding of institutional
finance.

There are many issues to be resolved in financing an institution of
higher education. What shall be the goal of an institution in providing
faculty salaries? What shall be the expected faculty workload and the
faculty-student ratio? What shall be spent for staff benefits and for
direct faculty support (secretarial assistance, equipment and supplies,
travel)? Shall separately budgeted public service be restricted to income generated by these activities? How much shall be spent for student financial assistance? How can the support (or overhead) expenditures be contained in the light of rising energy costs, the demand
for more student services, the increased requirements of institutional
reporting, and the trend to be involved in more and more litigation
costs?

The limitation on all costs within colleges and universities is income. It is not enough that institutions of higher education have
varied sources of income. The continuing challenge is what sources
shall be cultivated in order to expand their support of a particular
institution. Will increased tuition charges decrease enrollment and restrict educational opportunity? How can the political environment
be encouraged to increase institutional support, research support,
public service support, student assistance support? To what extent
can philanthropy be expected to provide greater support? Can the
sales and services of educational activities, auxiliary enterprises, and
hospitals be expanded? How can an institution generate greater
miscellaneous income? How can the cultivation of income from varied sources always remain supportive rather than subversive of the
exalted aims and responsibilities of an academic community?

Every such question involves value judgments. The conduct of all
higher education is an exercise in value judgments about the worth
of individuals, about social cohesion, about freedom and responsibility, about civic virtue, about the very meaning of American civilization. U.S. society up to 1986 has on the whole been well served by

U.S. higher education. We want our descendants to be able to make this same final judgment.

REFERENCES

Banfield, E.C. 1970. *The Unheavenly City.* Boston: Little, Brown.

Bowen, H.R. 1980. *The Costs of Higher Education.* San Francisco: Jossey-Bass.

Breneman, D.W. 1982. *The Coming Enrollment Crisis: What Every Trustee Must Know.* Washington, D.C.: Association of Governing Boards of Universities and Colleges.

Budget of the United States Government, Fiscal Year 1986. 1985. Washington, D.C.: U.S. Government Printing Office.

Bureau of Labor Statistics. 1980. *Occupational Outlook for College Graduates.* 1978–79 ed. Washington, D.C.: U.S. Government Printing Office.

Carnegie Commission on Higher Education. 1973. *The Purposes and Performance of Higher Education.* New York: McGraw-Hill.

Chronicle of Higher Education. 1985. "State Appropriations for Higher Education." 31 (October 30): 12–13.

Clecak, P. 1977. "Views of Social Critics." In *Investment in Learning,* edited by H.R. Bowen, pp. 388–427. San Francisco: Jossey-Bass.

Economic Report of the President. 1985. Washington, D.C.: U.S. Government Printing Office.

Ferrell, R.H., ed. 1985. *The Twentieth Century: An Almanac.* New York: World Almanac.

Hearn, J.C., and D. Longanecker. 1985. "Enrollment Effects of Alternative Postsecondary Pricing Policies." *Journal of Higher Education* 56 (September/October): 485–508.

Jencks, C. 1972. *Inequality: A Reassessment of the Effects of Family and Schooling in America.* New York: Basic Books.

_____. 1979. *Who Gets Ahead? The Determinants of Economic Success in America.* New York: Basic Books.

McCoy, M., and D.K. Halstead. 1984. *Higher Education Financing in the Fifty States.* Boulder, Colo.: National Center for Higher Education Management Systems.

Millett, J.D. 1984. *Conflict in Higher Education.* San Francisco: Jossey-Bass.

National Center for Education Statistics. 1984a. *Digest of Education Statistics, 1983–84.* Washington, D.C.: U.S. Government Printing Office.

_____. 1984b. *The Condition of Education: A Statistical Report 1984.* Washington, D.C.: U.S. Government Printing Office.

National Commission on Excellence in Education. 1983. *A Nation at Risk.* Washington, D.C.: U.S. Government Printing Office.

Statistical Abstract of the United States. 1981. Washington, D.C.: U.S. Government Printing Office.

_____ . 1985. Washington, D.C.: U.S. Government Printing Office.

_____ . 1970. Washington, D.C.: U.S. Government Printing Office.

INDEX

ABOUT THE EDITORS

Mary P. McKeown is finance coordinator for the Maryland State Board for Higher Education. She has bachelor's and master's degrees from Michigan State University and a Ph.D. from the University of Illinois at Urbana-Champaign. McKeown has held faculty positions at Eastern Michigan University, the University of Illinois, and Sangamon State University and conducted research in the financing of elementary and secondary education while serving as finance specialist with the Illinois State Board of Education. She also served as business manager for the University of Illinois Foundation and has been a member of the board of directors of the American Education Finance Association and the editorial advisory board of the *Journal of Education Finance.* She was coeditor of the 1985 AEFA yearbook and coauthor of *School Business Administration* and has written extensively in the area of education finance and management.

Kern Alexander was named president of Western Kentucky University in December 1985. Executive Editor of the *Journal of Education Finance* and author of more than thirty books and many journal articles, particularly on funding for higher education, school finance, and public school law, he is internationally known as a distinguished educational consultant. He has conducted major studies for governors, legislatures, and state educational agencies in more than half of the states and for numerous offices of the federal government.

Dr. Alexander was educated at Centre College, Western Kentucky University, Indiana University, and the University of Oxford, England. He holds an Ed.D. in educational administration and has completed post-doctoral studies with distinction at Oxford.

ABOUT THE CONTRIBUTORS

Sandra Allard is a finance analyst with the Maryland State Board for Higher Education. Her previous professional positions include assistant director for capital budgeting and assistant director for research and planning at the Tennessee Higher Education Commission and fiscal research analyst for the North Carolina General Assembly. She has conducted numerous studies in higher education finance and authored a variety of reports.

Elchanan Cohn is professor of economics at the University of South Carolina. He also is founder and editor in chief of the *Economics of Education Review*. A graduate of the University of Minnesota (B.A., M.A.) and Iowa State University (Ph.D.), he held faculty positions at the Pennsylvania State University before his current position. He has more than seventy-five publications, including books, articles, monographs, and reviews, and is the author of *The Economics of Education.*

O. Homer Erekson is associate professor of economics and director of graduate studies in economics at Miami University, Oxford, Ohio. He received his Ph.D. in economics from the University of North Carolina at Chapel Hill. His research in educational finance has focused on the relationship between public and private school financing, financial support of higher education, and financial analysis of intercollegiate athletics.

Carol Frances is a partner in the firm of Washington Resources, Inc. and an economic advisor to the National Education Industry Group of Coopers and Lybrand. She specializes in the economics and finance of higher education and serves as an advisor to colleges and universities, higher education associations, government agencies, and private firms. Her recent work includes studies of enrollment and college-going rates and reports on trends in the ability to pay for college.

Terry G. Geske is professor of educational administration and coordinator of the educational administration and educational research methodology program areas at Louisiana State University. He has published several articles on the economics of education and public school finance. He is coeditor, with Walter W. McMahon, of *Financing Education: Overcoming Inefficiency and Inequity.*

Howard Gobstein is a senior science policy analyst with the U.S. General Accounting Office in Washington, D.C. During the past ten years he has managed project teams and written on topics including the financing of research, research equipment needs, accountability for federal funds used to support university research, and the role of the White House Office of Science and Technology Policy in planning national science and technology policy.

Terry W. Hartle is a resident fellow at the American Enterprise Institute for Public Policy Research in Washington, D.C. He has been a research scientist at the Educational Testing Service and is coauthor of *Excellence in Education: The States Take Charge* and *The Great American Job Machine.*

Edward R. Hines is professor of educational administration and director of the Center for Higher Education at Illinois State University. He received an A.B. degree in zoology from Colgate University, an M.A. in higher education from Teachers College, Columbia University, and a Ph.D. in educational administration from Ohio State University. Hines' primary research activities have been in the political economy of higher education. He is coauthor, with L.S. Hartmark, of *Politics of Education* and, with J.R. McCarthy, of *Higher Education Finance.* He is editor of *Grapevine*, the monthly report of state tax appropriations for the operating expenses of higher education.

Frances Kemmerer, a research associate in the Center for Educational Research and Policy Studies and adjunct professor in the Department of Educational Administration and Policy Studies at the State University of New York at Albany, has written widely on efficiency and equity in the use of school-based resources and in the financing of education. Her published work appears in the Economics of Education Review, the Journal of Education Finance, and the Review of Education, among others. She also currently serves as coordinator for the U.S. AID Improving the Efficiency of Education Systems Project.

Lucie Lapovsky is director of finance and facilities at the Maryland State Board for Higher Education. She received her Ph.D. in economics from the University of Maryland. She has taught at Hood College and Morgan State University, has authored several papers on funding higher education, and is an expert on peer analysis of institutions.

John R. McCarthy is a professor of higher education administration at Illinois State University. His bachelor's degree is in European history and his master's degree is in American history. He also holds a Ph.D. in higher education from Florida State University. His most recent major publication was Higher Education Finance, with E. R. Hines. McCarthy's research interests include the finance and governance of higher education.

John D. Millett is president emeritus of Miami University, chancellor emeritus of the Ohio Board of Regents, and a life trustee of DePauw University. Millett earned both graduate degrees from Columbia University and did post-graduate work at the London School of Economics and Political Science. He was a member of the graduate faculty of Columbia University and vice president of the Academy for Educational Development, and has been an independent consultant since 1980.

Ralph Nichols is assistant vice president for academic affairs for the University of Michigan system. He earned a bachelor's degree in economics from the University of Michigan and a master's in educational research and evaluation from Wayne State University. He has served as assistant and associate registrar, director of institutional analysis, and coordinator of budget administration for the University of Michigan. Recently he was a member of the Michigan Higher Education Task Force on Formula Funding.

Douglas R. Sherman has been working as a management consultant in facilities through the Facilities Management Institute of Ann Arbor, Michigan, since his retirement as assistant vice president and director of capital planning for the University of Michigan. He received his B.S. and M.S. degrees from the University of Wisconsin-Stout and his Ed.D. from Wayne State University. He has taught at the high school, community college, and university levels and was director of capital programs at Wayne State University. Sherman specializes in research and consulting in the facilities area.

James B. Stedman is a specialist in education with the Congressional Research Service of the Library of Congress. He received his B.A. in history from Middlebury College and his M.A. in history from Harvard University. His areas of responsibility for the Congressional Research Service are analysis of legislative issues involving higher education, school reform, and school desegregation.

Alan P. Wagner is a research associate in the Center for Educational Research and Policy Studies at the State University of New York at Albany. He received his Ph.D. in economics from the University of Illinois, has taught at Purdue University, and currently is directing, for the Department of Education, a study of how postsecondary educational institutions package financial aid. He has published in the *Journal of Human Resources*, the *Economics of Education Review, School Review, Education and Urban Society,* and the *Review of Higher Education.*

Richard A. Yanikoski is associate vice president for academic affairs and chairman of the University Research Council at DePaul University, where he served previously as director of institutional planning and research. He is a former president of the Illinois Association for Institutional Research. For the past six years he has been tracking innovations in tuition pricing, most recently as director of a national study funded by the Exxon Education Foundation.

AMERICAN EDUCATION FINANCE ASSOCIATION OFFICERS 1986-87

Officers

President	James G. Ward
President-Elect	William E. Sparkman
Secretary-Treasurer	George R. Babigian
Immediate Past President	James L. Phelps

Directors

Robert Berne	Bettye MacPhail-Wilcox
William E. Camp	Van D. Mueller
Koy Floyd	Julie Underwood O'Hara
James Fox	Robert Perlman
Lloyd E. Frohreich	James Rose
Suzanne Langston	Joan Scheuer
Stephen B. Lawton	Deborah Verstegen
Kent McGuire	

Editor, Journal of Education Finance

Kern Alexander

Sustaining Members

American Association of School Administrators
American Federation of Teachers
National Education Association
National School Boards Association